THEATER
IN THE
AMERICAS

A Series from
Southern
Illinois
University
Press
ROBERT A.
SCHANKE
Series Editor

Other Books in the Theater in the Americas Series

Contemporary Latina/o Theater

Contemporary Latina/o Theater

Wrighting Ethnicity

Jon D. Rossini

SOUTHERN ILLINOIS UNIVERSITY PRESS
Carbondale

11 10 09 08   4 3 2 1

Library of Congress Cataloging-in-Publication Data

Rossini, Jon D., 1971–
Contemporary Latina/o theater : wrighting ethnicity / Jon D. Rossini.
    p.   cm. — (Theater in the Americas)
Includes bibliographical references and index.
ISBN-13: 978-0-8093-2830-7 (pbk. : alk. paper)
ISBN-10: 0-8093-2830-5 (pbk. : alk. paper)
    1. American drama—Hispanic American authors—History and criticism.
2. American drama—20th century—History and criticism. 3. Hispanic
Americans in literature. 4. Ethnicity in literature. 5. Hispanic Americans—
Ethnic identity. I. Title. II. Series.
PS153.H56R67 2008
812'.609928708968—dc22   2007036299

Printed on recycled paper. ♻

The paper used in this publication meets the minimum requirements of
American National Standard for Information Sciences—Permanence of
Paper for Printed Library Materials, ANSI Z39.48-1992.∞

For Paula,
with whom everything is possible

Contents

Acknowledgments

As a careful reader and wonderfully supportive mentor and friend, Jorge Huerta has been instrumental to the completion of this book from its very early stages. He is truly the godfather of Chicano theater studies. Tamara Underiner and Patricia Ybarra helped me through a crucial step in the revision process with insightful and incisive comments about the first chapter. Bob Schanke has made this a better book by insisting it be accessible to a wider range of readers. My colleagues at the University of California, Davis, especially Barbara Sellers-Young and Lynette Hunter, have provided intellectual and emotional support for the project.

I thank my colleagues and friends at Texas Tech, especially Madonne Miner and Scott Baugh for their careful readings and feedback, as well as Yuan Shu, Brian McFadden, and Jen Shelton for their collegiality and friendship. John M. Clum, at Duke University, was a wonderful role model and provided a supportive space from which to launch my scholarly career. He has continued to be an important mentor.

My graduate student researchers at Davis—Claire Blackstock, Darren Blaney, and Hope Medina—have been helpful in various stages of research and revision. Kristine Priddy and Wayne Larsen at SIU Press have been kind shepherds for the project. Thanks to Octavio Solis and Oliver Mayer for reminding me that playwrights care about what I am doing. Thanks also to Phil Esparza for sharing his thoughts and allowing me access to the El Teatro Campesino archives. Thanks to Salvador Guereño and Special Collections at the University of California, Santa Barbara; the San Francisco Performing Arts Library and Museum; and Elena Becks and the Committee on Black Performing Arts at Stanford University for providing significant research information. Funds to support research related to this book were provided by the UC Davis Committee on Research, the Big 12 Faculty Fellowship, and the University of California Institute for Mexico and the United States. Support was also provided by the UC Davis Office of the Vice Chancellor for Research and the Division of Humanities, Arts, and Cultural Studies. An earlier version of a portion of chapter 4 appeared as *"Bandido!*: Melodrama, Stereotypes and the Construction of Ethnicity" *Gestos* 25 (April 1998): 127–41.

Closer to home, my parents have been instrumental to this work. My father has encouraged me at every step of the way to say what I need to say. My mother's lifelong accomplishments in the face of many hardships have been an inspiration, especially for all of the discriminatory struggles she has overcome with perseverance and joy. She has always reminded me of what it means to be ethnic in the United States.

Finally, Paula M. V. Ramsay has been through thick and thin with me. My companion and support on a daily basis, she has dealt with my frustrations, anxieties, procrastination, and manic excitement. I never could have finished this book without her; consequently, it is dedicated to her.

Contemporary Latina/o Theater

Introduction: Writing, Righting, and Wrighting Ethnicity

Latina/o playwrights are uniquely positioned within contemporary culture to provide compelling ways of understanding the often vexed and oversimplified concept of ethnicity. As Latinas/os they are part of the second-largest ethnic group in the United States, one with increasing national visibility, as well as growing economic and political power. As playwrights they are not only creators of written texts but also collaborators in embodied, live performance in front of an audience. The unique power of this combination emerges from the vigorous public rhetoric and cultural assumptions attached to the label *Latina/o*, the sustained recognition of the importance of ethnicity despite the difficulty of defining it, and the effectiveness of theater and theatricality as structures for exploring contemporary social practice and identity. *Contemporary Latina/o Theater: Wrighting Ethnicity* unites an understanding of the complex aesthetic and cultural work of theater as a genre with the complex cultural positioning of Latinas/os as an increasingly heterogeneous and diverse group through the combination of two critical lenses: theater studies and ethnic studies. Theater studies attends to the semiotics of text and presentation and provides a complex understanding of the construction of identity through deliberate staging practices. The field of ethnic studies focuses detailed and careful attention on the material conditions of Latina/o lives. By bringing these two lenses together, *Contemporary Latina/o Theater: Wrighting Ethnicity* demonstrates the power of theatricality as a means of understanding, exploring, and rethinking ethnicity.

Writing Latina/o Ethnicity

Latinos in the United States have increasingly been recognized by the media and elected officials as a necessary and important part of the cultural and political landscape, even as their place in the United States is questioned. The spring 2006 controversy over the Spanish translation of "The Star-Spangled Banner" attests to the anxiety regarding the public performance of alternative forms of participation in U.S. culture created by Latinos. In late April 2006, "Nuestro Himno" ("Our Anthem"), a Spanish translation of the national anthem, hit the airwaves in support of immigrants' rights. Sung by a diverse group of artists, it was intended to "express gratitude and patriotism to the United States," as well as indicate solidarity with proimmigrant demonstrators.[1] The almost unanimous public response, however, was anger and negativity. Translating a sacred symbol of national culture into Spanish was viewed as a desacralizing gesture, a sign of disrespect, and a reflection of immigrants' refusal to assimilate into American culture. This resistance to the translation of a national cultural symbol reflects the perception that the increasing public use of Spanish as an everyday language in the United States threatens existing power structures and conventional ways of understanding identity and community. Implicit in this concern is a fear of the "other" maintained by a conceptual framework that posits an unbridgeable gap between self and other.

While a number of groups were represented in the immigration protests during the spring of 2006, in the mainstream public imagination (and on the basis of majority demographics) it was a Mexican issue. U.S.-Mexican relations have been troubled for more than a century and a half, dating back to attempts to grab Mexican territory by Anglo settlers and the forced sale of land by Mexico at the conclusion of the Mexican-American War. In 1848 the Treaty of Guadalupe Hidalgo made Mexicans who were living in the newly acquired U.S. territory citizens overnight. Puerto Ricans, whose country was acquired after the Spanish-American War in 1898, were made citizens through the Jones Act of 1917. In both cases, governmental action brought Spanish-speaking Latinos into the United States as citizens with full civil rights. The continued and growing presence of Latinos in the United States has transformed everyday life, and it is this very sense of change that appears most threatening to the unspoken but assumed allegiance to an America popularly composed of English speakers of European and, to a lesser extent, African ancestry. This threat manifests itself in the perceived danger of Latino bodies colonizing mainstream culture—conceptually endangering an entire way of life. In this way of seeing, the Latino body becomes a synecdoche for an emerging political resistance and the potential transformation of public space and everyday life, something that must be contained and controlled.

The growing population of Latinos with roots in a range of spaces beyond the physically proximate sites of Mexico and Puerto Rico creates a rich and heterogeneous cultural space where the concept of ethnicity is constantly called into question. According to a growing body of work by Latino sociologists and legal scholars, "[r]esearch on the social construction of racial identity among Latinos suggests that Latinos do not construct racial identity simply on genetic and physical characteristics but include social class, language, phenotypic variation within families, and neighborhood socialization. It is not that uncommon to find Latinos who claim a dual or tri-racial heritage, a combination of African, European, and indigenous ancestors."[2] This heterogeneity and multiplicity are also reflected in the confusion of government demographers. As of 1996 "most agencies of the federal government consider[ed] Hispanic to be a supplement to racial categories. However, some agencies collect data as if Hispanic origin was a racial category."[3] Suzanne Oboler and others have argued that this difficulty of marking Latinos as a specifically racial or ethnic other led to an absence of public discussion regarding this population and a blatant lack of attention to legal and civil protection, except on a regional basis where the overriding initial assumption was racial difference and the overwhelming practice one of discrimination.[4] Despite the historical reality that Spanish was spoken long before English in much of what is today the United States, the cultural mainstream seems increasingly willing to embrace a stance that the only acceptable Latino public behavior is English-speaking assimilation. The desire to maintain a form of national culture and a model of ethnicity that does not fully incorporate the experiences of U.S. Latinos makes it necessary to explore alternative conceptions of ethnicity that do not limit knowledge, civic participation, and culture.

The creation of the umbrella term *Hispanic* can be seen as part of this broader strategy of containment that must be contested. The term *Hispanic* was first used officially in the 1980 census to categorize Spanish-speaking persons and descendants of Spanish speakers in the United States from a variety of national and racial backgrounds. The category as articulated by the U.S. government is understood within a third-world paradigm of colonialism, since Spanish speakers from Spain are, though technically labeled Hispanic, not really the intended recipients of the label. Although there are individuals who prefer Hispanic as a label, others responded to this government decision by consciously employing Latino as an alternative umbrella term.[5] Like the label *Chicano*, which in its initial political reclamation in the 1960s marked an antiassimilationist identity for persons of Mexican descent who acknowledge their indigenous roots, *Latino* was intended as a means of collectively naming a group from within to promote collective thinking and action in opposition to the government-sanctioned census label.

Though the terms Latino and Hispanic moved into public prominence in the 1980s, they followed relatively closely on the heels of the larger category of ethnicity that reached prominence less than two decades earlier. While the adjective *ethnic* has a longer history, Richard Jenkins reminds us, "Historically speaking, ethnicity, for anthropology as for other disciplines, is a relatively recent term, coming into conventional usage in the 1960s. Within American anthropology in particular, this was in part the result of a gradual shift of analytical framework, from 'race' to 'culture' to 'ethnicity.'"[6] Increasingly during the mid 1990s, scholarly accounts of ethnicity called for a need to understand the complex plurality of definitions of the concept while simultaneously engaging in a discussion of its cultural importance. Reminding his readers "there is no necessary coherence between all the positions on ethnicity that have been advanced," anthropologist Marcus Banks argues that the abstract noun *ethnicity* functions differently than the adjective *ethnic*. Unlike the "adjective . . . that has largely entered public discourse," the abstract noun *ethnicity* "is an analytical tool devised and utilized by academics to make sense of or explain the actions and feelings of the people studied." Banks's model "locates ethnicity in the observer's head," placing a great deal of power in the spectator.[7] Though not unique to Banks, this model becomes a way of shifting the persistent conflict between essentialist and social constructionist (in anthropology, primordial and instrumental) conceptions of ethnicity.

Currently discredited in mainstream cultural studies, essentialism argues that there is an inherent "essence" that all members of an ethnic group share. A member is defined, from within and without, by a series of markers that range from language to cultural behavior to the semiotics of the body. The grounding of this identity is established biologically as blood connections through kinship or ancestry. Essentialism presupposes a unified understanding of cultural and political values based on shared cultural history and roots. Essentialism understands cultural behaviors as a product of roots and heritage, often leading to definitions of an authentic ethnic identity. The scholarly resistance to essentialism is based in part on the problems of limiting authentic ethnic identity, as well as a recognition of the danger of prescriptive racial or ethnic hierarchies that have emerged historically when value judgments are linked to essential differences.

Social construction, on the other hand, sees values shared among members of an ethnic group as products of participation in a network of relationships that shape behavioral responses. This network predisposes an individual to operate in ways that reinforce the cultural limits of a particular ethnicity. Popular conceptions tend to create a combination of the two models despite their potential tension. On the one hand, the possibility of shared values based on a cultural history allows for easy group identification, while on the other, the idea of prescriptive definitions of identity can be constricting. This tension is resolved by maintaining an understanding of the self as an essence that nonetheless plays a number of social roles, slipping between conceptual frameworks to naturalize any potential contradictions. This model of ethnicity is more congruent with theatrical understandings of the self than contemporary theoretical accounts of performative identity. Consequently, an understanding of theater and its practices is crucial to understanding this conception of ethnicity.

Theater's role in negotiating the conceptual complexities of ethnicity is clearly visible in the final scene of John Leguizamo's 1991 Obie award–winning one-man show *Mambo Mouth*.[8] The play presents a series of characters who explore conventional assumptions about Latino identity, playing with and against stereotypes. The final scene, "Crossover King," presents a motivational entrepreneur promoting the benefits of his self-transformation method, crossing over, to his seminar audience: "Crossing over is the art of passing for someone you are not in order to get something that you have not."[9] Referencing the language of racial passing more than the language of ethnic assimilation, this seminar purports to provide the tools to transform from Latino to Japanese. Replacing the conventional Euro-American target with Japanese rewrites the conventional narrative of assimilation in the United States while simultaneously highlighting the elevation of Japanese corporate strategies and management practices within the U.S. business community in the late 1980s and early 1990s. By ironically idealizing the

Japanese, Leguizamo points to the ties between essentialist thinking and stereotypes while questioning the culturally assumed connections between costume, physicality, ethnic identity, and success.

As the Crossover King critiques images of Latinos based on clothing, hair, and physical characteristics, he offers a solution in the form of alternative "crossed-over" corporate images of some of these same bodies. Presenting the transformation of "Rosa Herrera . . . welfare-leeching, child-bearing, underachieving, no-good Latina" into "Rose Hara, the timid, self-disciplined, lonely, constipated workaholic," he illustrates both the class assumptions attached to stereotypes of Latino identity and the losses that accompany the disciplining of a body within corporate capitalist culture. In extolling the virtues of his product, the Crossover King reminds his audience "nobody cares what *you* think. It's what *they* think that counts."[10] This reminder that identity is in the eye of the beholder echoes Banks's conceptualization of ethnicity in the mind. However, the possibility of acting to transform this thinking, even through the problematic process of crossing over, suggests that ethnicity emerges not simply from the mind of the observer but also in a dynamic interplay between observer and subject, audience and actor.

The multiple layers of ironic humor in Leguizamo's text extend from the questionable legitimacy of the seminar leader as a source of knowledge to his increasing loss of control over his self-imposed bodily discipline. The character's initial *"movements are controlled"* and *"his gestures are stiff,"* but his "Latino relapse[s]," the first of which is passed off as a dramatic re-creation, highlight the superficial nature of his crossover. By the end of the scene (and the show), the Crossover King's "Latino" physicality is completely restored, and he dances the mambo, first with his feet and then with his whole body, despite attempts to restrain it. He eventually *"Bursts"* and yells "Go Loco! Go Loco! Go Loco!" before ending the piece with "Sayonara. Hai! (*deep bow to the audience*)."[11]

This sequence initially appears to make the scene an allegory about essential Latino physicality and its ability to reemerge despite any self-destructive attempt to restrain it. The final language and gesture, however, play with and against an audience's easy assertion that the scene is about the impossibility of containing an essential Latino identity. The containment reading insists that to discipline the body is a betrayal of one's cultural roots represented less by selling out than by buying in, economic implications that are presented both in the corporate language and in the genre of the seminar itself. However, Leguizamo's multilayered performance evades a conventional reassertion of fundamental ethnic difference that implicitly reinscribes stereotypes. The use of Japanese and the accompanying physicality humorously punctuate the conclusion of the piece but also remind the audience of the work's status as theatrical performance. In doing so, these actions interrupt an audience's potential assumptions that the final "Latino relapse" has in fact stripped Leguizamo of any character and that he is now performing himself as a Latino. This conventional reading is suggested by the play's proximity to stand-up comedy and the performance of self as character in that genre, as well as the tendency to read ethnic performance as autobiographical rather than fictional.

But Leguizamo is also intentionally working against these presumptions. The performance of the mambo recalls the title of the piece, *Mambo Mouth*, suggesting that all of the characters somehow reflect the aesthetic range of the dance, a form with a complex cultural history. The physicality is more nuanced than may be assumed by the reductive reading of a dancing Latino body. The cry to "Go Loco!" also holds its own reference in the text, recalling a prior character, Loco Louie, an adolescent disappointed by his first sexual experience but explicitly covering his concern with macho braggadocio. Though the final dancing Latino body is still a character—the Crossover King in a state of public exposure of the failure of his bodily discipline—the ease with which this is forgotten suggests the facility with which an audience conceptualizes ethnicity as both a role and an essence. Crucially, "Crossover King" ends with a failed transformation not to reassert the possibility of an essential identity but rather to illustrate the dangers of capitulating too quickly to existing expectations; in doing so it illustrates the need to imagine an alternative that transforms not only the self but also the very structures of representation.

Rethinking Theatricality

The imposition of and resistance to the census label Hispanic in 1980 occurred at the same moment when the sustained, coherent, and widespread use of theatrical metaphor in the social sciences was acknowledged and the increasing "theatricality" of everyday life began to be critically articulated.[12] The use of anthropological and sociological lenses as the primary foci for discussions of ethnicity, combined with the increasing use of theatrical metaphors in these disciplines, is an important intersection that shapes contemporary rhetoric about ethnicity. Tracy C. Davis refers to this deployment of theatrical metaphors as "social dramaturgy," a category into which she groups sociologists such as Erving Goffman and Elizabeth Burns. Beginning with Goffman's *The Presentation of Self in Everyday Life*, social dramaturgs have used theatrical metaphors to describe a range of social situations. The growing ubiquity of this practice reflects the comfort that contemporary culture has in understanding social practice as theatrical practice. This comfort emerges from the power of theater as a space whose liminality is actually comprehensible and can thus conceptually contain the contradictions and paradoxes of postmodern life. The structural elements of theatrical performance, the layers of intention attributed to actors and characters, the conscious and sophisticated role-playing by actors, and the conscious staging and self-presentation of mise-en-scène parallel the conceptual frameworks used to understand the concept of ethnicity. This is not to suggest that U.S. Latino identities are equivalent to theatrical roles but rather to argue that the discourses used to talk about Latino ethnicity and identity are shaped by cultural understandings of the spatiality and conventions of theater. Consequently, theater that foregrounds the representation of ethnicity is perfectly positioned to offer alternative conceptions of ethnicity.

This intersection of theatricality and ethnicity manifests in part because of a recognition that the representation of ethnicity by an individual marked as ethnic is already an explicit performance for outside consumption. This basic concept of theatricality appears briefly in Elizabeth Burns's so-titled work on the sociology of theater when she quotes an essay, "Life as Theater," in which both Sammy Davis Jr. and Bernard Wolfe talk about the need to be "on" constantly as African Americans, assuming the presence of a constant audience gaze in everyday life.[13] This conceptual relationship with a spectator is at the heart of a range of definitions of theatricality and functions as a more benign form of the power of looking. The relationship can be fruitfully understood in relationship to Goffman's model of the frame as a means of organizing experience.[14] This concept of transformative spectatorship also haunts the idea of double-consciousness, Du Bois's classic account of black subjectivity in the United States.[15]

Critical arguments as diverse as Tracy C. Davis's discussion of Carlyle, William Egginton's discussion of the transition from medieval to early modern theater, and Timothy Murray's understanding of the term in French theoretical writing together demonstrate theatricality's relational dynamic.[16] These arguments illustrate, from a theater studies point of view, theatricality's function as a useful bridge between, on the one hand, poststructuralist thought and its emphasis on social constructions and performativity and, on the other, identity politics often grounded in essentialist discourses. Understanding theatricality and ethnicity as products of the intersection of subjectivity and spectatorship clarifies the importance of Latino theater as a means of exploring the operative dynamics of spectator, actor, and event.[17] Through theatricality, the other is positioned and understood.

Rather than merely conceiving of theatricality as the means through which the other is positioned and understood as a product of this spectatorial practice, it is possible to alter this dynamic. The playwrights in this study reimagine the shared structure of theatricality and ethnicity by granting agency to the object under scrutiny, by making observers self-aware of their habits of watching, and by providing multilayered and potentially conflicting accounts that open up the possibility for transformation. Self-conscious of the imposition of an external gaze on their work and the desire to position the other through an act of looking, these artists proactively engage in this positioning process, making it visible and exposing the unrecognized assumptions that allow spectators to elide their lack of understanding. This technique is manifest even in one of the earliest *actos* of El Teatro Campesino, *Las Dos Caras del Patroncito* (1965), which uses masks to expose the contingency of the identity of the boss. The central characters of "The Two Faces of the Boss," the boss, or *patroncito*, and the farm worker, or *campesino*, are both played by strikers—the only difference is the boss's pig mask. When the mask is removed and exchanged, the boss looks just like the *campesino* and the *campesino* easily becomes the new boss, immediately having access to his power and authority. Of course, rather than simply becoming the new boss, the farm worker rejects this very structure, walking away from it all, revising rather than capitulating to existing structures.[18]

Righting Latina/o Theater, Reimagining Practice and Politics

If *ethnicity* differs from *ethnic* in marking a relationship between spectator and actor just as *theatricality* differs from the adjective *theatrical*, then exploring this relationship offers the possibility of a new dramaturgy, a new way of knowing, a new theory emerging from the space between being or acting ethnic and ethnicity as an analytical tool. Ethnicity is always negotiated with the disembodied gaze of the spectator, the state, or other institution as audience, as a performance akin to theater. Thus it makes perfect sense that in the cultural moment when the theatrical metaphor is proliferating in the social sciences, there is a concomitant increase in attention to ethnicity as a category. Ethnicity as a conceptual space can be reclaimed by those being marked, thus exposing the fundamental tension in spectatorship and performance over the contours of this space. This tension can be understood through a distinction between the perceived and the conceived, what is seen and what can be imagined. Although these concepts are often conflated, the goal of the theater discussed here is to offer not the perceived but the conceivable as a way of shifting thinking about ethnicity.

To accomplish such change, the playwrights in *Contemporary Latina/o Theater: Wrighting Ethnicity* simultaneously correct and create, opening up possibilities of what can be conceived by exposing and transforming the structures of what is perceived. Aurally contained in this process of *wrighting* are the acts of writing and righting, the creation of texts that actively work to reconceptualize the structure of ethnicity. *Wrighting* invokes the sense of making theater that goes beyond but includes writing itself. Writing attends to the textual artifacts, acknowledging the intellectual labor in the practice of creation and demanding a close critical attention to the language of these works as a means of explicating their cultural and aesthetic power rather than reducing them to signs of ethnographic difference. This close attention to language also reveals the political and cultural positioning enacted by the process of righting—correction, orientation, and revision—contained within these works, often in dialogue with or contradistinction to the visual information presented. Wrighting is thus a simultaneous process of correction, revision, and cultural repositioning in the act of creating a new conceptual framework.[19]

The processual structure of ethnicity has been devalued in part because of the predominant use of the prepositions *by, for, about*, and *near*, first articulated in W. E. B. Du Bois's 1926 essay on the Krigwa Little Theater:

> The plays of a real Negro theatre must be: 1. About us. That is they must have plots which reveal real Negro life as it is. 2. By us. That is they must be written by Negro authors who understand from birth and continual association just what it means to be a Negro today. 3. For us. That is, the theatre must cater primarily to Negro audiences and be supported and sustained by their entertainment and approval. 4. Near us. The theatre must be in a Negro neighborhood near the mass of ordinary Negro people.[20]

In a disciplinary environment saturated by postmodern thought that continues to celebrate the constructed, the contingent, and the provisional, *by*, *for*, *about*, and *near* remain associated with an essentialist politics that argues for a fundamental difference. Du Bois was writing within a political and cultural moment that could argue for an essentialist politics without apology, but the continued utility of his statement reflects the importance of maintaining a space for racially and ethnically marked theater within the United States in the face of a language of multiculturalism that sometimes works to erase difference. These terms allow one to talk about the process of theater making for a community by taking the definition of that community as a given, something the playwrights here do not.

Though the content of each of these terms has shifted in the eighty years since Du Bois's articulation, both American Indian playwright Hanay Geigomah and Chicano playwright Luis Valdez have used these terms to help define their theater and implicitly delineate the playwright's ethical responsibility to his or her community.[21] This responsibility is grounded in a clearly defined identity politics based on essentialist identity formations, often in support of separatist politics, and consistent with the ideals of the diversified civil rights movements from the mid 1960s to the mid 1970s. The operative assumption was that a cultural worker who identified with a particular community ("by") was in fact creating work "for" and "about" that community, and there was a strong sense of the role of the artist as one who not only gives voice to the political concerns of his or her people but also shares in their struggle ("near"). In this vein, playwrights developed theater with a political function, exposing social injustice, recuperating history, raising consciousness, and carrying the message of political activists to new audiences.[22]

This shift was part of a general movement toward an investment in the representation, practice, and politics of identity that has been central to theater in the United States since at least the 1970s. While ethnic theater, especially in languages other than English, had a powerful following in the first part of the twentieth century, it was primarily intended as a pedagogical and community-building activity structured within the paradigm of assimilation.[23] With the resurgence of broad-based ethnic theater and performance as an articulation of communal resistance in the 1960s, this paradigm shifted to an assertion of visibility and political rights. The plays that were born of this resurgence worked in parallel with the performative demonstrations of the civil rights movements of the 1960s and 1970s, when issues of experiential difference based on the body became organizing principles for political action. This sense of body politics, manifest most articulately through the feminist movement, was central to the initial stages of contemporary identity politics—the practice of shared politics based on markers of identity such as race, gender, or ethnicity. These political actions largely shaped the theatricality of contemporary culture as they became manifest in the spaces of the street and on the backs of flatbed trucks at public demonstrations, marches, and gatherings. The interplay between political concerns and theatrical aesthetics is visibly recorded from the late 1960s through the 1970s, and even a traditional account such as C. W. E. Bigsby's overview of U.S. theater displays an understanding of the centrality of this political spectacle to the cultural work of the period.[24]

During this period the practice of identity politics was central to theater, performance, and everyday life. Stemming from race, gender, and ethnic rights movements, the basic premise of identity politics is that one's politics and political platform are driven by one's identity. Under critical assault in the 1990s and slowly being recuperated, the practice of identity politics allowed previously unheard cohorts to gain a voice in the public arena by dint of establishing a coherent political platform based on personal identification with a particular group—women, blacks, Chicanos. The power of this movement also leads logically to a validation of difference in the act of creating space for representation. Participants recognized that the public arena and the supposedly universal practice of art and culture were in fact the products of those who had access to the means of production and the power to disseminate their ideas—predominantly white men. To counter this situation, a call went out for a reconsideration of culture and history to document and celebrate the contributions of marginalized groups. Practitioners of identity politics also encouraged a unique sense of contribution that leads logically to the construction of a fundamental or essential difference between groups. And, of course, validation of this model of essentialism allows for a positive assertion of specific traits that contribute to a larger whole, helping to shape a sense of identity, community, and belonging.

This implicit association between shared ethnicity and shared values is a legacy of the political power of social movements based on identity politics. *El Movimiento*, the Chicano movement, depended initially on an essential definition of Chicano identity based on biology and grounded in the history of colonialism and conquest. For individuals in the movement, the choice to be labeled Chicano was not only an acknowledgment of indigenous roots but also an acceptance of a new political and ethical sensibility based on a sense of *mestizaje,* or mixture. This self-labeling countered the dominant language of assimilation to "Anglo" culture that was represented by Mexican American identity but was predicated purely as a racial or ethnic identification. Unfortunately, Chicano identity as part of a radical unified political movement was established initially on a relatively limited conception of identity, not accounting for gender and sexuality as important political elements. This restriction occurred because the most efficient means of agreeing on a politics of identity is to limit that identity so as to establish a baseline of coherence for a political platform. Identity heterogeneity gained greater force in the late 1970s within civil rights spaces as women of color began asserting the need for attention not only to women's issues within the movements for ethnic rights but also to issues of ethnicity and race within the feminist movement. Chicana lesbian feminists Gloria Anzaldúa and Cherríe Moraga were among the most articulate organizers and promoters of this transformation in thinking in the early 1980s.[25] With this critique in place, Chicano identity from the 1980s on has been seen more as a cultural and political position than an essentialized identity, even as gestures of essentialism have been articulated through the construction of *mestiza* identity itself as a new "ethnicity."[26]

During the resurgence of ethnic performance in the mid 1960s, theatrical groups directly participated in the street-level transformations of politics and articulated their aesthetic platforms in explicit opposition to mainstream practice. In his "Notes on Chicano Theatre" from 1970, Luis Valdez argued that Chicano theater, which existed to explore Chicano reality and to deal with specific social issues, was a departure from the "antibiotic (anti-life)" productions of the professional and university theater.[27] In the same way, theater emerging from Puerto Rican, Boricua, or Nuyorican experience was concerned with the specific social and material circumstances of that community and with developing aesthetics to engage it. As groups and individuals achieved greater success and broader attention, they began to move in the direction of what might be called mainstream professional theater. The movement from the theatricalization of public spectacle in the United States during the 1960s—during which group demonstrations and theater were seen as an essential part of the practice of radical politics—to the theater in the late 1970s and 1980s has appeared to some as a depoliticization of ethnic drama.

According to Alberto Sandoval-Sánchez,

> Latino theater production proliferated in the 1960s and 1970s as a political theater of social consciousness that centered on issues of ethnic hybrid identity, discrimination, oppression, exploitation, underrepresentation, and misrepresentation. Since the 1980s, though, attention in Latino theater and (mainstream) regional playhouses and productions has been drawn to marketing, accessibility to the general public, theatrical and artistic professionalization, identifying targeted audiences for sponsorship, and crossing over in order to cater to Anglo-American audiences in English only.[28]

This shift is accompanied by the cultural and institutional recognition of *Hispanic* as a category of identity in the 1980 U.S. census.

The history, however, is not a story of "crossing over" but one of doing politics differently. The shift toward professionalization within Latino theater at the very moment of widespread recognition of Hispanic presence seems to confirm a shift away from radical politics to a platform of inclusion and assimilation. This trajectory, however, oversimplifies the cultural developments that make such a narrative possible and that are countered by the playwrights in this book. By the late 1970s, the radical claims of civil rights movements based on separatist and oppositional politics lost a great deal of their unified cultural energy. Participants in *El Movimiento* and the Puerto Rican Liberation movement moved away from cultural nationalist platforms toward a politics of affiliation and cultural celebration that privileged difference as a site of knowledge and understanding.[29] This shift occurred not only because of demands from within the movements to recognize the plurality of experience but also because of the emerging power of a Hispanic middle class intent on maintaining a positive mainstream representation connected to a politics of assimilation.

A second shift was manifest in the movement from a more politicized articulation of ethnic difference to a broader language of multiculturalism through a misapplication of the knowledge generated by ethnic studies. Ethnic studies departments, initially the product of activist demands during the rights movements, had demonstrated the importance of embodied knowledge within ethnic communities and insisted on understanding ethnicity as a way of knowing. These programs aided in the recuperation of cultural histories and often championed the argument that assimilation is a historically and culturally specific mode of engaging with U.S. culture rather than a universal or even necessarily desirable process. However, this valuation of ethnically specific epistemologies was transformed into a broader multiculturalism, in which participants in mainstream culture are expected to embrace difference as a means of expanding their own cultural horizons.

This problematic model sees ethnic knowledge and cultural production as supplements to a mainstream agenda rather than as sources of creativity and power. Difference is valued in a way that makes it safely consumable by mainstream audience members, allowing them a safe visit to the exotic and an unquestioned assumption of cultural understanding instead of an experience that forces them to reevaluate the very terms through which they engage with the world. In this transformation the reductive model of the melting pot is replaced by alternative culinary metaphors for cultural mixing that describe cohabitation of cultural space in which each group maintains a distinct flavor (tossed salad, for instance). It is not incidental that ethnicity, culture, and food are tied together in the multicultural project, since the preparation and consumption of food is the ethnic performance most easily commodified and appropriated to create a fictional sense of inclusion and community. Engaging theatrically with this mainstream multiculturalism without questioning it thus runs the risk of depoliticizing the theater, of "crossing over."

For El Teatro Campesino, the archetypal model of Chicano theater, the movement away from strictly agitprop theater, which was directed toward a specific political outcome through collaborative and collective creation, to a different and often more poetic theatrical language and aesthetics was neither a denial nor a turning away from political theater. Rather, political theater was reconceived as one that places less value on articulations of specific and immediate politics and more emphasis on politically informed multivalent theatrical presentations that contest the very practices of representation. Since the mid 1970s, Latino theater and public spectacle have been somewhat separate from revolutionary idealism and have in turn inspired notions of political effectiveness that recognize the importance of a broader audience willing to work for change. The emergence of the regional theater movement has clarified the possibility of political efficacy and consciousness-raising on a local level that leads to national understanding. To accomplish this consciousness-raising, the terms *by*, *for*, *about*, and *near* are being expanded to account for a heterogeneous and inclusive conception of the audience and political aims of Latino theater.

The Broadway production of Luis Valdez's play *Zoot Suit*, whose entrance into the mainstream was seen by many as a betrayal of the values of Chicano theater, marks the first step in this transformation.[30] The values that were broken in this act were predicated on a political consciousness of theater and an expectation that theater serve a unified group identity, an ethnic identity that was equated with a political and cultural position. Despite a lack of radical change in the overall social system, by the late 1970s Chicano theater as a movement paralleled the fragmentation of the larger Chicano movement, as issues of gender and sexuality were used to question the larger monolithic concept of Chicano identity. Implicit in this critique was an understanding that the shared community and values were masculinist and heterosexist, values that Alicia Arrizón and Lillian Manzor argue were still present in Latino producing spaces at the beginning of the 1990s.[31]

As suggested, one of the aids to the perceived depoliticization of Latino theater has been the co-optation and mainstreaming of multi-culturalism and diversity as two economically valuable terms. Main-stream multiculturalism became, and still is, a tool for transforming difference into something that can be easily consumed, thus avoiding the transformations that may result from serious and sustained mix-ing of cultures. However, this mainstreaming has also resulted in real economic support for the development of Latino playwrights and their plays. Various forms of funding helped projects such as the South Coast Repertory Hispanic Playwrights Project and INTAR's Hispanic Play-wrights in Residence workshops led by Maria Irene Fornes.[32]

In the 1980s writers tended to produce work that satisfied the de-mands of both a Latino community and a mainstream community searching for "universal" values about the relationship of identity and home. What emerged as a series of new languages of the theater were too quickly critically subsumed under a sloppy imposition of the aes-thetic category of magical realism; regrettably, the constraints of the association of magical realism with Latino cultural production remain in force. The 1990s saw an explicit shift for many artists from self-defi-nition as a Latino playwright to a playwright who is Latino, an implicit acknowledgment of the assumed but incorrect attachment of marginal-ization, tokenism, and ghettoization to the status of ethnic playwright. By the mid 1990s, many playwrights had clarified their discomfort with reductive notions of ethnic affiliations and were willing to question the "by" and "about" categories of ethnic theater through works ranging from Diana Son's *Stop Kiss*—a much more difficult play to label "ethnic" than her anthologized short work *R.A.W.*—to the founding document of the Campo Santo ensemble, based in San Francisco, that no longer insisted on a genealogical authenticity to provide legitimacy for a playwright's voicing of ethnic concerns.

With the awarding of the 2003 Pulitzer Prize to *Anna in the Tropics* by Cuban American playwright Nilo Cruz, the critical and contextual understanding of the importance of *for* and *near* is understood primarily in metaphoric and symbolic terms. At the same time, the tribalism and cultural nationalism firmly visible within the original conceptual space of *for* and *near* become contested political positions. Political radicalism is understood as a necessary step in political achievement, not a sustainable political practice. *For* is expanded in consensus-building gestures that invoke the term *Latino* to appeal not only to the established Puerto Rican, Cuban American, Mexican American, and Chicano communities but also to new immigrants from Mexico and other parts of Central and South America. These terms provide categorical limits that help define the shape of aesthetic and cultural reception, but they also appear central to a necessary cycle of evolution and renewal.

While the nascent stages of an identity politics of theater demand the protected incubation of a mode of writing contained through *by*, *for*, *about*, and *near*, these markers either disappear or acquire new definitions to keep from limiting the possibilities of creation. Thus, the continued use of these terms requires a sustained engagement that allows their meanings to shift to reflect changing cultural realities and intellectual models. Keeping these terms as an element in the dialogue helps us realize the ongoing shift from the immediacy of the perceived and the lived as reflected in the theater to the space of the theoretical and conceptual. This movement to the conceptual is necessary in part to counter the unfortunate effect of a Pulitzer on the contemporary state of Latino theater. The supposed moment of arrival marked by Nilo Cruz's *Anna in the Tropics* has become a justification for the removal of regional support for Latino theater outside specific Latino producing organizations.[33]

This prize illustrates the complexity of the representational issues at stake. While Cruz's play is an impressive piece of work and deserves its accolades, it is ironic that a play so deeply invested in the process of reading would win such an award. This irony shows up on a couple of levels. While individuals have speculated that the only Latino play that could win a Pulitzer has a Tolstoy novel as a central character, it is clear that some of the potential political radicalism of the social space Cruz documents, the socialism of the tobacco factory workers, is not made visible. While documenting the radicalism was not the intent of his play, the more interesting issue is that of reading. On the one hand, the fact that the Pulitzer jury awarded the prize without ever seeing the play attests to the power of language.[34] However, from another point of view, by only reading the play, the jury members not only placed it in the familiar realm of something to be read rather than fully produced (as too often happens with Latino theater) but also avoided dealing with the real complexities of casting and representing Latino bodies on the stage. The Latino body could stay safely in the space of the imagination.

What has been neglected in this account of a genealogical shift away from politics to a mainstream accessibility is that this history is a constant process of *wrighting*. Rather than merely reflecting the contemporary debates, the theater challenges and moves beyond these debates, creating alternative models and exposing the limits of existing ones. While the contexts of these claims shift, assumptions about the political elements of the theater are often limited to subject and content rather than structure and form. If indeed the work becomes more accessible and more acceptable, it is a product of the fine line that the playwrights negotiate in their acts of *wrighting*, correcting, revising, and restructuring the intersection of spectator and actor in the act of creating theater. This fine line is exemplified in the craft of bilingual writing that remains accessible to a monolingual audience. Playwrights employ techniques that range from questions in one language and answers in another to repetition of words in one language in the replies of another character, and in a tour de force, José Rivera's *Cloud Tectonics* motivates the possibility of repeating a central monologue in both English and Spanish. While this repetition is a form of capitulation to an English-speaking audience and a desire for mainstreaming, it is also a recognition that some Latinos are monolingual English speakers and, more important, it can be seen as an exercise in the pedagogy of Spanish, exposing readers and audience to language in translation, providing them the tools to learn.

Wrighting Ethnicity

The intersection of identity politics and theater has made increasingly clear that the stage is an ideal space in which to explore a multiplicity of cultural identities, to understand new possibilities for cultural formation, and to draw attention to the continued tension in the embodiment of any given identity. However, race and ethnicity as categories of identity and analysis within the theater have received systematic and sustained scholarly attention only since the 1990s, at the same moment when the anthropological and sociological communities began more clearly articulating the contested nature of ethnicity itself. While there has certainly been significant scholarship prior to this period, the majority of it was invested in documentation and thematic exploration.[35] Despite a long history of attention to racially and ethnically marked characters in the theater (as foreigners, as others, etc.), these characters have been primarily understood as thematic elements or symbolic functions of difference, as types, rather than as integral and central figures of analysis.

The need for a shift to ethnicity as a central focus of critical analysis is articulated cogently in the introduction to Josephine Lee's groundbreaking *Performing Asian America*, where she both defends the specific limits of her investigation and asserts that the scope of her analysis is shaped by the nature of the artists' preoccupations based in part on their specific cultural position. Her argument that "[w]e can no longer assume that the canonical classics can be evaluated according to supposedly universal or objective aesthetic standards, with works by artists of color added to the repertory solely to ensure political representation" clarifies the need for a different way of thinking through the aesthetics of her texts. According to Lee, the works she deals with

> share . . . certain theatrical strategies that make issues of performance, dramatic form, and audience response inseparable from considerations of ethnicity and race. Traditional theories of theatrical presentation have not allowed for a discussion of how the perception of race and ethnicity affects cognition and meaning in the theater. In order to understand the emerging ways of constructing not only what is Asian American, but what is more generally racialized or ethnicized, I suggest we begin by developing a more complex critical vocabulary and a theoretical position from which to talk about the theater.[36]

Lee's insight points towards a similar issue in all theater in which ethnicity is marked. She calls for a new "theoretical position" that can account for what is actually happening in the theater and the ways that it engages with the complexity of life practice and representation. *Contemporary Latina/o Theater: Wrighting Ethnicity*, however, takes a different approach to this moment of analysis, in part because, although there are strategies for attending to race and ethnicity, as well as increased attention to these issues, the attention they receive rarely moves beyond acknowledgment of their existence as a reflection of cultural difference. Ethnicity is not fully understood as something that produces a space for experience, generates cultural knowledge, and offers alternatives to models of identity consistently trapped within a representational paradigm. Nor is ethnicity fundamentally understood as something structured in the same mode of analytic framework as theatricality itself. To understand the possibility of this connection we need not a new position but rather a new framework that enables an audience to recognize not only the creation of aesthetic and emotional pleasure through theatrical art but also the creation of theoretical alternatives for thinking of and through ethnicity. Latino playwrights use the theater to materialize new models of ethnicity, often doing so ahead of theorists who discuss cultural practice.[37]

Playwrighting is a powerful space for the articulation of materially grounded theory whose comprehensibility is heightened not only by the process of staging but also through the conventional and widespread understanding of the complexities of the genre of theater itself. The complex mode of reception demanded by theater and historically labeled the "suspension of disbelief" by Coleridge is not often recognized for its intellectual complexity. Retaining knowledge in a suspended state and keying the experience to recognize the not-really-real status of intention on the stage are just two of the activities taken for granted by the accessible aesthetics of psychological realism. Of course, one of the primary goals of mainstream realism in the United States is to do everything possible to train the actors to convince themselves that what they are doing is exactly what they want to do at that moment—constructing motivations and objectives based on the characters they are playing.

However, even as we see a character or a chair in a play, we also see the body of the actor or the specific architectural design and color scheme of the chair. The chair is chosen to match the overall design of the set, helping to establish the cultural context, the socioeconomic status of the characters, and the nature of the stage space. Depending on the extent to which it is a chair that probably would not appear off-stage, it also reflects particular thematic, characterological, or conceptual traits within its design. With a chair on stage the audience has the freedom to determine, from the nature of the play, that any or all of the aspects of the chair have meaning. For example, scale and ostentation relative to the bodies on stage might effectively shift the status of characters in relationship to their environment. Like the chair, the bodies themselves can be read for all of their various parts, and here ethnicity becomes legible in the theater. Even while accepting the agreed-upon convention, the audience never forgets that the actor is both the character and the actor simultaneously. Though perfectly obvious, the very impatience with rehearsing this structure erases the mental complexity of sustaining this multiplicity of identity that, in the space of written articulations of critical theory, requires the use of complex new articulations of thinking.

In realism, the dominant U.S. cultural form of representation, ethnicity is marked by a visual literality indicated by skin color, eye shape, and other physical features, as well as language use, costume, and gesture. The farther the play moves from the space of realism, the less sociological pressure is placed on the significance of ethnicity in the body of the actor. However, even when there is clear sociological pressure to create an accurate and authentic representation based on shared ethnicity, there is a great lack of clarity about its actual meaning as a significant marker of identity. This uncertainty is typically disguised by employing stereotypical assumptions about cultural behavior, usually explained away as common sense, while always carefully adding the liberal piety that each person is a unique individual regardless of her or his assumed position within a cultural group. However, since objects and bodies on the stage represent both themselves and the sign of themselves ("this man" and "man" in general), the burden of representation attached to ethnically marked bodies, in which an individual is assumed to represent a group, is heightened in the space of the theater. Thus, a Latino man is representing a Latino man in addition to his character. And this is precisely what allows an audience to read the Crossover King as a model of essential Latino identity. However, it is important to retain possibilities and keep the question of meaning open. What does it mean to represent a Latino, and how can playwrights create the texts in which this question can be explored?

Ambivalence and multiplicity are sustained by the very nature of theatrical space. As a liminal space the theater enables the conventional suspension of disbelief that allows us to replace the body of the actor with the body of the character. However, this replacement is in many ways suspended in the moment of its realization—no one ever forgets the reality of the actor's body. Still, the meaning of that body is too easily assumed to be a further example of an increasingly codified and stereotyped version of identity—it stands in for what is already known. The average spectator for theater is accustomed to processing the reality of a character overlaid on an actor and allowing those two images to blend together into an experience that is never fully settled. This same conventionally trained spectator intuitively understands the complexity of the postmodern experience of identity that insists on fragmentation, division, lack of authenticity, and most important, a situation in which an individual is both X and Y. This "both/and" logic is built into the multilayered representation and reception of theater itself in a manner accessible to individual spectators. Thus, theater becomes a powerful means of illustrating and examining the sustained paradoxes, doublings, and excesses used to explicate the complexities of contemporary identity, doing so in a manner familiar to spectators comfortable with the conventions of both the genre and the space.

For this transformation to occur, ethnicity must be understood as something that can be made and remade, not just a fixed relationship. Otherwise, the practice of objectification may be reasserted, that is, an object of study may be based on an assumption of a category rather than a willingness to chart the contours of what is actually presented. This limiting practice of reception grounds a practice of perception in which the stereotype becomes an efficient shorthand for gaining cultural knowledge in a complex and increasingly intertwined cultural landscape. This tendency to reduce, to assume, and to limit is not always practiced from the outside, as Latino communities have also found themselves narrowing their focus, deemphasizing the complexity and the ambivalence of their position to achieve a reasonable sense of political efficacy. This efficacy, however, is directly opposed to a practice of *wrighting* that engages and embraces complexity.

Rather than passively responding to and deconstructing cultural assumptions placed on them, the playwrights represented in this book are actively crafting new forms of ethnicity from their understandings of identity and community and manifesting them through various forms of theatricality. This act of *wrighting* allows a focus on the processual dynamics of ethnicity as performed and witnessed. The plays here illustrate the structures that attempt to shape the production and reception of ethnicity in the theater and in everyday life. In doing so, they demonstrate the limits of conventional thinking about ethnicity. To accomplish this aim, the playwrights interrogate ambiguities that

emerge and are sustained in the construction of identity and foster recognition of the complex cultural forces that help shape the literal and
metaphorical staging of identity and community. Symbiotically creating
and correcting, revising and reorienting, they highlight the edges of
existing conceptual frameworks to point to a space beyond.

The necessity of reconceptualizing ethnicity through *wrighting* is exemplified in *The LA LA Awards* by Latins Anonymous. First produced
in 1992, this work is intended as *"a satirical up-to-the minute look at
the Latino presence in Hollywood."*[38] *The LA LA Awards* questions
how Latinos are represented in the media and interrogates the crisis of
representation of Latinos through parody. The play carefully details
each scene to allow the audience to understand the complexities of
representation and to question the structures of power that enable
specific forms.

This hilarious piece critiques a number of cultural assumptions, but
its most explicit reference to *wrighting* is demonstrated in the "live reenactment clip" of the nominee for "'Best actress in a movie starring
a bleeding-heart liberal who wants to act in a mainstream minority
project.'"[39] The two nominees, María María and Meryl Estripada,
perform a scene from "'Cry Me over the Border'" in which "María,
a young urban Latina" is forced to perform an impoverished third-
world identity to satisfy Mrs. Wright's demand for a "maid, er . . .
housekeeper." Mrs. Wright's self-correction demonstrates how political
correctness in language merely changes the word and not the cultural
assumptions behind it. Mrs. Wright is looking for someone to whom she
can provide not only employment but also an act of charity. To enable
this act, Mrs. Wright demands a specific performance from María: she
must embody a stereotypical disadvantaged immigrant. Mrs. Wright
becomes a writer, scripting María's performance just as the playwrights
themselves create this explicit act of writing.

The placement of both actresses in competition for the award not
only allows for reenactment of the scene but also foregrounds competing ideas about Latina identity. María's performance (as Maid María)
involves the development of an accent, as well as an increasingly ri-
diculous and contradictory family history that exaggerates a range of
stereotypes placed on the Latina body, beginning with the assumption
of third-world status, poverty, and terror summed up in the demand
for "[i]ntrinsically oppressed indigenous brown people." Mrs. Wright
expects a María who fulfills all of her preconceptions, and out of economic necessity, María performs this role for the sake of employment,

reinscribing the stereotypes and reassuring Mrs. Wright of her "rightness." María's rights are subordinated to her economic need, and yet she also wins the award, suggesting both the success of her acting and the pleasure that critics derive from this particular performance. María María might initially appear to be safely separated from the implications of her actions—she is, after all, acting—but she accepts the award in the braids that aided her supposed transition from urban Latina to impoverished, rural Mexicana. They become the reason for her victory: "I just want to thank my braids who made it all happen."[40] Her clear understanding of the power of extrinsic visual markers (hairstyle) as a catalyst for success leads to a question regarding María's own professional agency outside the performance of visual stereotypes. Her sheer joy in accepting the award also increases the irony of the situation.

Even more important than this irony is that Mrs. Wright is played by a Latina actress who ventriloquizes the voice of power, demanding conformity to her personal stereotypes. While María's transition is still ambivalent, Mrs. Wright's function as the villain of this piece reaffirms the importance of *wrighting* as a simultaneous act of creation, correction, and cultural positioning. The assertion of the stereotypical frames of Latina and bleeding-heart liberal in the actress who plays Mrs. Wright (and remember that María is one as well) makes liberalism an empty escape from the problem of representing Latinas in an adequately complex way. It fails to attend to the reality of their presence as professionals, as members of the middle and upper classes, and as citizens of the United States whose pedigree may be longer than those of the majority of people who assume they are immigrants. Understanding the challenges posed by Mrs. Wright's representational practice requires a new conceptual space. In the process of making space for a sustainable conception of Latina identity and community, Latins Anonymous heightens the multiple layers of ambiguity to chart both the necessity and the conceptual difficulty of offering an alternative framework to the unexamined and self-centered investment of the Mrs. Wrights of the world. Because Mrs. Wright is Latina herself (and even more powerfully, second-best actress in her category), the easy assumption of a demand for a specific kind of Latina performance by a supposedly Anglo audience is complicated because of the voice that demands the stereotype. The critique of the stereotypical bleeding-heart liberal who wants to rectify a social problem but who can do so only through the creation of a stereotypical problem also makes clear that merely being visible and vocal does not change the situation.

Cultural expectations from both within and outside cultural groups continue to shape what one can do and say and still obtain the job or the award. And, more important, the assumption of representation attached to liberal guilt is disguised as a form of generosity that is really less about correcting a social problem or aiding an individual in need than it is about increasing the giver's self-esteem. Unfortunately, this patronizing gesture is the most visibly practiced alternative to a complete lack of acknowledgment. The assumption that a Latina must take on an immigrant identity to obtain an acting job is not absolved by the presence of a bleeding-heart liberal, despite the assumed conservatism of blithely imposing immigrant status on a Latina body.

The only way out of this impasse is to create a new space not just for representing but for thinking and doing. The complexities of representation, here presented ironically but accurately, require the transformation of reception and performance at multiple levels. Preexisting forms of representation must be questioned and the limits of their assumptions revealed through critical irony or an alternative narrative, but more important, there must be a space for an alternative structure. While this scene does not fully wright a new conceptual framework, it nonetheless implies the imaginative possibility of an alternative in which performance is not transformed on demand. Instead, it calls for a space in which a young urban Latina character, a Latina actor, can speak for herself rather than in the ventriloquized voice of an identity or a politics imposed on her.

Documented in the remaining pages of *Contemporary Latina/o Theater: Wrighting Ethnicity* are playwrights who engage in this practice; that is, they speak for themselves. Theirs is not merely an act of writing, of giving voice to the issues, or of righting, of correcting assumptions and revising limited models of identity and history. It is an act of *wrighting*, of creating something new in the process of correction and revision that moves beyond cultural assumptions that limit thinking and place Latinos in demarcated cultural spaces. Moving beyond the demands for authenticity, the limits of fixed definitions of ethnicity, and the well-intended gestures of multiculturalism that insist on honoring Latino contributions as long as they are both comprehensible and comfortable, the playwrights here expose the structures that shape our reality and offer energizing and transformational alternatives.

Miguel Piñero's Theatricality: Fear, Respect, and Community

So here I am, look at me
I stand proud as you can see
pleased to be from the Lower East
a street fighting man
a problem of this land
I am the Philosopher of the Criminal Mind
a dweller of prison time
a cancer of Rockefeller's ghettocide
this concrete tomb is my home
to belong to survive you gotta be strong
you can't be shy less without request
someone will scatter your ashes thru
the Lower East Side.

    —Miguel Piñero, "A Lower East Side Poem"

To be a man whom others respect and to be respected is another
of the basic demands of our masculinity. Although respect is not
exclusive to men, since women also give and demand respect, we
see the demand on men with a certain particularity, because encounters between men are basically influenced by mechanisms of
power; on occasion power and respect become synonymous. . . .
Respect is taken to mean the appropriate comportment in social
encounters, in both the manner of behaving and the reaction to
how others behave.

    —Rafael L. Ramírez, *What It Means to Be a Man:*
    Reflections on Puerto Rican Masculinity

From the Streets to the Theater

On Sunday, August 17, 1969, a five-foot-high wall of burning garbage blocked all six lanes of traffic on Third Avenue in El Barrio, the Puerto Rican neighborhood in East Harlem. This spectacular culmination of a political protest begun on July 27 was designed to draw attention to the Department of Sanitation's failure to provide adequate service in the neighborhood. Organized by the New York chapter of the Young Lords Party, a radical left Puerto Rican organization working for liberation on the island and within the United States, the "Garbage Offensive" moved from sweeping the streets to burning the garbage piles. According to Miguel Melendez, one of the organizers of the event,

> Every single Young Lord threw a match. Every single person of our community who had helped, threw matches. In a matter of minutes it was like an ancient ceremony, with flames high into the skies, reaching to touch our gods. It was a collective cry of "¡Basta ya!"—"Enough!" As the garbage burned and the flames grew, people nearby cheered spontaneously. We all felt the spirit of winning, the triumph of good over evil, where justice, in this moment, prevailed. I remembered the revolutionary and spiritual marriage with the people. The dominoes players, the doñas, and the Young Lords had all found themselves in the middle of the garbage protest. At that moment we knew we were victorious. Indeed it was a theatrical scene. Flames went up spectacularly as people started to scream with joy.[1]

The theatricality of this communal act of resistance marked the beginning of a series of highly visible and controversial actions performed by the Young Lords with varying degrees of community support. These actions included the occupation of the First Spanish Methodist Church and Lincoln Hospital with the intent both to redirect the resources of these institutions toward the real needs of the community and to hold the institutions responsible for the well-being of the community. For example, the church, occupied on multiple occasions, was transformed into the People's Church to provide health care, food, clothing, and cultural activities.

The Young Lords' insistence on reclaiming the resources of the community for the material needs of its inhabitants provided a concrete focus for their political action. These events drew media attention and catalyzed responses from administrative officials, but they were contro-versial both inside and outside the community, and the revolutionaries were unable to maintain unified support for their radical activities. These spectacular actions did not generate the sustained impact their instigators hoped for, and political energy shifted to a larger concern with colonialism on a global scale.[2] The period of radical, theatrical intervention, labeled the "era of radical barrio politics" by Pedro Guzman, came to an end by 1973 as "a result of both internal factionalism and external pressures," including harassment by the FBI. This era was followed by what political scientist Sherrie Baver calls a period of "expanded participation and new pragmatism" involving more traditional strategies of mainstream electoral politics: a transformation in the political landscape from guerrilla activism to new modes of articulating the needs and pursuing the cultural and political aims of the community.[3]

This movement toward mainstream political action occurred simultaneously with a corresponding transfer of energy from radical street politics to radical street aesthetics that situate, explore, and celebrate the experiences of Puerto Ricans in New York. The focus shifted away from a Eurocentric investment characteristic of Puerto Rican belles lettres on the island to acknowledge the central role of urban, mainland experiences in Puerto Rican identity, culture, and politics. Products of personal experience, as well as analysis of the lived conditions that provoked political protest, these emerging works were deeply infused with the politics of the existing cultural milieu but at the same time were resistant to the perceived dogmatism of revolutionary organizations. According to Pedro Pietri, poet and playwright whose poem "Puerto Rican Obituary" forms the front material for the 1971 Young Lords' book *Palante*, "In 1971, after the Young Lords disbanded and the Black Panthers were on the wane, that's when I got into theater. Because all those political organizations—the Black Panthers, the Young Lords, the Movimiento pro Independencia [Movement for Independence]—wanted to control your mind. . . . [I]t was the people in the theater that got back my trust in human nature."[4] Pietri's entry into the world of theater at the waning of guerrilla politics exemplifies the larger shift of community action from political outlets into artistic creation through poetry and theater. His rejection of the implicit dogmatism of the radical groups is not an abandonment of the political aim to make specific voices heard but rather a redirection of energy into the complexity of aesthetic representation.

This new aesthetic movement was labeled Nuyorican, a conflation of a location, New York, and a national and cultural identity, Puerto Rican. The term references both the people and the aesthetic. According to Nuyorican poet and scholar Miguel Algarín, the name emerged from an experience he and Miguel Piñero shared in the San Juan airport:

> . . . then I heard the word *newyorican* but I did not know they were talking about Piñero and me. I did not understand. Finally, when we were waiting for our bags I paid attention: *new-yo-rican*, that is, New York and Puerto Rican. They were looking down on us, as if we were nothing. We were Puerto Ricans talking in English, and that to them was contemptuous. . . . Then, when we got back to New York, I found that William Morrow had sent me a contract for an anthology that was published in 1975 and that they wanted to call *Puerto Rican Poets in English*. And I said to Piñero: "Why don't we give the title of *newyorican* to this anthology?" Piñero said: "But I am not new anything, I am not *neo*, that is an intellectualism." So I asked him, "What are we then?" And we both said, "We are *nuyoricans*." We spelled it like that, and we said it like that and in less than six months after the anthology was published the word connected and now has currency all over.[5]

Nuyorican acknowledged for the first time the specific cultural experience of Puerto Ricans in New York, validating it through an aesthetic whose hybrid and street-inflected language reflected the everyday lives of this community. *Nuyorican* celebrates the cultural and linguistic forms that emerged from an identity tied not to the island of Puerto Rico but to a diasporic identity reflected through the urban realities of New York neighborhoods. This label was quickly attached to the theatricality of the street and embraced communally and publicly in the "circa 1973" founding of the Nuyorican Poets Café by Algarín and the newly titled *Nuyorican Poetry: An Anthology of Words and Feelings*.[6]

Even before the publication of this anthology and this wrighting of Nuyorican identity, Piñero had already received significant critical acclaim for his prison drama *Short Eyes*, the first Latino play on Broadway.[7] In addition to this famous work, developed with the help of Marvin Felix Camillo's theater group The Family, Piñero wrote a number of plays, poems, and television dramas and had brief stints as an actor on stage and screen.[8] Because of his phenomenal success with

Short Eyes and his centrality to the articulation of the Nuyorican aesthetic, Piñero is often considered the seminal playwright within New York Puerto Rican theater in English.[9]

Piñero left few written records beyond his published works, in part because he defined himself as a countercultural figure whose street credentials provided the creative energy and vision for his theater. Consequently, a great deal of the biographical history that illuminates Piñero's cultural and aesthetic investments is based on the anecdotal recounting of a life on the edge. His biography reflects many of the sociopolitical realities of being a part of the Puerto Rican underclass in New York, including poverty and underemployment. Migrating to the mainland at a very young age, he worked and stole to support his family, passing in and out of various legal institutions before finally receiving a longer sentence for armed robbery in Sing-Sing (Ossining Prison), where he was introduced to Camillo and wrote his first poetry and theater. Piñero's choice of subject matter—a representation of life in the barrio, in prison, and among people hustling for a living on the streets—reflects his personal experiences. His urban theatricality celebrates the poetry of the everyday life of the street and wrights a new form of ethnicity that embodies the political and cultural realities of being Puerto Rican in New York.[10]

Because Piñero began writing for the theater while incarcerated, his work that explores criminalized identities is the product of what Antonio Gramsci would call an "organic intellectual," one whose sensibilities and political projects arise directly from the circumstances that developed his consciousness. Understanding Piñero as an organic intellectual helps displace the dangerous representational practice of reading ethnic cultural production as sociological, merely autobiographical, or slice-of-life from the spaces he inhabited, an especially dangerous possibility with Piñero, whose work often engages naturalistically with the underclass. In the early 1970s reviewers often invoked adjectives such as *raw*, *immediate*, and *documentary* to describe his work, words that, unfortunately, displaced and disempowered Piñero's original insights in their attempts to understand the aesthetics of a new voice.[11]

Piñero's cultural legacy, beyond his published texts, includes the traces of his presence in the stories of the artists he influenced, stories whose passion helps to shape the critical response to his engagement with the world. The practice of storytelling about Piñero reflects the same aesthetic of embodied presence demonstrated in his poetry and theater, a gritty materialism that acknowledges the pleasures and survival strategies of an urban underclass. His biography is filled with the artistry of everyday life performance, an aesthetic also present in Leon Ichaso's film biography *Piñero*. The stories of those who had the privilege (and often the frustration) to know and work with him include one by choreographer Alvin Ailey who reminisced about riding with Piñero in "a long black limousine, late-thirties vintage, with an open top. Miguel and I would often drive through the Lower East Side, standing on the backseat of the limo, with our heads and bodies out, waving to the people in the street. They would yell 'Hey, it's Mikey. Hey Mikey!' They didn't know who I was. We were waving like the pope, both of us totally spaced out of our minds."[12] Ailey's anecdote recalls not only Piñero's celebrity status in the Lower East Side, a predominantly Puerto Rican neighborhood at the time, but also his fondness for engaging directly with his audience. Lois Elaine Griffith recalls an earlier and more specifically theatrical moment that reflects this same sense of engagement: "It was 1973 when Miguel Piñero taught me about theater. Mikey could stand on a street corner, gather a crowd around him, and spit out a poem that induced action from an audience—an audience completely unaware that their response was creating a drama about the intensity of everyday life."[13]

An exploration of the Puerto Rican community in New York, *Nuyorican Stories* (1999), by the Chicano comedy troupe Culture Clash, offers another document of his performance energy. Richard Montoya, one of the members, relates the following anecdote about Pinero's response to his own question posed to a group of Chicano poets standing on a New York street corner in 1974: "'What is the greatest Chicano poem ever written?' They thought about it. No one said anything. Then, Piñero lifted up his shirt sleeve and there tattooed on his arm, were three words . . . 'Mi Vida Loca.' . . . My crazy life. That, Piñero said, was the greatest Chicano poem ever written."[14] This moment not only serves as a strong reminder of the similarities between these two movements in which aesthetics and cultural identity politics were often closely aligned but also emphasizes the centrality of lived experience to Nuyorican and Chicano theatricality.

A later passage in *Nuyorican Stories* reinforces the transitional nature of Puerto Rican intellectual and cultural life in New York in 1974, the year *Short Eyes* premiered. Speaking nostalgically in a theoretical vein Piñero himself would never have used, Miguel Algarín recounts, "I think the most important part about '74, young man, was the fact that I came to the realization that we were living in an age of no theories. No socialism, no communism. They had all fucked-up and died, so in an age of theory (or lack of theory), there was nothing left but lust."[15] What is intended to be a pessimistic statement about the failure of liberationist politics is in fact the implicit articulation of a new form of embodied theory. If there is "nothing left but lust," then lust itself, desire, becomes the material for wrighting identity.

While Algarin bemoaned the lack of theory in 1974, Piñero stepped forward at this moment, employing his lust to live life to the fullest, to shape not only many of his central characters but also his own life practice. Desire for life and the creative valuation of lived experience provide the genesis for his writing. This writerly aesthetic is made explicit in two of his one-act plays, *Cold Beer* and *Tap Dancing and Bruce Lee Kicks*, through the character of Mike Poor, a *"Beer-bellied poet"* who functions as an avatar for Piñero himself. *Cold Beer* is Poor's story of writing on demand in which the events of the day combine with his imagined encounters into a single piece of theater written with "movement . . . rhythm." Two darkly humorous real events—a visit by a cop asking him to stop pissing on the neighbor's dog and two young kids looking for attention—are split by an imagined visit by a salesman offering him a blowjob. These encounters form the subject of the play Mike is writing. The last image in the play is the sound of *"Typing . . . heard all over the Echo Park district of Los Angeles that night."* In *Tap Dancing*, a series of scenes in three different apartments, Mike is found in the middle scene writing for a commission. He writes a central character who "wished he had it inside himself to capture all the sounds that invade his privacy" because "[t]hey painted a picture only a Michelangelo could create." This desire to make art out of life is an explicit articulation of Piñero's practice of wrighting, most successfully achieved in his play *Short Eyes*.[16]

Short Eyes: Losing Community through Fear

Piñero's most celebrated play, *Short Eyes* tells the story of one day in "the House of Detention," exploring the ethical dynamics of community in a total institution.[17] The prison functions as a microcosmic mirror for exploring codes of interethnic interaction in the broader social macrocosm, as Piñero himself indicated: "Prison is a society within a society. It's a reflection of life in the streets. The jargon may be different, but we think and feel the same as on the streets."[18] *Short Eyes'* naturalistic aesthetics follow the traditional unities of time, place, and action, and chart the disruption of an established community through the entrance of an outsider followed by a restoration of order. The outsider, Clark Davis, a white, middle-class pederast, is placed with a small group of inmates who have established a pattern of interaction in keeping with the larger structures of the prison. Clark is killed after he resists an attempted rape and threatens to turn the perpetrators in to the authorities. The only character who refuses to participate in this abuse is Juan, a Puerto Rican whose crime is never named but who has a chance to return to the streets rather than serve hard time upstate. He becomes the ethical voice of the play and, through his willingness to listen, is placed in the awkward position of father confessor to Clark, a man whose crime places him outside the race-based networks of affiliation that structure life within the prison.

There is only one location in the play, a "Dayroom . . . in the House of Detention,"[19] an institutional space that functions as a transitional space. The inmates have not yet had their cases resolved—they are awaiting bail, sentencing, and conviction. The oppression and control of the institution is materialized for the audience through the disembodied voices of authority demanding an accounting of the prisoners. The constant noise and absence of personal space free from scrutiny are heightened in the film version, shot in "the Tombs," a Manhattan house of detention no longer in use. This oppressive structure establishes a framework for the explicit assertion of power and the inmates' various forms of resistance.

As in the rest of the prison, the population of this dayroom is divided racially, and the emerging tensions are articulated primarily through this nexus, though geography and personal politics trouble the easy establishment of racial groups. Throughout the play, sexual and intraracial tensions are consistently shifted into interracial tensions. For example, even before Clark's arrival, tension has been established through the desire of some of the inmates for Julio, nicknamed Cupcakes, to become sexually available, to turn "stuff." Since he has no "plexes," no psychological complexes, there is no reason, in the logic of prison life, why he can't be penetrated by the other men, be the bottom in a male-male sexual encounter; however, he refuses. As usual, from the moment Cupcakes enters the dayroom, the teasing begins, but this banter quickly shifts into racial tension made explicit by El Raheem, a black Muslim who is trying to use his prison time to better himself. He castigates Omar, another black inmate, for "deliberately acting and thinking out of your nature . . . thinking like the white devil, Yacoub," before quickly shifting his attack to Longshoe Charlie Murphy, the only

33

white inmate. Their verbal conflict results in a fight that is restaged as a "fair fight" with the support of Mr. Nett, an old-school white prison guard much closer to the inmates than his superiors would like him to be. This fight explicitly illustrates the inter-racial tension and establishes Nett's sense of control over the inmates.[20]

Clark's initial entrance is also racially marked, as the inmates, while playfully insulting him, call on Longshoe's responsibility, based on a shared whiteness, to introduce his "kin."[21] The newcomer draws attention away from Cupcakes, who exploits the distraction so as to divert attention from his own body as a site of sexual interest. Although the discourses of ethnic identity and sexual availability are operating in dialogue in this play, creating interplay between the politics of identity and the politics of lust, they are actually operating in different realms. Ethnicity and race are fixed, while sexual practice has an element of choice.[22]

The conception of ethnicity is made clear in the "program," the model of prison life that Longshoe explains to Clark. According to the "Glossary of Slang" at the end of the published play, a program is

> The do's and don'ts of prison life. Programs are ethnically determined: they are different for whites, blacks, Puerto Ricans, etc. Programs are not enforced by prison authorities; they are determined by the prisoners themselves. The program for the whole prison population regulates the way in which members of different ethnic groups relate to one another in specific situations. It rigidly governs who sits with whom in the mess hall; where people sit in the auditorium; who smokes first; etc. It is the first thing a prisoner learns when he enters an institution. Failure to follow the program is a sure way to have trouble with fellow inmates and will result in physical reprisals—sometimes death.[23]

According to the program, ethnic identification not only is fixed but also directly determines behavioral options and choices. Ethnic disloyalty is the gravest possible offense against the community. It is possible to establish and maintain the hierarchy of a functioning society only through careful negotiations carried on with a full awareness of racialized groupings. White men are the minority in this world, which means their very existence rests on a precarious negotiation between two much larger groups, African Americans and Puerto Ricans. This inversion of the world outside is unfortunately an accurate reflection of the population behind bars.

The program can be read as either a divisive product of institutional colonization or a productive strategy of resistance. On this particular floor it appears to be a strategy of resistance based on an established model of communal discussion: "Anything that would affect the whole floor . . . we would hold council on it, right?"[24] Ice, a black inmate, reminds Juan. While in agreement, Juan also insists, "The council was set up to help, not to destroy."[25] Even in the institutional space of prison, community is a possibility, but maintenance of a healthy and productive one is difficult. While this racial system is problematic, it parallels the practice of identity politics in which networks of affiliation are assumed on the basis of shared markers of race and ethnicity. Clark's entrance and crime displaces this structure, and through this displacement "Piñero exposes the constructedness of deviant identity."[26] The nature of Clark's crime stretches the limits of this community, as he is placed outside the racialized structure of the prison.

Clark's crime is exposed by the deliberate comment of a disgusted Nett. Nett's action not only asserts his power over Clark but also reinforces his ability to manipulate the inmates, a power already demonstrated by granting Longshoe and El Raheem a "fair fight." Nett knows what the other prisoners will think of Clark's transgression, and by publicly naming it, he ensures that Clark will lose the protection of the established inmate community. This absence of protection eventually manifests itself as Clark's availability as stuff, demonstrating the way Piñero shifts personal responses to the hierarchy of power into questions of desire. Clark's crime justifies the inmates' behavior in their own mind, and the institutional condemnation voiced by Nett provides legitimacy to their swift and brutal rejection of him, establishing a sense of community and identity predicated on the negative practice of exclusion.

Clark's crime is not only the source of the play's title but also a label that carries an etymology steeped in ethnicity and sexuality. According to the glossary in the play text, *short eyes* is the term for a child molester, the lowest of the low. The crime is looked on with disgust and is given its own particular prison label.[27] Although the reaction to Clark's crime reframes the sexualized joking prior to his introduction, an alternative etymology of *short eyes* forges a stronger link between the inmates' sexual behavior and his crime. In an interview with Norma

Alarcón McKesson, Piñero suggested that the title came from the Puerto Rican pronunciation of the term for pornography, "short heist."[28] This slippage between the official and the personal account of the term echoes the slippage in the play between the official line and the personal explanation for behavior. If the Puerto Rican pronunciation of a slang term for pornography is the same as the slang term for child molester, then the detailed attention to sexual desire and pornography that the inmates share establishes a clear connection between their behavior and Clark's transgression. Through this intimacy Piñero questions the extent to which community is brought into being by defining the "other" as more distant from the self than is actually the case.

A confessional scene at the center of the play draws attention to the intersections of ethnicity and desire. While confirming the premeditated nature of his activity, Clark uses racial and ethnic categories to distinguish differing attitudes toward sexuality. Left alone with Juan, he indicates awareness of the horror of his transgressions in the eyes of a broader culture, though he is unable to view them as such. He is in denial about the destructive power of his lust as he relates the story of his primal scene, a moment of flashing his little sister's Hispanic friend. His next two encounters were with Puerto Rican girls, one of whom becomes a regular victim. Clark relates, "I always told them to meet me in the very same building they lived in . . . On the roof or their basements or under the stairs . . . Sometimes in their own home if the parents were out . . . The easiest ones were the Puerto Rican and the black girls . . . Little white ones would masturbate you right there in the park for a dollar or a quarter . . . depending on how much emphasis their parents put in their heads on making money . . . I felt ashamed at first . . . But then I would rehearse at nights what to do the next time . . . I couldn't help myself."[29] Though molesting Puerto Rican girls allegorically replicates the colonial rape of Puerto Rico by the United States, this political statement is not Piñero's central project. Instead, he chooses to explore Clark's "professional" knowledge to wright the audience's understanding of the location of criminality, shifting it from men of color to the specific body of a white, middle-class family man, the ultimate representation of domestic stability and cultural power in the U.S. imaginary.

Clark freely explains that different types of girls are differently accessible, as if this knowledge somehow legitimizes his crimes. Unlike other groups, the white girls understand the activity as a commercial exchange. In his account this preadolescent prostitution is poignantly condoned by the parental valuation of money. The introduction of money seems intended to make the transgression less invasive, because the request for money implies at least a minimal awareness of notions of exchange and self-awareness. The girls are both actively involved in the process and able to stymie the chance of being penetrated; they are being paid for a service. Ironically, the amount paid is based not on the value of the service but on the importance of money to the individual, which results in a transaction that devalues the body.

Distinctions of color are made to indicate a criminal complicity on the part of the girls of color. They are "easy," and their imputed stereotypical sexual availability seems to limit Clark's responsibility, at least in his own mind. If they are willing to meet him in their own houses, then his behavior is allowed by their actions. The logic of this description echoes the "white" logic of displacing criminal transgression on the body of color. Clark's confession, which increases the audience's disgust even as it humanizes him, illustrates his inability to recognize his transgressions as violations against community standards.

The return of the rest of the inmates to the dayroom becomes an opportunity to explore the nature of ethnic loyalty through a discussion of Omar's responsibility to Ice. The extended dialogue generated by Ice's request for a favor exposes the realities and the limits of black solidarity. Ice asks Omar "to look out for [him]" because they are "homeeeeeys" and is reminded that in fact they are not from the same neighborhood; they may share a borough, but they are from the very different spaces of Coney Island and Bed-Stuy. As the conversation progresses, it becomes clear that their racial solidarity was predicated on oppositional isolation, "nothing but Whiteys on the floor," and that Ice stood with Omar because he "no wanna die alone," a personal decision rather than an expression of community. Omar turns the table by suggesting a contract, a more formalized exchange, between the two of them; Ice's resistance to this attempt to raise the stakes culminates in his playful buttering up of Omar: "you'll always be my main nigger." Omar's response is to demand "a softshoe," rejecting Ice's approbation as pure self-interest. Ice complies with a minstrel performance, calling Omar "boss, captain, your honor, mister, sir," clarifying the power hierarchy that is created in the act of minstrelsy—a performance of a subservient self. This final exchange escalates the situation to an ironic master-slave dialogue as a means of establishing power, leaving the rhetorical combatants no further safe ground for negotiation. Therefore, immediately after Ice's acquiescence, which can lead nowhere but intraracial derision and conflict, Omar shifts his attack to Clark, claiming he is a "freak" who is occupying his personal space. Once again, intraracial tension is deflected through an alternative scapegoat. The other inmates follow Omar's lead, forcing Clark to stand by the toilet, the most dehumanizing location within the spatial confines of the dayroom. Although Juan asks them to back off, he is chided by Ice for "[going] against your own people," reinforcing the reality that Omar's attack on Clark was a necessary rhetorical shift to maintain the existing race-based social structure within the prison.[30]

Despite Clark's awareness and admission of his prior guilt, he is incapable of changing his behavior because he is "just ashamed" of and not "disgusted" with himself. Although he realizes that exposure of his guilt places him irrevocably outside society, he cannot imagine himself in such a position and is thus incapable of understanding his behavior as sufficient justification for the dehumanization practiced by his fellow inmates. Continuing to believe in his rights, he claims he is "not going to stand for this treatment" when his space in the dayroom is restricted to the toilet. Unable to understand that he has violated any code, Clark reads the inmates' behavior as inappropriate. His sense of self-righteousness is clarified in the ease with which the other inmates trap him rhetorically.[31]

Clark's revulsion at Longshoe's request to hold his penis while he pisses makes clear his limited fetishism of sex. His willingness to practice a certain form of "sexual education" with young girls does not mean he can imagine himself outside a limited white-collar identity. Thus he becomes an easy victim of the other men, who accuse him first of ethnic disloyalty and then of various misrepresentations of Longshoe's racial identity. By refusing to hand over his chain at Longshoe's request, Clark sets up a no-win situation wherein the black prisoners join in the accusations that he is calling Longshoe a "quadroon" or a "passer"—insulting him by "deny[ing] his whiteness."[32]

Clark is incapable of understanding the importance of the claims against him in this scene. His identity as white, outside the House of Detention, has allowed him freedom from self-reflexivity. He has no conception of himself except as a "professional degenerate,"[33] an identity that suggests he conceives of himself primarily in occupational terms. That he has time for molestation implies he is fairly well-off economically, but his social position leads to his arrogance about the space in which he has found himself. This rhetorical entrapment eventually leads to physical abuse, and at the close of act 1, Paco, Omar, and Longshoe ram Clark's head into the piss-filled toilet.

When the other inmates are about to rape him in act 2, Clark threatens to complain to the authorities, basing the potential success of his complaint on his family's wealth. His gesture, however, echoes the cultural logic of the white girls who prevent their own violent penetration by recasting the encounter in economic terms. Because the other prisoners are unwilling to face further incarceration, his threats of retribution from the authorities lead to his death rather than a reprieve. Clark has managed to place himself outside the code of the prison and consequently has lost all hope of survival.

Part of the inmates' willingness to make Clark into stuff arises from Cupcakes's challenge that Paco is afraid of Clark because he is white. In a parallel to the early exchange between El Raheem and Omar, Cupcakes uses this racialization of sexual power to deflect Paco's interest away from him, creating an interethnic rather than an intraethnic conflict. During Paco's encounter with Cupcakes in the shower he speaks in Spanish, using the language to indicate intimacy and emotion. Paco's offer to "go both ways," however, is made in English. This highlights the intersection of sexuality and power, presenting the possibility of an equal relationship and suggesting that Paco's desire might be more than simple lust.[34]

Act 2 begins with Longshoe's unwillingness to meet with his visitors of the day because of his fear that the destabilizing presence of Clark might change the way his own life is conducted both inside and outside the jail. Longshoe's fear highlights the danger that Clark represents. Even though he has destroyed the sense of community in the dayroom, Clark still believes he has rights. While Juan is horrified by Clark's actions, he nonetheless stands up for him against the other inmates. They read Juan's concern as a desire to keep the stuff for himself, but he is in fact trying to maintain a sense of humanity in this prison space—something Clark's very existence undermines. Juan's project, ironically echoing Paco in his final offer to Cupcakes, is not to eliminate desire but to practice it outside a destructive space based on fear and power. Unfortunately, the transformative power of Clark's crime, twisting desire into perversion, is not contained, as the second act ends with his death. Cupcakes's final comment, "Oh my God . . . is this really us" reflects not only Clark's murder but also the impending conflict between the other inmates.[35]

Cupcakes's cry of despair illustrates the difficulty of maintaining identity and community in this institutional space. Unwilling to understand how he had become the fantasy of other men, Cupcakes constructs a racist model that shifts the inmates' prurient interest to Clark, whose status as an easy mark is validated by the nature of his criminality. Cupcakes's decision to use Clark's isolation to deflect Paco's pursuit breaks the code of the prison. Rather than dealing with his own intraethnic issues, Cupcakes instead manipulates the very structure of the program. While El Raheem and Omar make similar gestures, they are willing to take on the consequences of their actions personally rather than manipulating another to act for them. Cupcakes's dismissal of Paco's willingness to create a reciprocal relationship is a failure of humanity, made clear not only by Clark's death but also by Juan's final pronouncement that jail had taken his soul. Piñero, through Juan, makes it clear that if the individual and the community are to survive, identity cannot be predicated upon destruction and dehumanization of the other.

Part of *Short Eyes'* power as critique rests on the exposure of the complicity of white authority with the white aggression that leads to Clark's death. Longshoe, the actual perpetrator of the murder, could never be imagined to be the guilty party by the prison authorities; consequently, he is asked to give his account of events. Of course, the entire group was watching *The Dating Game* when Clark killed himself, even though the television was broken. The irony of the situation is that Juan, the only one unwilling to participate in the abuse and murder, was the only one with proof of Clark's guilt. And, even more disturbing, he was the only one to understand Clark's thoughts about the racialization of sexual availability. By his actions, his willingness to understand, Juan is able to reach out; he does not place himself "above understanding," thus avoiding Cupcakes's final failure.[36] Through understanding Clark, Juan frees himself from the guilt of a murder more justified than the other inmates knew. In doing so, he protects himself from the fear manifest by the institution and its social dynamics.

In contrast, the other prisoners have begun a process of policing based on a politics of fear by placing themselves above understanding, denying their own humanity, and dehumanizing Clark. They allow their fear of his potential power over them on the outside to shape their behavior. To create this scenario, they imagine an unbridgeable gap between themselves and Clark by denying the parallels between his behavior and their own: Ice's story of masturbating to Jane Fonda, their constant perusal of pornography, and most damning, their willingness to make Cupcakes stuff. The final mutuality of the prisoners' denial as they rescript Clark's death as a suicide is symptomatic of the process of denial and displacement sustained by the institutional structure whose codes they adopt. Instead of merely following the program, they allow an officer of the House of Detention to categorize Clark as suicidal on the basis of his crime, and not recognizing the similarity of their own practice, they kill him for his unwillingness to accept the consequences of his actions.

Juan's awareness of Clark's guilt and his refusal to divulge this information to the other inmates becomes a conscious choice that complicates the ethical universe of the play and the relationship between ethnicity and other forms of identification. Juan cannot condone Clark's release, yet he is unwilling to kill him to prevent it. Juan's desire for Clark to be kept off the streets emerges directly from his knowledge that Clark will continue on the path he has established for himself—he is incapable of internal policing, and society will not place limits on someone of his class and racial background. Yet Juan watches, along with the audience, as the other men carry out the sentence he is unable to deliver. Ironically, the possibility remains that Clark's behavior was an act of "involuntary suicide," attaching a level of truth to the false claim. Perhaps because he was unable to police himself, he put himself in a position to be killed.[37] In any case, Juan's ethical refusal to participate allows him to retain his humanity despite the demands of the total institution, while Clark's death becomes a way for the audience to avoid the highly charged problem of allowing him to go free, knowing what they know. In claiming that the institution has transformed men into animals and taken their souls, Juan attaches the responsibility for this transformation to the place itself, quietly asserting a structural argument of institutional responsibility.

By beginning both the first act and the epilogue with a "count"—the disembodied responses of prisoners to their cell designations, Piñero reminds the audience of the institutional space he has created, one in which dehumanization is central to maintaining order. This structure is sustained by Captain Allard's destruction of a television repair order to maintain the fiction of Clark's suicide for the outside world. Allard is forced to destroy the order after he fails to elicit cooperation from the prisoners, in part because the two most likely informants, Longshoe and Cupcakes, are the two most responsible. The attempt to secure information from Longshoe fails because Allard, banking on ethnic loyalty, wrongly assumes that "every offense that has been committed against a young white boy in this place has been perpetrated by the blacks and the Puerto Ricans."[38] Piñero inverts the assumption of the institutional authorities: the offense is committed by Longshoe and condoned by Nett, himself a part of the white power structure.

While Longshoe is being interrogated, Juan and Cupcakes discuss his interrogation among themselves in Spanish. Paco joins this conversation, while Ice and Omar are on the catwalks, speaking "in 'ism' language."[39] Both Spanish and "ism" language shift the cultural practice of politics through language. These two ad-libbed conversations frame the central lie being perpetrated and clarify that the truth is available but only in languages tailored to specific groups, languages that are inaccessible to those in power. This practice echoes the general bilingualism in Piñero's wrighting, wherein code switching occurs not only in the movement between English and Spanish but also between "playing" and everyday language, between "isms" and other forms of dialogue. These specialized languages, made clearer by their displacement to the margins of the stage are forms of resistance in this institutionalized space. This freedom of communication, silenced by the authorities but never really understood, allows resistance to sustain itself. In this case, the resistance is manifest through the unwillingness to share the truth about Clark's death. Ironically, the authorities do not know they have been saved the trouble of releasing a guilty man who simply could not be identified as such.

Piñero places the audience in the position of father confessor through the onstage body of Juan and implicates them in the desire to both condemn Clark and remain free from making the choice to participate in his death. Because values in prison are different from those on the outside, Clark as a middle-class white man has lost all of his institutional power unless he can be placed directly in the presence of the highest authority, Captain Allard, who must maintain a connection between exterior and interior values. Not understanding that presence, not merely the implied threat, is crucial in this world, Clark cannot understand the literalization of divisions that operate in opposition to his notions of the world. He is destroyed both because he breaks the code of moral conduct and because he can never establish his own value in this world. The obvious horror for a bourgeois white audience is the recognition that the power structure they hold so dear is contingent on environmental conditions. Change the status quo, shake things up just a little, and access to controlling narratives becomes impossible. The subtler message about the politics of fear is that institutional authority maintains this form of control, and ironically, cultural separatism based on race becomes a means of creating a safe space through which communal dialogue can occur.

Piñero's wrighting thus forces an audience to come to terms with the contingency of representational power. However, in acknowledging the reality of structures of power founded on ethnic solidarity, the play also exposes the limits of this political practice at the very height of its emergence within the Puerto Rican community. Like the Young Lords' insistence on working with and for the community, Juan's critique of his fellow inmates insists on their failed responsibility to a communal ideal. Juan's crossing of communities, his empathy, is enabled by a moment of communication free from institutional strictures. This valuation of anti-institutional communication implicitly makes an argument for the space of theater, of art itself, as a medium through which to begin to understand institutional structures in a new way.

Short Eyes demonstrates the danger of institutional power that is structured through fear. Fear allows the acceptance of an external policing that separates the responsibility of community maintenance from the individual members and places it in the hands of agents who solidify the legal codes and cultural practices that harden communal boundaries. Piñero recognizes that the institutional demands that create a community based on fear can only be destructive and insists on the possibility of understanding, forcing the audience to recognize an alternative possibility of community not based on ethnic lines. If indeed Cupcakes's "fear of this place stole [his] spirit,"[40] then safeguarding one's spirit requires resisting institutional power and asserting one's fundamental humanity against both the politics of ethnic separatism and institutions of white power.

From Fear to Respect

Piñero's *The Sun Always Shines for the Cool*, which premiered in Washington, D.C., June 3, 1977, explores a world that operates on a model of respect. Issues of intention, esteem, and respect for people and space are at the core of this value system, manifest theatrically in a player's bar. One's position within this self-selecting community is predicated on the ability to both garner and grant respect. Players are self-made men, actors in the life of the street who adhere to their own codes of conduct while doing what is necessary to survive. While they may be pimps, petty thieves, or whatever they have to be to hustle a living, they nonetheless maintain a code of respect that establishes community.

Sun extends over one evening in Justice's bar, a space for the hustlers and players who work the streets, one where both drug pushers and revolutionaries are unwelcome. The action is a series of conversations and encounters that establish the ethics of this community and emphasize the importance of storytelling through extended speeches that function like jazz solos. These monologues help craft identity, describe ways of knowing, and articulate philosophies of life. The language of the play is the poetry of the street, and rhetorical ability is a respected skill. Even more important than the linguistic virtuosity of the players is their willingness to follow through on any play that is made. With the use of language and, only rarely, action, masculinity and respect are negotiated through the parallel spatial politics of the street and the bar.

Spatial politics gain a different valence when articulated through a Nuyorican lens. The Puerto Rican diaspora reflects a larger politics of movement, of migration that cannot be neglected in any account of Puerto Rican identity. Along with this sense of movement, the street itself becomes an important space for the performance of Puerto Rican masculinity. In the 1970s, the street was one of the real homes of the Puerto Rican underclass in New York's urban landscape and is the space where Piñero's players do the majority of their work. In Piñero's case the space is specifically Loisaida, the Lower East Side, which, as Liz Sevcenko writes, "was about more than claiming space as Puerto Rican. The Loisaida movement, as it came to be called, constructed a neighborhood-specific discourse of puertorriqueñidad born from its *political relationship to urban space*" (italics added).[41] Ševčenko further argues that the naming process itself insists on a kind of action, and becoming a part of this space requires an ideological citizenship.

Miguel Piñero's "Lower East Side Poem" reflects his awareness of this urban geography. The excerpt that serves as an epigraph to this chapter articulates the intersection of space and identity in a Nuyorican body that threatens a bourgeois establishment. Piñero supplements the physical "street fighter" with the careful invocation of "the Philosopher of the Criminal Mind," the lover of wisdom aware of the possibilities of the criminal as a site of generative knowledge. His philosopher-fighter negotiates the streets through language, explicitly aware of the juridical reading of his identity as a "problem of this land." The speaker's status as a problem exists only within a particular geographical, cultural, and temporal context: "the Lower East Side" and "Rockefeller's ghettocide." He is a product of this institutionalized violence, a process of urban renewal based on a politics of fear of the "other" and the under-class that destroyed Piñero's neighborhood ecology.[42]

The use of the street as a space for the negotiation of power and identity is also articulated in a more abstract way in sociologist Michel de Certeau's work on everyday resistance, *The Practice of Everyday Life*. In a late chapter titled "Spatial Stories," de Certeau articulates his concept of "delinquent narrativity." De Certeau presents a world in which an entire way of life, of being in the world, becomes a resistant act through "taking the story literally . . . making it the principle of physical existence where a society no longer offers to subjects or groups symbolic outlets."[43] Through his players, Piñero wrights this delinquent narrativity. Reading delinquency in Piñero's work allows a reciprocal reflection: the term *delinquent* is clearly an imposition produced by the prescriptive gaze of the outside spectator. His players are delinquent only to the extent that bourgeois culture is understood as the normative standard. That the delinquency rests not in the player himself but with the interpreter foregrounds the establishment of a relation between spectator and actor, a theatricality, through which criminality, mas-culinity, and ethnicity are understood.

Piñero's plays work against a reductive understanding of these con-cepts because, despite their legal transgressions, the inhabitants of his theatrical spaces operate by strict codes of behavior based on respect. Respect, the ultimate ideal and marker of social standing within this world, emerges from control: control of self, of language, of emotions, and of reception. Although not exclusively a Puerto Rican value, respect is considered a core value by scholars working to understand Puerto Rican masculinity. This chapter's epigraph from Rafael Ramírez's book on Puerto Rican masculinity stresses the significant role that respect plays in male-male interaction within Puerto Rican culture. Ramírez suggests that respect emerges out of an "agrarian society" that necessitates a "reciprocal obligation" to enable negotiations between power differentials.[44] Anthony Lauria Jr. argues that although the no-tion of respect is clichéd, it nonetheless functions as a primary feature of interpersonal interaction, and a failure to grant respect is one the most often cited causes of violence. According to Lauria, "Respeto . . . signifies proper attention to the requisites of the ceremonial order of behavior, and to the moral aspects of human activities. This quality is an obligatory self-presentation; no Puerto Rican is considered properly socialized unless he can comport himself with respeto."[45] The relation-ship between respect and morality is crucial to an understanding of the communal ethics that lie at the heart of Piñero's representation of playing. Because players are positioned on the fringes of hierarchies of power, the preservation of a code of respect becomes central to the maintenance of community. While outside this space players may generate power through fear, within this space the community insists on a form of power and a sense of self that are predicated on respect.

In *The Sun Always Shines for the Cool* the semiotics of playing and its crucial intersections with respect are most clearly articulated through the conflict between Viejo and Cat Eyes over the future of Viejo's daughter, Chile Girl. A highly respected veteran of the world of players despite his stint as a drug dealer, Viejo has just left jail and is in a position of self-reflection and evaluation, attempting to understand his position in the world free from the demands of an institutional space. His desire to connect with Chile Girl after his long absence is at the center of this transformation. Viejo knows that whether or not he can establish a real emotional relationship with his daughter, he can nonetheless employ the skills he possesses as a player to protect her from the machinations of the world he knows so well.

Cat Eyes, a much younger player, is unwilling to recognize the basic rules of comportment and respect within this environment. Cat Eyes's inability to understand the world in which he operates is made clear from his first entrance. The play begins with one of Cat Eyes's girls, Phebe, showing disrespect by turning her back on the bar. Justice, the bartender, decides to run the bar on him, make him pay for everyone's drinks, because "all [his] customers are players, and they go with the rules . . . the same ones that are out in the street apply here. One . . . the major, is respect . . . you don't disrespect the place . . . and if you disrespect . . . you pay."[46] Rather than respecting the "play," Cat Eyes overreacts and takes it as a personal assault. In fact, for him everything becomes personal, a problematic practice in a space where personal value is contingent on respect for the community's laws, harsh as they may be. A precocious player, Cat Eyes cannot understand this foundational concept that allows for the formation of community in the absence of institutionally sanctioned codes of behavior. He values only the personal acquisition of power and his own performance: "they don't like me, cuz they all know that I'm swifter than any of them were at my age . . . my rap is strong and my words are never wrong. I'm young and faster than a streak of lightning and a ball of heat."[47]

Cat Eyes's willingness to destroy everyone around him signals to the other players that he cannot and does not understand the world they live in. His concept of history is a forgetting of his own history except as a record of his meteoric rise to importance within this community, and his easy dismissal of his relationship to the other players makes clear that he does not really understand the rules of the game. He cannot understand community in any form, reflected in his disturbing means of negotiating family relationships and love—pimping. Having pimped his own sister and lover, Rosa, Cat Eyes has no compunction about doing the same thing to his current lover, Chile Girl. Although most of the players are pimps like Cat Eyes, they make a distinction between their professional and personal lives. Chile Girl believes that Cat Eyes loves her and is in the process of self-improvement and lifestyle transformation; she is naively unaware of his plan to pimp her out. Ignorant of Viejo's paternal relationship to Chile Girl, Cat Eyes shares his plan. Because Chile Girl will not accept Viejo's advice, since he has failed as a father in her eyes, Viejo has no choice but to kill Cat Eyes to prevent her from being used.

Viejo's sexual encounter with Rosa, a gift from Jr. Balloon, is the one break from the neoclassical unity of the play's location. The encounter with Rosa not only allows Viejo to wright his individual masculinity in opposition to Rosa's assumptions but also clarifies the importance of language. The proper use of language is essential to respect, as exemplified by Viejo's concern about Rosa's constant reference to him as "old man." Although, as she points out, "old man" is the literal translation of his name, it does not have the cultural significance of the experience attached—the act of translation makes the history disappear. *Viejo* marks his survival to a certain age despite the immense risks of a player's life, while *old man* is a literal rendition of his current state of being. The power of translation as an act of disrespect reinforces the importance of specific identities in the player's world. Rosa's misunderstanding of Viejo's failure to perform sexually leads her to be abusive, because her pimp "can't do anything unless you insult him . . . unless you make him feel like he ain't shit." His response clarifies that her mistake is an assumption about the homogeneity of players: "That's Junior, that's not Viejo. Viejo is Viejo. Junior is Junior. If junior is a freak for shit like that, that doesn't mean that every player in the life is the same way."[48] By clarifying the different possibilities, Viejo articulates his way out of a crisis of masculinity.

Viejo's nostalgic account of a player's life suggests his rejection of the new street life that has changed the values of masculinity. As an alternative he invokes the possibility that a player plays with and against hegemonic masculine ideology. Waxing poetic in response to Rosa's concern about his desire to kill Cat Eyes, Viejo insists

> I'm only going to do what man has done for centuries and what others have avoided doing . . . what every player and hustler know they must do when they enter a new town or a new prison. You stop the action before it starts . . . you go for broke in any situation that threatens to take control of your game or take control of something you consider valuable enough to fit and live for. . . . Every player is a poet . . . an actor . . . a statesman . . . a priest . . . but most of all he's a player. You go out there and meet the world of suckers . . . the world of greed and whatever other names have been defined for those that seek something outside the acceptances of their society . . . and you stand with your balls exposed in this jungle of fear . . . and you battle . . . and you fight the hardest fight of your life, each day out there in them streets that demand blood to nourish its own energies.[49]

This narrative, while ostensibly a traditional account of competence, virility, and violence, also clarifies the importance of playing in the space of the street.

Viejo's conception of masculinity points toward machismo and violence, a configuration that seems conservative rather than innovative. However, even in revisionist accounts of Puerto Rican masculinity there is difficulty imagining a masculinity that moves beyond a macho/nonmacho binary. After going through a careful deconstruction of reductive and culturally imperialist impositions of machismo, Rafael Ramírez provides an account of Boricua masculinity in practice that echoes the very terms he critiques. Rather than asserting a lack, or a sense of abjection, Ramírez presents a picture in which there is no easy alternative to hegemonic masculinity. Similarly, Piñero's text insists on the practice of what appears to be hegemonic masculinity as an alternative to the ideology of hegemonic masculinity; it is a conscious choice manifest in a specific space and time, not a default into stereotypical action.

Piñero wrights the identity of the transgressor as the sucker, not the player, who is "seek[ing] something outside the acceptances of their society." Though the player is also operating outside the bounds of society, his ability to slip in and out enables control of the staging for both himself and for the "sucker." The con game and prostitution both contain a substantial element of theatricality, and though either activity can potentially succeed economically despite inadequate performance, repetition and continued success depend on staging. The sucker, through the theatricality of the gesture, is placed "outside" without ever realizing it.

The identities of the players here reflect a Lower East Side space privileging persons of color. Certainly Viejo and Cat Eyes are Puerto Ricans, but the only labeled "gringo" in the text, Willie Bodega, has an ethnic identity conferred on him to accommodate him in this space. Bodega's story, tied carefully to economic exchange, explains the emergence of his nominal Puerto Rican identity from his choice of language during a stint in prison; being constantly asked to supply various goods by his fellow inmates, he responded, "You motherfucker must think I'm a fucking Bodega."[50] Cat Eyes's description of him as a "whitey that raps like a nigger" moves beyond a simple naming to an observation of culturally specific praxis. Although the term *like* seems to (dis)place Bodega, his retort that "that ain't nothing, man. I just rap this way cuz that the way I raps" insists on his personal style and leads into his critique of Cat Eyes's response to Justice's running the bar on him.[51] This move illustrates the importance of attending closely to the sequence of conversation in Piñero's work, as shifting dynamics became important markers for reinforcing communal values, similar to the rhetorical avoidance of intraracial conflict in *Short Eyes*.

Here it is clear that one must learn both respect for personal style and a clear understanding of acceptable behavior. Bodega tells Cat Eyes, "All you had to do if you think yourself as being what you are, a man, is, man, that you apologize to the place and accept the play, man, to you . . . that's all. . . . The run of the tab on you was just a way of Justice letting you know that you blew it in here with him and that you should be aware of it. Like on the streets a knife in your gut or a bullet in your head would have been the respond and I guess that's what you think you are supposed to respect, the force, and fuck the rest of the real attitude."[52] By giving Bodega the voice to critique Cat Eyes's flawed understanding of his community, Piñero demonstrates his participation within it. Bodega's critique also reiterates the explicit concern with foregrounding the active creation of masculinity in this space.

Bodega's account of Cat Eyes's failure to distinguish anything but a violent response is one of his two indications of the way in which Viejo will deal with Cat Eyes. The second is the longest account of masculine performance in the play, Bodega's account of his brother's death. The story celebrates death as rebellion, romanticizing his brother as the rebel living after death: "He looked like a young god taking his anger out on the fucking world. That was his power. That's why they had to kill him three times after he was dead."[53] This willingness to die, combined with a righteous anger, a performance of power that goes beyond the simple fact of having a gun, illustrates an ideal end of life performance. It is, as Piñero demanded, the crazy life wrought in full.

Viejo's final confrontation with Cat Eyes, the moment the entire second act anticipates, begins with a literal threat to Cat Eyes's masculinity as Viejo holds a .357 on him under the table. Recognizing that he cannot convince Chile Girl of her danger by himself, Viejo extracts a confession from Cat Eyes under the threat of death, gaining the support of the other players by having Rosa reveal her relationship to Cat Eyes. Though Chile Girl demands that he die rather than beg for pity, Cat Eyes is emasculated through begging for pity from the man holding the gun on him, going so far as to call him God. While Viejo's performance verges on the melodramatic and is clearly homophobic, within the traditional space of dominance he offers a different sense of masculinity predicated on space and community, a community that itself might be read as ethnic. The rules make the community, the rules of the player, and without these safeguards the community cannot function.

Crucially, Viejo makes a distinction between playing and acting, the latter being a false space:

> Faggot, don't you know that out here in this jungle if you are caught acting, you are one dead player? Out here you go for broke . . . you take it to the streets on all levels and you took it to the level that's gonna cause your death. This ain't the semi-truth world of the tennis hustler or the pro golf pusher, this is the real world of the dreamer strung out. But you can't understand that. Are you listening, Chile Girl? He ain't shit. He's a phony being, a fake . . . even his lies are false. You blew this the moment you thought you were the only player in town that made the rules. I invented the game. You can't hustle off a hustler. You can't play on a player. You gave yourself no out. You put yourself in solitary confinement, baby.[54]

Players don't act, or at least they don't get caught doing it. When forced through a combination of ethnoenvironmental factors to perform, the process becomes one of wrighting. There is a creative act of making that is theatrical but that transcends the mere dramaturgy of self-presentation. Understanding this world involves a clear recognition of class positioning and location—on the street. Here the model is "the real world of the dreamer strung out," a paradox in which a double filtering process brought on by dreaming and drugs is necessary to encounter the real. The stakes are higher and more immediate than in other economic environments. This insistence on true playing makes sense within an already theatricalized reality in which visible acting becomes a failure of the compact between player and audience. While every player is constantly wrighting identity, each of these gestures has real material consequences. Failure to back up claims with action is deadly.

However, Cat Eyes's failure is not merely a failure of action; it is also a failure of understanding. His failure to understand echoes both Juan's comment to Cupcakes in *Short Eyes* and Viejo's previous attempts to clarify for Cat Eyes a methodology for approaching life: "I know that there's a lot I don't know . . . and I also know that the only way I am going to learn the things I need to know is if I admit that I need to know these things."[55] Cat Eyes's refusal to admit his ignorance through a dismissal of Viejo's advice is part of his continued failure to understand.

In the end, Viejo commits suicide rather than killing Cat Eyes. This gesture echoes Bodega's brother's gesture of rebellion; it becomes in and of itself a creative act and a means of maintaining self-identity by taking control over the one thing that is left, his own life. Though Viejo's act is respected as an admirable play, the significance of his choice to leave Cat Eyes alive at the end and kill himself goes deeper than that. One explanation for his choice is that leaving Cat Eyes alive allows him the chance to experience the lesson Viejo is trying to teach him. If he kills Cat Eyes his function as a teacher disappears. He also acts to show Chile Girl the limits of her existing perceptual framework. By killing himself he also gains the respect accorded Bodega's brother for dying in the line of duty and no longer has to account for his actions or risk a failed reconciliation with Chile Girl.

The most compelling reason for this self-destructive choice, however, is a desire to maintain and reconstruct community in a way that would be impossible without his death. Though Viejo certainly recovers his masculinity in a traditional sense by doing his duty as father to protect his family, he could have achieved that effect without killing himself. And killing Cat Eyes would have ensured that he could not harm Chile Girl. However, in teaching Cat Eyes a lesson about respect, he completes Bodega's attempt to show him that not only is violence not the only response but that establishing violence as an alternative to respect destroys the very community respect engenders. Although his suicide could be seen as a disrespectful gesture to his position within the community, it is a necessary decision. If Viejo needs a gun to ensure that respect retains its role as the modus operandi for communal interaction, then the notion of respect is destroyed. Sustaining respect through violence transforms it into a politics of fear.

By killing himself, Viejo not only teaches but also absents himself from the position of enforcer, making respect a value in its own right. Cat Eyes's failure of respect has isolated him from the rest of the community. However, rather than making Cat Eyes a scapegoat, closing him out of the community and creating rigid boundaries, Viejo's suicide affirms a much more fluid sense of space based on voluntary participation. In this model, joining a community is achieved through a proactive gesture in support of the community, regardless of how "delinquent" such a community may be. Thus, respect becomes the means through which wrighting is possible. Respect informs masculinity and ethnicity so that all three become central to the space of delinquent theatricality of the player situated between "acceptable norms" and the violent inscription of masculinity.

Sun suggests that the player's performance demands an active creation and maintenance of community rather than a passive assumption of its existence. This demand can be seen in the 1989 *Nuevos Pasos* version of the play in which Justice "*holds* CHILE, *faces her towards* CAT EYES" before his final comment. Although Justice's embrace can be seen as a gesture of comfort protecting the woman from the sight of her dead father, it is also a chance for her to see in stark contrast the masculine relationship to respect. Rather than closing off community, this version of the play ends with an epilogue with "*five flashback freezes*" that move from a focus on Cat Eyes in a prostrate position to the entrance of various characters. The expected isolation in a final scene of violence is inverted to insist on communal coherence.

This community, positioned both within Justice's bar and on the streets, insists on a behavioral practice that respects the space. This primacy of space as a vector of community and individual identity clarifies the anxiety that turning your back to the bar creates. While the gesture itself is a mark of disrespect in a general communicative ethos where assumptions about direction, distance, and eye contact are crucial to communication and interpersonal connection, it also places the individual in the space in a particular way. And that space, itself distinguished precisely by the refusal of violence against the other, becomes a space for players to wright the street. The street is a space of violence against the other, in part because it functions as the space of interaction between different societal groups, but the bar, even as a player's space on the fringes of society, is a protected space of community. Viejo's choice not to kill Cat Eyes becomes a mark of respect for the space itself.

In its liminal location as theatrical space for the players, the bar ties together the streets and the theater into a unique communal space for wrighting identity. In the 1989 text, the play begins with a prologue in the form of a street scene of pimps and prostitutes. And, to bring the audience into this world, not only do they *walk about the stage as if on the street,* the prostitutes actually *proposition the audience.* According to Kanellos and Huerta, "JUSTICE's *tavern, more than a mere 'player's bar,' is a stage; it offers the spotlight to the people who play their lives out on the streets as they come in and perform for each other as well as the audience which is invited, no hustled, in the Prologue of the play.*"[56] This account provides a careful revision of the invitation into a hustle, a shift between the theatricality of the stage and the theatricality of the street; however, in the 1984 version the very first stage directions are "Actors come in from hustling on the streets with the audience."[57] This one line provides a rich blurring between actors and hustlers, shows access to the streets, and places the audience in the strange position of being either temporally and spatially "with" the actor/hustler, or even more interesting, participating in the very practice of hustling.

Perhaps the safest reading of "with" is a spatial proximity. However, even that reading suggests the possibility of community "with" the actors, making the entire theatrical event a frontier space. The audience is invited to be a part of the active creation of community. Rather than being hustled by the hustlers or played by the players, the invocation to community suggests that the spectators themselves become players helping to stretch the bounds of this liminal space, freeing us from our relationship to delinquency and arguing that for all of us, identity must be "played . . . to the bitter end."[58]

El Pachuco: Myth, Theatricality, and Ambivalent Community

> What is Chicano theater? It is theater as beautiful, rasquachi, human, cosmic, broad, deep, tragic, comic, as the life of La Raza itself. At its high point Chicano theater is religion—the huelguistas de Delano praying at the shrine of the Virgin de Guadalupe, located in the rear of an old station wagon parked across the road from DiGiorgio's camp #4; at its low point it is a cuento or a chiste told somewhere in the recesses of the barrio, puro pedo.
>
> Chicano theater, then, is first a reaffirmation of LIFE. . . . The characters and life situations emerging from our little teatros are too real, too full of sudor, sangre, and body smells to be boxed in.
>
> —Luis Valdez, "Notes on Chicano Theater"

> In summary, the Pachuco argot may be said to have two main social functions in the Tucson community. The first . . . is its function as the private language of groups of boys who find themselves not fully accepted in either American or Mexican society. As such, Pachuco transmits a set of values which runs counter to the accepted social order and tends to isolate the users from the type of social contacts which would assist in their assimilation into American life. . . . To the extent that Pachuco persists as a private language in Tucson, it might be taken as symptomatic of the continuing disorientation of one element of the younger Mexican generation.
>
> —George Carpenter Barker, *Pachuco: An American-Spanish Argot and Its Social Functions in Tucson, Arizona*

As I joined the line to enter the theater on a warm August Sunday afternoon in San Jose, California, I could feel a palpable excitement. We were going to witness the twenty-fifth-anniversary revival of Luis Valdez's play *Zoot Suit*, directed by his son Kinán and presented at the Center for Employment Training in San Jose, California. The audience was eager to participate in the re-creation of an almost mythic event of Chicano theater history. According to Jorge Huerta, "The success of *Zoot Suit* in Los Angeles became a watershed moment in the history of Latino theatre and of all theatre in the United States. . . . *Zoot Suit* proved popular across ethnic, class, and cultural lines in Los Angeles but most importantly, while that play was being performed in the theatre, while El Pachuco strutted nightly across that stage, that space belonged to La Raza. Luis Valdez had ushered-in the era of professional Chicana/o theatre and the theatre would never be the same."[1] A revival more than an interpretation, the goal of this production was to re-present and celebrate the success, power, and influence of a work that has been widely studied and discussed as drama and film but rarely performed live in the theater. *Zoot Suit* forms a nexus in a cultural debate about the nature of Chicano identity and cultural production that is echoed in the work itself. At the center of the play is El Pachuco, the physical incarnation of a cultural icon imbued with dramaturgical power. The image of Edward James Olmos as El Pachuco—red shirt, black zoot suit, and porkpie hat, one leg bent, the other stretched out and his back rigid at a nearly forty-five-degree angle—and Ignacio Gomez's poster of the figure have become iconic in Chicano culture. However, Olmos's El Pachuco can never be freed from an association with the historical pachucos who occupy an ambivalent position within the Chicano history of Los Angeles.

Chicano Theater, CorpoReality, and the Audience

Besides his success with *Zoot Suit*, Valdez is traditionally seen as the principal organizer and founding figure behind El Teatro Campesino, a collective theater ensemble that arose in Delano, California, in 1965 in conjunction with the strikes of the United Farm Workers (UFW). Accounts of El Teatro's three basic structures—the *acto*, *mito*, and *corrido*—are defined with his voice.[2] The initial dramatic work of the ensemble, *actos* performed along the picket line and from the back of flatbed trucks, led to a pragmatic aesthetic. The *acto* is designed to present the reality of the Chicano's life and ideally promote change and social justice. Valdez defined the form thus in 1970: "Actos: Inspire the audience to social action. Illuminate specific points about social problems. Satirize the opposition. Show or hint at a solution. Express what people are feeling."[3] The performances are a form of street theater with accessible language, hyperstylized characters, improvisation, stereotypes, and masks. The aesthetic contains elements of Brecht, commedia dell'arte, and Mexican popular performance aesthetics from the tent show, or *carpa*. Some of these techniques were familiar to Valdez from his work with the San Francisco Mime Troupe; others he learned through a study of Brecht at San Jose State, and a great deal was also brought into the productions through the contributions of *campesino* performers who had personal experience with Mexican popular performance traditions.[4]

These popular roots led to a Chicano theater in which there was no significant distance between actor and audience; theatrical elements were seen as organic products of a communal aesthetic, not outside impositions. During the powerful resurgence of Chicano theater in the mid 1960s, the need to separate theater and real life was not a problem for theater workers and audience members. Many actors were amateurs pulled from everyday life, and their images and characters often directly reflected their immediate, lived experiences. In the original *actos* the community itself was doing the acting. This privilege continues today in the work of El Teatro Campesino, most visibly in its alternating annual December productions of *La Pastorela* and *La Virgen de Tepeyac* in the Mission in San Juan Bautista, California, in which multiple generations of community members participate.

Valdez was initially heavily influenced not only by his work in street theater but also by his readings of Mayan philosophy. Indigenous religious ritual and spectacle became logical precursors of a theatrical tradition working against Eurocentrism. Articulated both through pragmatic Catholic practices and indigenous religion and philosophy influenced by Domingo Martínez Parédez, spirituality formed a core element of the aesthetics. Mayan and Aztec spirituality were considered central to an understanding of Chicano political, aesthetic, and social identity, and not oppositional to an exploration of real material issues. This intersection is explored in Valdez's poem *Pensamiento Serpentino*, written in 1971 and subtitled "A Chicano Approach to the Theatre of Reality."[5]

However, for many of Valdez's critics more heavily invested in the real fruits of social revolution (and often more explicitly Marxist), an investment in spiritual and philosophical origins was a dangerous distraction from the work at hand—the need for social transformation. This political crisis could be averted as long as the aesthetic aims of the group did not interfere with the political exigency of community organizing demanded by the realities of the strikes. Valdez realized that these exigencies were placing limits on the artistic development of his theater workers, and thus the choice was made to separate from the UFW, a separation that led to the development of new forms, including the *mito*, a celebration of Chicano mythology and philosophy invested in indigenous ideals of the land and Mayan conceptions of circular time, and eventually the *corrido* and the *historia*.[6] The separation also allowed for an expansion of the political exploration of the group from strike issues to education, the Vietnam War, media representations, and the politics of *El Movimiento*, the Chicano movement.

Written to articulate the cultural, political, and aesthetic values of this emerging form of socially conscious protest theater, Valdez's "Notes on Chicano Theater" is a product of revolutionary fervor within the space of post–civil rights battles for ethnic empowerment. It separates Chicano theater from mainstream conceptions of theatrical practice by supplementation and excess. One of the most important aspects of Chicano theater is the ability to bring real life into the theater, to move beyond an academic form framed by a proscenium arch. According to Valdez, "A demonstration with a thousand Chicanos, all carrying flags and picket signs, shouting "CHICANO POWER!" is not the revolution. It is theatre about the revolution. The people must act in *reality* not on stage (which could be anywhere, even a sidewalk) in order to achieve real change."[7] While theater is not the revolution, it cannot be divorced from the difficulties of daily life and the various forms of discrimination and mistreatment encountered by both migrant workers and urban Chicanos.[8] Valdez insists on an embodied practice in which the immediacy of the performers has a direct, visceral impact on an audience community who are full participants in the process of performance. As he wrote in 1970, "Audience participation is no cute production trick with us; it is a pre-established, pre-assumed privilege."[9]

Valdez's investment in lived material conditions parallels the contemporary concern with an emerging identity politics in the 1960s and 1970s, embodied in *El Movimiento*. During this period, some participants in *El Movimiento* envisioned a radical separatist project centered on the recuperation of the Chicano homeland, Aztlán, in keeping with the separatist politics articulated in contemporary forms of Black Nationalism. Other members emphasized a focus on civil and human rights, equal treatment before the law and in educational practice, and increasing attention to the contributions of Chicanos and other persons of color in the cultural and political history of the United States. As Harry Elam Jr. argues in his comparison of El Teatro Campesino and the Black Revolutionary Theater, these two ensembles created a space for the articulation of ideas and ways of being in the world for blacks and Chicanos, "revitaliz[ing] their cultural consciousness, and agitat[ing] in that unique historical moment for social action."[10]

El Teatro Campesino's national and international successes helped define a Chicano theater practice predicated on a necessary relationship between a community and its theater. This relationship also fostered a theatrical model in which excess is central to the form, counteracting the traditional Aristotelian reception practice that attempts to limit the transformative power of theater. While the danger that conventional assumptions of an audience might erase the radical elements of theater was less imminent in a local audience community whose values may have been shared by the performers, the movement into a mainstream space with a conventional disjuncture between stage space and audience changed these dynamics. This change became visible with the increasing mainstream success of *Zoot Suit*.

Valdez's counterstrategy to the constraints of mainstream audience reception, the refusal to be "boxed in," insists on a specific *corpo-reality* that reflects the lived experience of Chicano actors and their audience. Like Ramón Saldívar's Chicano narratives, Valdez's plays "shape modes of perception in order to effect new ways of interpreting social reality and to produce in turn a general social, spiritual, and literary revaluation of values."[11] By instantiating community that can be experienced by the body of the spectator, the theater can create space in which new ways of knowing become available; the possibility exists to construct an alternative reality connected to the lived experience of the audience.[12] This unmediated experience is too often assumed to reflect a naïve or unsophisticated audience, demonstrating the implicit convention in theater reception that a gap between audience and production should be maintained. Valdez wrights the possibility of a community that can bridge this gap while always acknowledging the powerful forces working against it.

Contextualizing *Zoot Suit* and El Pachuco

Gordon Davidson, artistic director of the Center Theater Group, first approached Valdez about the possibility of writing a play on the Zoot

Suit Riots as an attempt to understand the history of discrimination in the city of Los Angeles. The riots occurred over a period of eleven days in June 1943, during which servicemen beat and stripped youth wearing zoot suits and ducktail hairstyles, publicly burning their clothing with apparently tacit approval from civilian and military authorities. In return, Valdez offered Davidson the 1942 Sleepy Lagoon murder trial in which a group of twenty-two youths, organized and named by their geographic proximity on Thirty-eighth Street ("gang" was added by the media) were indicted for a single murder. Seventeen of the twenty-two were convicted. Though their conviction was eventually overturned through the efforts of Chicano community activists and other progressives supported by several well-known Hollywood figures, the convicted youths spent almost two years in San Quentin before an unbiased trial could finally be held.[13]

At the center of both of these events is the fascinating, ambivalent, and iconic pachuco. Created through style and performance, the pachuco's highly theatrical identity resists an assimilationist ideal that would erase the in-between identity of Mexican Americans caught between U.S. and Mexican culture, considered *pochos* in Mexico and Mexicans in the United States. The intersection of a hybrid language, elaborate style of dress and movement, and outlaw status are a part of the representation of the pachuco as a historical figure; however, this self-conscious performance, both creative and transgressive, also satisfies the prurient interest of the academic researcher. Feared, loved, and despised, often by the same groups, the pachuco represents a creative space for the formation of an identity in between cultures. Ironically, this very creativity is presented as countercultural and often criminal behavior.

George Carpenter Barker's *Pachuco: An American-Spanish Argot and Its Social Functions in Tucson, Arizona* (1950) provides an introduction to the historical roots of the language practice of pachucos that reflects the sociological discourse during the historical moment Valdez explores in his play. Arguing "that Pachuco borrows heavily not only from Mexican slang, but from American slang as well," Barker documents literal translations of English expressions, Spanish pronunciations of English words, and transformations of syntax and meaning, form and content of Mexican Spanish and its various dialects to create a new linguistic space.[14] The language practice itself creates a space between cultures through a series of creative and original translations, influenced by, and partially articulated within, the cultural and linguistic constructions of American English and Mexican Spanish.

Perceived to be outside two communities, the youthful linguistic innovators instantiate a culture that is positioned simultaneously within and outside both Mexican and U.S. culture.

The history of the language practice is attributed to *caló*, the "argot of the Mexican underworld," taken from the word used by gypsies in Spain to refer to their own language.[15] Each moment in the description of this linguistic history is one of social marginalization, from gypsies in Spain to the Mexican "underworld" to "marijuana smokers and peddlers" in El Paso. This marginalization is read as a priori criminalized, and though in his summary of the social functions of Pachuco, Barker presents the antiassimilationist practice as countercultural rather than necessarily criminal, he includes a staged Pachuco dialogue that illustrates the latter.

Barker provides a clear social context for this staged dialogue but seems strangely unaware of the possibility that the performance presented by people he has just met might be an attempt to satisfy or titillate the voyeuristic demands of a researcher. Careful not to tell the youths he was making value judgments while studying the language, Barker believed he was receiving a value-neutral performance; however, his choice to show the practice of this language in context as an assertive masculinist performance is crucial. One can imagine that the countercultural youths were aware (and proud of) their "criminal" reception and attempted to create a dialogue that lived up to these ideals. In this particular case, the anthropologist had only known his informants for a few hours, ninety minutes of which involved recording a dialogue in "an imaginary pool room setting." From his brief observation, Barker is willing to make claims such as, "the smart pachuco gets the girl to pay for his dinner (que paguen las chavalas)" based on his informants' comments.[16] Though he includes only one of six staged dialogues, Barker chooses one with a physical fight between gang members, perhaps indicating less about his methods than about contemporary cultural assumptions.

It is significant that Barker recognizes the contingent and theatrical nature of this entire activity. He claims, "It is of course open to question as to what extent the writer's ten gang participants subscribe to the system of values implied in their records and their recorded conversations. The point cannot be denied, however, that they set up these conversations as fair samples of Pachuco talk. It seems fair to assume that the habitual use of Pachuco implies the substitution of such Pachuco values for the more conventional ones of Mexican and American society."[17]

Values are "substituted" rather than practiced, indicating potential access to other values. Barker assumes the idiom and value structure are freely chosen; at the same time, he makes a second argument connecting "habitual use" and identity construction: continued practice suggests (and potentially creates) an alternative moral universe. This conclusion is particularly interesting given the theatrical nature of his encounter; he acknowledges the young men are acting, playing improvised roles for a spectator, though he does not recognize the possibility they are negotiating between youthful braggadocio, academic expectation, and their real lived experience.

The pachuco also caught the attention of Octavio Paz, whose *El Laberinto de la Soledad* contains an essay translated as "The Pachuco and Other Extremes." In this essay, based on a visit to Los Angeles, Paz argues that pachuco identity arises from denied entry into the social milieu and functions as a cry for attention. Recognizing like Barker that the pachuco constitutes only a small portion of the population, Paz claims, "It is not important to examine the causes" of the pachuco's conflict with North American society, thus eliding any sense of the progressive power of the identity.[18] Many critics of Paz's essay object to his reduction of pachuco sensibility to an adolescent one, an "empty gesture," because it does not draw directly on traditional Mexican forms of self-expression.[19] Unable to understand that the pachuco invalidates any call for a return to Mexican values and traditions, Paz describes a masochistic and sadistic self-fashioned identity both paradoxical and self-destructive.

From Paz's perspective, North American society is a closed door and the pachuco becomes one means of entry, albeit a dangerous one:

> I believe that the North American's irritation results from his seeing the *pachuco* as a mythological figure and therefore, in effect, a danger. His dangerousness lies in his singularity. Everyone agrees in finding something hybrid about him, something disturbing and fascinating. He is surrounded by an aura of ambivalent notions: his singularity seems to be nourished by powers that are alternatively evil and beneficent. . . . The *pachuco* is impassive and contemptuous, allowing all these contradictory impressions to accumulate around him until finally, with a certain painful satisfaction, he sees them explode into a tavern fight or a raid by the police or a riot. And then, in suffering persecution, he becomes his

true self, his supremely naked self, as a pariah, a man who belongs nowhere.[20]

Paz reflects the very "irritation" he ascribes to the North American vision of the pachuco. Forgetting that his own exploration of identity was catalyzed by his very status as "other" in Los Angeles, he envisions the pachuco's lack of a home because he cannot conceive of hybridity in spatial terms.[21] Ironically, the hybridity that Paz recognizes as an extreme, the middle ground of betwixt and between, is now a common contemporary trope of ethnicity understood in theatrical terms. Calling it an "extreme," he refuses to recognize the innovation and creativity at its core.

The public spectacularity of the pachuco's rebellion appears to irritate Paz more than the rebellion itself. The pachuco "knows that it is dangerous to stand out and that his behavior irritates society, but nevertheless he seeks and attracts persecution and scandal. It is the only way he can establish a more vital relationship with the society he is antagonizing. As a victim, he can occupy a place in the world that had previously ignored him: as a delinquent he can become one of its wicked heroes."[22] Paz's reading presents this identity as both a potentially destructive force and a necessary first step in the procession of redemption; however, redemption may occur only after a cyclical process in which a ritual stripping down allows for potential reintegration. His understanding that being pachuco is a style as much as an identity, and that the trappings are not peripheral but essential to such a transgressive identity, ironically places Paz firmly in the mindset of the Anglo servicemen who felt it psychically necessary to strip down the pachuco during the Zoot Suit Riots.

Although many progressive critics argue against the relatively pejorative construction of the pachuco presented by Paz, his recognition of the paradoxical symbolic possibilities parallels the figure's own life within various Mechicano communities.[23] For the *Mexicano* community this figure makes absolutely no sense, arising out of a tradition of the values of the "*norteamericanos*." For parts of the Mexican American community, the pachuco is dangerous, because the association with violence and transgression he represents may be symbolically mobilized to envelop an entire community. For the Chicano community, the powers of self-naming and cultural resistance that cannot be reduced to a nationalized subjectivity reflect their own cultural positioning. By divorcing himself from the myth-making act, Paz attempts to defuse the power he gives to the pachuco as both "disturbing and fascinating." As a cultural ideal the pachuco embodies both of these concerns, illustrating the inherent tension between the potential power of the myth and its imputed pathology. Problematic as it may be, this identity offers an alternative to mainstream conceptions and as such becomes the site of conflicted imagination around which community can manifest itself. The pachuco becomes a space of myth paradoxically in dialogue with the lived realities of Chicanos wearing zoot suits—an intersection of icon and corporeal beings.

Forming Ambivalent Community: *Zoot Suit* as Performance

Though Luis Valdez employed the pachuco in both *actos* and *mitos*, his most sustained representation of the figure is in *Zoot Suit*, the beginning of Valdez's transition into the representational politics of the 1980s. *Zoot Suit* exemplifies his use of theatricality as a means of wrighting a nuanced and complex ethnic identity whose identification with a larger ethnic community is not assumed a priori. Like much of Valdez's work for the theater, *Zoot Suit* explores the conflicts brought on by the burden of representation created by an assumption of speaking "for" a community. Valdez explores the representational pressures placed on both the Chicano (and Latino) playwright and the individual performer on the stage and in everyday life. Valdez's work not only highlights important moments in Chicano history but also is an aesthetic autobiography exploring a deliberately constructed outlaw status. In this manner he creates spaces that disrupt mainstream interpretation while constructing an alternative form of community. In Valdez's theater, the performing Chicano body becomes a visceral site of resistance, creating representational excess that threatens traditional categorization.

Despite his movement into the mainstream, Valdez remains committed to Chicano theater issues, especially the crucial conceptions of reality and corporeality that form the framework for the political interventions of El Teatro Campesino. Exploring the dynamics of representation, Valdez exposes the external and internal limits that fix and stereotype Chicano masculinity by focusing on the effects of a variety of cultural and generic frames.[24] Going beyond Goffman's basic idea of the frame as a way of organizing and making sense of behavior, Valdez uses the stage as a site to explore the more explicit institutional power structures of a racist press and judicial system. Rather than simply acknowledging the presence of a representational "boxing in" by the media and the legal system, Valdez provides a means by which Chicanos can act, disrupting the often invisible practice of framing the ethnic body. This disruption is most explicitly manifest through the theatrical staging of El Pachuco, the iconic and mythical form of the historical pachuco and the nodal point for a constellation of legal and media attempts at control. In *Zoot Suit*, the body of El Pachuco becomes the primary locus through which Valdez wrights community and the possibility of a new identity for Chicanos. In doing so, he never forgets the framing activity that writes the pachuco as a criminal figure.

This paradox is clear in the media coverage surrounding the amazing success of *Zoot Suit* in Los Angeles in 1978–79. Valdez himself recalled, "I knew two Pachucos early in my life—one my cousin, Billy Miranda, and the other, his close friend, Cesar Chavez."[25] We are unfamiliar with Billy because he was killed in the mid 1950s, but the very different histories of these two men serve as a cautionary tale to anyone overly eager to limit the possibilities of pachuco youth. In an April 1979 article charting various generational and political responses to the representation of pachucos, Richard Vasquez crystallized the cultural possibilities through two photos of Mike De Santos, a California Highway Patrol officer, one in uniform and one in his zoot suit. The irony of this situation was not lost on the CHP brass conflicted about the circulation of this representation. On the one hand, some officials argued that "those who wore the zoot suit . . . during the 1940's were in flagrant violation of the war effort," but others further up the chain of command saw this as an excellent opportunity to assist in the recruitment of diverse officers.[26]

As a play, *Zoot Suit* shows an understanding of the broader representational battle taking place through the representation of the Chicano body in the Sleepy Lagoon murder trial and the Zoot Suit Riots. The plot operates outside linear chronology, beginning after the death at the Sleepy Lagoon and relating the events leading up to it as if for a trial jury. In its later and more stylized incarnations (including the published version of the text), the character of the Press and various spoken accounts of newspaper stories lend a Brechtian air to the work, and piles of newspapers serve as furniture and occasionally frame the scene to further emphasize the media saturation that haunts the world of the play.[27] The only character capable of standing up to the figure of the Press is El Pachuco, whose corporeality is manifest not only through the sustained physicality of the stylized action but also in the seductive power of his dramaturgical control over staging.

The play begins with El Pachuco's symbolic action of slicing through media representation by using a giant switchblade to separate a drop curtain, painted as a newspaper front page from June 3, 1943, the first day of the Zoot Suit Riots. Valdez provides explicit stage directions about the gestural language of El Pachuco as he enters, elaborately garbing himself in costume and finally "assum[ing] a Pachuco stance."[28] Based on the representational choices in the text and the anniversary production, El Pachuco is not so much a character to be interpreted as a physicality to be replicated. The invocation of "a" pachuco stance should now perhaps be "El Pachuco's stance," as the figure of Edward James Olmos in his red shirt and black *tacuche* and the image of El Pachuco on Ignacio Gomez's poster for the show have become cultural icons, sharing space on wall murals with *La Virgen de Guadalupe*.[29]

Valdez's narrative figure has a dialogic relationship with the leader of the Thirty-Eighth Street Gang, Henry (Hank) Reyna, whose non-archetypal status as pachuco heightens the mythological quality of El Pachuco. The protagonist of Valdez's play, Reyna is a "construct of fact and fantasy" who stands in for the historical Henry Leyvas.[30] Undergoing an existential crisis, Hank Reyna tries to determine his own identity within the various frames imposed on him by the legal system and the media. Theatrically, El Pachuco is used to both question and support Hank, commenting on and controlling the flow of action on the stage. But unlike the film version, the play is El Pachuco's.[31] After Hank's initial incarceration, El Pachuco asks him, "Haven't I taught you how to survive?" El Pachuco's concept of survival involves a community allegiance, an allegiance to *la raza*, the people, but not a nationalist identification with the United States. In belittling Hank's decision to join the Navy he insists, "[T]his ain't your country. Look what's happening all around you . . . the Mayor of L.A. has declared an all-out war on Chicanos. On you! . . . Your war is on the homefront." Uncertain how to proceed with this new agenda, Hank is assured by El Pachuco that he should "Fight back! Stand up to them with some style. Show the world a Chicano has balls." Hank's resolve is embodied by the stage direction *"Assuming the style"* in which his attitudinal transformation is instantiated by a style.[32] He takes on the iconic physical mannerisms of El Pachuco in an act of conceptual transformation, in which an identity enables agency and a way of knowing at the moment when it is most explicitly theatricalized. By tying together resistance and style with masculine authority and power, El Pachuco makes clear one vision of pachuco identity.[33]

As many critics have recognized, primarily in relationship to the film, style itself is central to understanding *Zoot Suit*; yet what is absent from many of these accounts is the question of El Pachuco's spiritual function, as opposed to his psychological function. Many critics equate style with the mythological construction of El Pachuco as a sign of Chicano essentialism and cultural nationalism. For example, echoing criticisms by Tomas Ybarra-Frausto and Yvonne Yarbro-Bejarano, Granger Babcock argues, "Valdez's essentialization of Chicano identity in *Zoot Suit* was a historically necessary political act to give, as he says, 'a disenfranchised people their religion back.' However, this reduction of identity ultimately produced an impasse because it marginalized lived social conditions and other possible identities."[34] Babcock's concern about essentialism is limiting here, in part because he does not see the very playing of the iconic and mythic role as a means of personal and social empowerment. He is trapped, like Paz, in the mode of limiting the myth rather than accepting its political power. Thinking theatrically about the practice of character, the very act of rehearsal—the embodiment of a social actor—can instigate a process of social transformation beyond the space of the play, especially when the representation has the power of El Pachuco.

Though not attending to the marking of the body through rehearsal and performance, Marcos Sanchez-Tranquilino and John Tagg reiterate the potential power of this cultural creation that brings about a "third space" between two nationalized spaces. According to Sanchez-Tranquilino and Tagg, "*Pachuco* culture was a survival strategy not of purity, of saying *less*, but rather of saying *more*, of saying too much, with the wrong accent and intonation, of mixing the metaphors, making illegal crossings, and continually transforming language so that its effects might never be wholly assimilable to an essential ethnicity, to a 'social ecology' of delinquency, or to the spectacle of multicultural and commodified diversity."[35] Here, the pachuco gains stylized power through rhetorical and spectacular excess, two concepts employed by Valdez in the theatricalization of El Pachuco. Following this argument, the pachuco and El Pachuco become producers of "delinquent narrativity,"[36] much like Miguel Piñero's players—creating worlds and stories that embody the border and the spaces in between.[37] El Pachuco's excess is something that cannot be fully categorized by means of conceptions of ethnicity; Valdez is wrighting a conceptual space beyond essential or constructed, a kind of experiential transformation that, while literally constructed through experience, becomes something beyond the limits of an individual identity.

However, if Valdez's theory of transformation is taken seriously, then the shift is even more profound. The interplay of pachuco as mythic identity, as social individual, as group identity and language practice, as *nahual* (spiritual double), and as psychological interiority, fuels much of the critical discussion around the play. Yarbro-Bejarano and Ybarra Frausto suggest, "Historical and mythical *Pachuco* are opposed, and anyone who has seen the show knows which one dominates the play. . . . The audience reacts so positively to El Pachuco that no critical examination of his qualities is possible."[38] This anxiety about the sensual allure of the theatrical performance is working against the very power of the genre. In El Pachuco's function as *nahual*, Hank's "other self," he provides a space for the potential fragmentation of Hank's identity and an understanding that this splitting is not necessarily disempowering.[39] The competitive aspects of the relationship between Henry and El Pachuco are predicated on stylistic issues.

> HENRY: (*Furious but keeping his cool.*) Mira, ese. Hank Reyna's no loser. I'm coming out of this one on top. ¿Me entiendes, Mendez? (HE *walks away with a Pachuco gait.*)
> PACHUCO: (*Forcefully.*) Don't try to out-Pachuco ME, ese! We'll see who comes out on top.[40]

The idea that El Pachuco is not only resistant to the incarnation of his mythic status but also potentially threatened by such an act allows for competing notions of pachuco identity. El Pachuco is not merely an expressionistic character who brings Hank's unconscious to life. Instead, this relationship explores the possibility that control is a question of style, as Hank assumes the style precisely to enable his social agency on, and perhaps beyond, the stage. Unable to control how one is being read, it is still possible to maintain some control over what is being read, over the visual semiotics of the character and its perceived relationship to community.

In a controversial moment read cinematically as the conflation of myth and an essential Chicano identity, El Pachuco is stripped of his zoot suit by rioters and is left in a "small loincloth." El Pachuco "turns and looks at HENRY, with mystic intensity. HE opens his arms as an Aztec conch blows, and HE exits backwards with powerful calm into the shadows."[41] At this moment El Pachuco becomes most easily read as the essential Aztec at the heart of every pachuco (and perhaps every Chicano as well), but the physical embodiment and presence of this symbol within a theatrical context work against this reading. Rather than seeing an essential self, what remains is still a role, still a costume, and the power of the moment comes from the sounds of the conch, the power of his gaze, and of the actor's calm exit. Though Valdez certainly invokes an extended history of resistance that includes indigenous culture and knowledge, the space of the theater makes the assertion of an essential self a near impossibility, as is clearly evidenced by the power and presence of socially constructed identities. The actor's body contains and performs the essential identity, thus ostending or pointing to this as an act. This is not the practical emptiness of everyday gesture but a meaningful act that contains the power of spirituality and ritual. This power is sustained by the actor's presence, developed in part through the physical training for the role.

The tension created by the conceptual space between the actor's body and the character's body serves as a counter to any easy assumption of essentialism, even as the conventions of theatrical semiosis mark the body as standing in for a general category. In his liminal space, El Pachuco mythically transcends and controls the stage, but this identity is still clearly one constructed by the space of the stage itself, making theatricality itself generative of power. The critical resistance toward this theatrical moment is indicative of an antitheatrical prejudice that resists the material nonreality of the theatrical space. In the search for a class-based reality, or out of fear of an essentializing discourse of identity, critics have forgotten that it is in fact theater they are watching (and in fact many are watching the fixed and disembodied space of film), and they have reduced the body of the actor to the character portrayed, losing the necessary and always present distance that allows for potential transgression and transformation.

More important for Valdez's project, his recuperation of an urban Chicano spirituality through the ambivalent figure of El Pachuco can be rooted in a myth-history previously erased from cultural representation. Not necessarily arguing for an essential Aztec at the heart of the pachuco, he is nonetheless acknowledging the indigenous roots of the intercultural resistance and conflict embodied in the Chicano; and, in doing so, he makes an implicit argument regarding the anxiety produced by this representation, a form of media containment whose hysteria makes sense only in relationship to the construction of an archetypal threat. In a sense, Valdez is articulating the ambivalent power that emerges from the construction of the fear of the other. The problems with this form of empowerment are clearly articulated through the contentious vision of El Pachuco as a central iconic figure around which community is manifest.

The criticisms of Valdez's potentially archetypal figure also do not take sufficient account of his insistence on style as a transformative force; physical and linguistic gestures create a multiplicity of possibilities, opening up space rather than fixing it on a particular identity. El Pachuco's cynicism and linguistic playfulness ironically distances him from any fully fixed sense of self, even as he is articulated in mythic terms. He is

> A mythical, quizzical, frightening being
> precursor of revolution
> Or a piteous, hideous heroic joke
> deserving of absolution?
> I speak as an actor on the stage.
> The Pachuco was existential
> for he was an Actor in the streets
> both profane and reverential.[42]

Explicitly stating the logic of both/and, the self-characterization of El Pachuco creates excess passing by through a series of poses. El Pachuco is an "actor on the stage" through his own self-referential naming, but one who is attempting to represent and articulate the possibility of "Acting" on the streets, a gesture that heightens everyday behavior into a self-conscious construction that offers the possibility of its own frame. If a person on the street is an "Actor," there is an implicit demand for the framing activity of an audience invested in witnessing what will transpire. Everyday gestures gain the semiotic significance of stage action, and on the stage the heightened style of El Pachuco is central to the theatricality of the play as a whole. With the construction of pachuco identity as a character, as a dramatic role that can be placed upon the body of a Chicano actor, becoming an "Actor in the streets" offers the real possibility of a theatrical self within the everyday world. Valdez's creation of this role was literally an act of empowerment, providing a model not only for the actor playing the role but also for audience members who could now imagine the possibility of occupying this position of ambivalent power.

The reverential space articulated by El Pachuco also echoes the spiritual practice inherent in the dramaturgical vision of El Teatro Campesino and Valdez. According to Broyles-González's account of the Theater of the Sphere, one theoretical framework developed and employed by El Teatro Campesino, the spiritual practices inherent in their dramaturgical vision do not impede an analysis and awareness of the social real but rather function "as a model of human liberation indispensable to the larger social struggle."[43] This potential for theatrical space as "liberational praxis" is an inherent part of Valdez's project. By articulating the potentiality of El Pachuco through a Chicano actor whose very role is the embodiment of this claim, the transformative theatrical power of the pachuco on stage offers the possibility of transformation beyond the stage.

In his reading of the film version as a combination of Aztec and Brechtian imagery, Mark Pizzato reminds us that Valdez presented El Pachuco as an incarnation of the Aztec god Tezcatlipoca, and that he understood the appeal of the play to rest in the power of this invocation. In his discussion of the Aztec rituals surrounding the worship of Tezcatlipoca, Pizzato states, "For the feast of Toxcatl, in honor of Tezcatlipoca, a captured warrior, dressed in the symbols and colors of the god, was sacrificed at the top of a temple pyramid. But first that captured warrior was trained by temple personnel and performed the character of the god for an entire year."[44] Ironically, though, despite reminding his readers of Valdez's desire to return a level of spirituality to the people, he reduces that spirituality to a psychological abstraction through the lens of Lacanian psychoanalysis. In addition, he elides the second crucial aspect that he highlights, the literal training of the captured warrior necessary to perform the role of the God. This training is central to *Zoot Suit*; the representation of El Pachuco is not a space for improvisation but rather a stylistic ideal whose representational power alchemically produces agency not only on stage but on the streets as well.

Returning the stage to its theological state, Valdez performs a dramatic and spiritual gesture that Pizzato recognizes but limits by connecting it to Artaud and his attempts at presence. Valdez is constructing a spiritual truth that manifests itself physically in the liminal space of the stage and literally transforms El Pachuco into an icon of resistance. This spiritual component explains Valdez's lack of concern with criticism that he misrepresents or misses an opportunity to represent the historical realities of the moment in a naturalistic model that reflects even more effectively on the Chicano. It also accounts for his increasing focus on theatricality, which critics such as Richard Eder condemned.[45] In the most extreme version of this reading, the historical presentation of events becomes merely a context for the emergence of El Pachuco as a mythical site through which a different model of Chicano agency can be articulated. The act of acting in this space and the audience's role in witnessing this incarnation allow a shared moment of community, one grounded in a spiritual power that reflects everyday lived practice of contemporary Chicano life.

El Pachuco's agency, his power to transform representation, exists in his capacity to function as a stage manager controlling the flow of events but is contingent on the physical style and gesture of the Chicano embodying the myth. Though dramaturgical control is central to the theatricality of the style, the materiality of El Pachuco's body is at the center of the power of this play and the style of his performance is central to a successful performance. During rehearsals for the twenty-fifth-anniversary revival of *Zoot Suit*, a great deal of energy was engaged in training the actor's body to replicate the gestural language first manifest in the body of Edward James Olmos and canonized in contemporary Chicano popular culture. This work both validates the importance of stylization and performance in the corporeal manifestation of this myth and recognizes that miraculous transformation is in fact a product of human labor. The body as transformative agent gains its power through training and development of a particular style of movement and presence attached to the costume of the zoot suit. The gestural language and bodily iconography of El Pachuco are not idiosyncratic choices of actor psychology but rather are integral and fixed parts of the role. From this vantage point, there is a substantial parallel with Brecht's gestus, especially Fredric Jameson's reading of the term as an example.[46] Given the pedagogical implications of Brecht's theater, Valdez is in fact using the gestus differently, teaching a physicality that enables transformation rather than using gestus to merely mark a social position.

This literal transformation enabled by El Pachuco can be seen in Edward James Olmos himself. The one sustained critical success of *Zoot Suit* in its first move from Los Angeles to Broadway was the reception of Edward James Olmos as El Pachuco, a magical role that helped launch his film career, defining him as an actor and an Actor with the potential for transformation from the margins and the mainstream.[47] According to Broyles-González, "His sensual sliding gait, his staccato speech and honeyed speaking voice were among the characteristics that gave him a distinctive personality."[48] Olmos received a World Theater award for his work with the play, was lauded for his "comic ferocity" in the role in New York City, and received a Tony nomination for his work. He also received an American Theatre Wing award for the representation of a "quintessential American character," an award shared by Lee J. Cobb's Willy Loman and Marlon Brando's Stanley Kowalski.[49]

Rather than charisma leading directly to power, El Pachuco demonstrates that certain styles hold representational power, an argument for the enabling power of style to grant agency—a trope literally accomplished through the transformation of Edward James Olmos. The energy attached to his acting and the compelling quality of the portrayal insist that the embodiment of the style itself retains its force as a node where the emotional energy of the audience can be invested, giving El Pachuco the "license" to manipulate the stage and perhaps the larger world. According to a typed biography intended for release as part of the promotional materials for *The Ballad of Gregorio Cortez*, "Three weeks after [*Zoot Suit*] premiered in Los Angeles, the actor received a phone call requesting him to address an assembly of students as Roosevelt High School. Overwhelmed by the teenagers' positive reaction to his message, the encounter sparked Olmos's interest in community involvement and helped launch his national speaking tour."[50] Over the next several years, he spoke to youth in prisons and reform schools, always encouraging them to develop the discipline necessary for self-transformation. This self-transformation parallels Olmos's own role in *Zoot Suit*, one that provides the power to take charge and change the world.

Though the extreme form of this change is utopian, it is enabled by the invocation of style, theatricality, and myth as a space for transformation. In a sustained analysis of the alterations in *Zoot Suit*, Broyles-González demonstrates a gradual shift away from the naturalist beginnings of the text toward an increasing theatricality. She argues that this move toward abstraction is partially due to increased mainstreaming, a move away from the material history that works against the politics of the piece. This transformation was also noted by Richard Eder in a review of the Broadway production; he expressed concern about the move away from realism during the early phases in Los Angeles toward what appeared to him to be a much more diffuse piece in New York.[51] However, this movement toward theatricality may in fact clarify the sustained contingency of the history of the pachuco as an identity always articulated in highly theatrical terms.

One of the central points of exploration in the existential coming-of-age story of Hank Reyna as a protagonist in *Zoot Suit* is the extent to which his maturation will be figured in relationship to the mythical El Pachuco. As a character Hank offers a material limit and counter to the myth, exposing in his conflict with El Pachuco the divided and ambivalent attitude toward the figure in various Mechicano spaces. In this sense, Hank becomes a sign of the conceptual limits of the Pachuco as an actor on the streets. Though he has choices, they are constrained by the critical assumptions of those around him and the various narratives and historical events that frame his identity. Valdez's ability to wright these frames is dependent on shifting from the historical tendency to understand pachuco style as a form of delinquency to a recognition of the style as a radical self-assertion and manifestation of cultural power.

In his reading of the film, Carl Gutiérrez-Jones argues, "In addition to his complex role as a paranoid reader, then, El Pachuco acts as a paranoia-inspiring panoptic force in his own right. The play and the film in fact begin with his transgression of theater's traditional visual flow; he literally turns the gaze back on the audience, making it the object of his amusement. In both the cinematic and theatrical versions, the control suggested by this change in dramatic gaze is then exercised by Pachuco through various extradiegetic manipulations of scenes."[52] Although for Gutiérrez-Jones these are primarily events in the cinematic version that have no direct parallels in the dramatic text, there are two particular moments that are important to reexamine.

During a fight in act 1, El Pachuco freezes the dramatic action on stage, telling Hank, "That's exactly what the play needs right now. Two more Mexicans killing each other. Watcha . . . Everybody's looking at you."[53] With the *caló* "watcha" he breaks the frame of the fourth wall and directly references the audience. As much as the actual content of the moment, his use of code switching here invokes a particular Chicano audience capable of understanding this tableau as a potential moment for a mainstream audience to reinforce its learned prejudice of violent Chicano masculinity. In this moment, he uses an English word conjugated as a Spanish verb that implies the doubled possibility of *mirar*—to watch and to look. "Watcha" is a caution that draws attention to two acts of watching—Hank's glance at the audience and the audience's scrutiny of Hank. In this moment of critical recognition, the boundaries of these two acts are blurred in an explicit manifestation of theatricality as a relationship between spectator and actor.

Operating in the linguistic world of *caló*, aurally performing his identity, El Pachuco is able to slide across boundaries and perform analytic work while simultaneously undermining the very binaries that might describe this movement. The content of this metatheatrical moment calls attention to the spectatorial allure of intra-Chicano violence while satirizing its problematic status as an Anglo cliché. By preventing the killing while drawing attention to the desire of a particular audience formation, El Pachuco contradicts the narrow-minded and violent racist essentialisms of documents such as the Ayres report, read during trial proceedings, that maintained racist beliefs about a Mexican proclivity toward violence based on an Aztec past. The audience is imputed to possess a voyeuristic desire to see the "other" kill the "other" in a space framed so that the self is not in danger. Making an even larger indictment about literal audience investment, El Pachuco emphasizes, "That's exactly what they paid to see. Think about it."[54]

In this moment of consciousness-raising, El Pachuco invokes an audience who pays to witness a safe death of the "other" on the opposite side of a proscenium arch. By crossing the proscenium with his words, he implicates the Chicano audience itself in this moment of mainstream reception, explicitly asking them to think about their own position vis-à-vis what the hegemonic gaze has "paid to see." Here, the crucial questions of who is for sale and how much this form of representation costs echo themes of the oft-anthologized El Teatro Campesino *acto Los Vendidos* (The Sell-Outs or Those Who Are Sold). Stopping the action provides a moment of self-reflection for the audience; they may be caught in their enthusiasm for a moment of violent excitement whose racial politics might otherwise be invisible precisely because of the frequency of the representation of brown-on-brown violence. This dramaturgical control is more powerful than a simple critique of stereotypical criminalized representation, because it exposes the audience's emotional investment in the moment.

A second important Brechtian moment emerges when El Pachuco replays the Judge's statement, "The zoot suit haircuts will be retained throughout the trial for purposes of identification of defendants by witnesses."[55] Relying on a historical record that indicted the original trial judge for exactly this racist behavior, this moment shows not only the assumption of style as a marker of criminality but also the slippery chain of signification by which "Mexican" is transformed into criminal, while simultaneously exposing the very contingency of its manifestation by legislating the "retention" of specific style markers. Without retaining their clothing the boys would no longer be recognizable as "criminals"; yet this insistence that the clothing literally makes the man exposes an anxiety about the contingency of identity.

If a pachuco can be identified only by his suit, then what is the prosecution to make of Tommy Roberts? Roberts, the Irish pachuco, makes clear his allegiances despite claims by his *carnales* that his ethnicity (seen here as specifically outside his pachuco identity) will get him some form of preferential treatment.

> HENRY: There's not a single paddy we can trust.
> TOMMY: Hey, ese, what about me?
> HENRY: You know what I mean.
> TOMMY: No, I don't know what you mean. I'm here with the rest of yous.
> JOEY: Yeah, but you'll be the first one out, cabrón.
> TOMMY: Gimme a break, maníaco. ¡Yo soy Pachuco!
> HENRY: Relax, ese. Nobody's getting personal with you.[56]

Joey's insistence on a privilege system predicated on Tommy's "paddy" identity is rejected by Tommy's insistence of his pachuco identity. This gesture, underwritten socially by his presence in the cell, forces Hank to counter that no one is "getting personal." The traffic in identities is understood to be depersonalized; consequently, no one need be offended. Hank is in fact forced through the play to rethink his categories of identification, producing an alternative notion of community emerging from the self-transformation of performance enabled by pachuco identity.

The original conflict that leads to the trial in the stage version—the supposed murder of Jose Diaz—comes in part from the confusion between the Thirty-eighth Street Gang and the Downey Gang. Because there are twenty-two defendants, an entire gang on trial for one action, there seems to be a transformation of the term guilt by association into the idea of guilt as association: claiming a collective identity is in and of itself a dangerously illicit act. The confusion of identities exposes the prosecution's inability to clarify what is being looked at. It is very clear they are in fact blinded by an ethnic stereotype placed squarely on a real ethnic body. With this use of stereotyping, the real is evacuated and the remainder is an essentially interchangeable ethnic other. If the lawyer George Shearer is right, "All the prosecution has been able to prove is that these boys wear long hair and zoot suits."[57] If style is criminality is ethnicity, then the essentialist roots of the racist harangues that convict these boys are put into question.

Valdez's final gesture in the play breaks open the possibilities for Hank Reyna's future. The Press appears to have the final word, providing a biography with loose echoes of Henry Leyvas, the historical Henry, and his narrative statement is accepted as the conventional close of the play. In the twenty-fifth-anniversary production, audience members began clapping, only to be interrupted by El Pachuco calling on other members of the cast to provide alternative futures for Henry. By the end of the play El Pachuco has opened up the symbolic space of representation enough to rewrite history beyond the scope of partial facts, insisting on the transformative choices of everyday life, on the possibility of wrighting ethnicity. Though critiqued by some as a refusal of the material realities of Henry Leyvas's life, these multiple endings are necessary to continue the possibility of transformation engendered within the space of the play. El Pachuco's interruption forces the audience to recognize their willingness to accept a problematic future and implicates them in the necessity of finding a new one. By working communally to tell the possible trajectories for Hank Reyna, as each character provides a different story in the space El Pachuco has opened, he once again enables the possibility of moving beyond the theater even as this agency only emerges through his theatrical power and the voice and space of the community in the theater.

4

Bandidos to Badges: Criminality and the Genre of Ethnicity

Building upon his wrighting of the ambivalent figure of the pachuco, in *Bandido!* and *I Don't Have to Show You No Stinking Badges*, Luis Valdez continues to focus on the intersection of criminality, history, and representation. From the bandido, the historical bandit, to the cholo, the contemporary cousin of the pachuco, Valdez takes seriously the claims of Alfredo Mirandé that

> [t]he criminalization of the Chicano resulted not from their being more criminal or violent but from a clash between conflicting and competing cultures, worldviews, and economic, political and judicial systems. . . . Chicanos were labeled as *bandidos* because they actively resisted Anglo encroachment and domination but lacked the power to shape images of criminality or to articulate sociological/criminological theories. The *bandido* image served to reinforce or legitimate their economic, political, and legal exploitation.[1]

This construction of criminality through control over representation is crucial to understanding Valdez's investment in historical Chicano male subjectivity. In the process of wrighting an alternative relationship between Chicano identity and community, Valdez draws his audience's attention both to their own processes of interpretation and to the construction of an individual's communal and cultural position. Valdez makes use of two popular genres, nineteenth-century stage melodrama and television situation comedy, as aesthetic frames to render visible the audience's mainstream and restrictive cultural assumptions.

Bandido! and the Melodrama of Ethnicity

In *Bandido!*, subtitled *The American Melodrama of Tiburcio Vásquez Notorious California Bandit*, Valdez recuperates the legendary figure of the *corridos*, or folk ballads. Reviled by authorities but celebrated by average citizens, Vásquez "was the last man to be legally, publically executed in California."[2] Because he was daguerreotyped and interviewed, Valdez is able to place Vásquez's historical narrative and the melodramatic stereotype of journalistic sensationalism in dialogue.

The published version contrasts two representational frames, realistic theater and melodrama, effectively wrighting both the bandido and melodrama itself. The scenes alternate in their presentation between these two aesthetics, and the realistic play is constantly aware of the existence of the melodrama; the presentation of the latter is placed within the realistic frame, and it functions, with the mixed blessing of Vásquez, to help defray the costs of his legal defense. This metadramatic construction is the central trope of the published play, its main point of interest, and the site of its potential undoing. By subtitling his play "*The American Melodrama*" Valdez situates it within a cultural tradition. Melodrama was the dominant aesthetic of nineteenth-century U.S. popular theater but has rarely been understood as a mode of sophisticated aesthetic entertainment. Literally referencing the musical underscoring that allowed British theatrical producers to evade theatrical patents, melodrama is typically seen as the epitome of Romantic notions of character development, as well as the home of spectacular visual effects.

However, through the work of Bruce McConachie and Jeffrey Mason, nineteenth-century American melodrama has been recuperated for its important cultural work. McConachie's method is to study what he calls "theatrical formation" in which "groups of spectators and theatre performers produce each other from the inside out as artists-to-be-experienced and audiences-to-be-entertained."[3] According to McConachie, melodrama's function is to create a social identity capable of reading and understanding the social constructs imagined on the stage in front of them. Similarly, Mason argues for the dialectical influence of the genre within a particular historical configuration, "to elicit its operation in relation to ideology, myth, and representation." Mason's description of the function of melodrama is particularly useful in understanding Valdez's play:

Each melodrama must satisfy its audience concerning the nature not of virtue, but of evil. . . . By its very nature and method, melodrama must satisfy its audience's expectations rather than present a confrontation with belief and value. The strength of the melodramatic imperative betokens a lurking, covert fear that can drive the machinery. If society can change, if it can evolve or change into something new rather than experiencing restoration to its former condition, then it is possible for such change to leave the subject behind, rendering him marginal, rejected, and out of place. This is the fear of erasure or displacement, of being cast aside and left alone.[4]

Valdez employs melodrama's implicit myth-making project not to transform the inherently conservative cultural politics of the form but rather to expose the restrictive conservatism practiced by the genre's implied spectator.

If, as Mason argues, melodramatic ideals are a mainstay of American cultural history and western mythos, then trafficking in such discourse is an ideal cultural space in which to wright the representational history of Chicanos. At the same time, melodramatic language and characterization verge on the creation of types or stereotypes, and given the ethical dimensions of this genre, those types are marked as indisputably good or evil. The deployment of melodrama to deconstruct or rewrite history thus runs the risk of creating new forms of stereotyped and conventional history in the process, not to mention reinforcing a reductive moral binary.

Peter Brooks argues that melodrama arises at the same moment as "the very anxiety created by the guilt experienced when allegiance to a sacred system of things no longer obtain." Instead of "illumination and recognition in terms of a higher order of synthesis," which is the concluding moment of tragedy, melodrama produces "clarification and recognition of the signs in conflict."[5] Brooks concludes that melodrama, in its attempt to return to a synthetic conclusion, is productive only in the moment of failure. Though the form exposes rather than resolves cultural anxiety, the very act of revealing this anxiety is productive. This dynamic echoes Louis Althusser's argument about materialist theater in his essay on the Piccolo Theatre. Describing a situation parallel to the multiple frames of Valdez's play, Althusser explores the potential ideological critique manifest in a work containing multiple irreconcilable temporalities. He argues that the "silent confrontation of a consciousness" infused with one model of dialectical reality "with a reality which is indifferent and strange to this so-called dialectic . . . makes possible an immanent critique of the illusions of consciousness."[6] Valdez's critique is manifest in the interplay between the character of Vásquez, in his various staged manifestations, and his historical record, itself melodramatic. Never transcending reality except in melodramatic terms, Valdez exposes the chains that bind this potential moment of wrighting.

Though Vásquez was still young when California became a part of the United States, he was old enough to understand and recognize the transformations taking place: the undesirable occupation of California by Anglos. Until the 1840s, Anglo movement into the region had been primarily peaceful and the new inhabitants were willing to mingle with and adapt to the ways of the old, but as the decade progressed, the westward-moving population became increasingly uncomfortable with adapting to the Californios, the Mexican inhabitants of California. By the time of the Treaty of Guadalupe Hidalgo in 1848, which ended the Mexican-American War, and the discovery of gold at Sutter's Mill, American-Californio relations had become strained. Monroy explains, "Californios perceived a difference between the first Americanos, as they called the Yankee immigrants to Mexican California, and those who came after the early 1840s. 'Many settled among us and contributed with their intelligence and industry to the progress of my beloved country,.' . . . 'Would that the foreigners that came to settle in Alta California after 1841 had been of the same quality as those who proceeded [sic] them!'"[7]

The newcomers "sought not to join Californio society . . . but to fashion American settlements within California." After the Mexican-American War, "the Californios soon found themselves and their ways placed outside the new Anglo-American laws."[8] According to Monroy, the most telling signs were legal justifications for the removal of "foreign" miners, and the Land Act of 1851, which reevaluated Californio land ownership according to Anglo legal codes and bureaucratic machinery. Early on, a distinction emerged between the upper class, landed Californios who were considered Spanish, and the lower-class "Mexicans," who were cultural scapegoats for racist bigotry. Under the aegis of this so-called "Spanish Fantasy," as Carey McWilliams labeled it in *North from Mexico*, one class was allowed the possibility of assimilation into the new American society despite radically different attitudes toward land ownership and means of production. Landed Californios were merely indolent and wasteful in the minds of the occupiers; Mexicans, however, were collectively criminalized as class lines became increasingly racialized. Lynchings by transplanted Texans and the presumption of Mexican guilt resulted in this class-based cultural separation based on class lines, which in turn led to a growing resistance among the occupied population. According to Monroy, "a very small number took to the hills and began a life of crime against the white Americans. Such actions further convinced the Americans of the criminal nature of the Mexicans. The Mexicans themselves looked to these bandidos as avengers, materially supported them, and gained vicarious revenge through them."[9]

In one oft-quoted exchange, Vásquez describes his personal experience of oppression to justify his transgressive activities.

> My career grew out of the circumstances by which I was surrounded. As I grew to manhood I was in the habit of attending balls and parties given by the native Californians, into which the Americans, then beginning to become numerous, would force themselves and shove the native-born men aside, monopolizing the dance and the women. This was about 1852. A spirit of hatred and revenge took possession of me. I had numerous fights in defense of what I believe to be my rights and the rights of my countrymen. The officers were continually in pursuit of me. I believed we were unjustly and wrongfully deprived of the social rights that belonged to us.[10]

Although his attitude might seem overly flippant at first glance, "[d]iffering cultural customs," Burciaga explains, "can mean everything in such situations. While to 'cut in' was perfectly normal conduct for a Yankee, to the Californio it was an insult, a personal affront. 'Cutting in' is still considered a dangerous practice in many parts of the Southwest, Mexico and Latin America. Machismo is not necessarily the negative Anglo-American interpretation. To a Latino male, machismo can also be an honest self-assurance to defend country, women and honor with their very life."[11] Even more important than the potential threat to one's pride is the potential threat to one's identity, an identity transformed from national to ethnic. If the Californio women are "taken away" by the newcomers, then the genealogical roots of identity are endangered along with their property. Defending the right to your dance partner becomes not only a question of honor but also a symbolic site to contest the future of the territory.

Vásquez's outlaw career was interrupted by two jail stints in San Quentin, and though he was well known to contemporaries, historical amnesia forms part of Valdez's interest. The disappearance of Vásquez from public mythology did not result from an absence of published accounts of his life, capture, and death. Among the several written accounts were *Vásquez, or the Hunted Bandits of the San Joaquin* by George Beers, the man responsible for wounding the bandido in the shoulder during his capture.[12] All of the accounts agree that Vásquez first fell on the wrong side of the law in 1852 for his involvement in the slaying of a constable ostensibly restoring order at a fandango in Monterey County. Vásquez's association with Anastasio Garcia, an older bandido, is offered as the explanation for his entry into banditry. His notoriety became widespread in the early 1870s, mostly because of his robbery of the town of Tres Pinos during which three people were slain. Despite multiple accounts of the murders and a guilty court verdict, Vásquez maintained his innocence of murder while simultaneously bragging about his robberies.

It is clear from undoubtedly embellished interviews that he was determined to cultivate the media personality of a gentleman bandit. Monroy calls him "the classic social bandit,"[13] and Broyles-González goes further, calling him a "social activist,"[14] emphasizing his revolutionary claims over his criminal activities. Though presumably romanticized, his choices to refrain from taking items with sentimental value, to not take a life, to never abuse women, and to occasionally lessen the inconvenience of his prisoners are reported in interviews and accounts. The media recorded a philosophical poet whose generosity and respect for his captors was worthy of admiration. This image prompted women to venture to the jailhouse for a glimpse of the notorious bandit. A sophisticated student of self-representation, Vásquez made pragmatic use of his public allure. He sold photographic cards with a short history of his exploits to interested parties for fifty cents apiece, close to nine dollars in today's money, in order to assist with his defense.

The two generic modes of realism and melodrama form a doubled vision that Valdez makes clear in the initial stage directions: "This realistic framework of the jail . . . serves as the infrastructure for the gilded melodrama stage into which it transforms. . . . The contrast of theatrical styles between the realism of the jail, and the *trompe l'oeil* of the melodrama is purely intentional and part of the theme of the play.

Their subtle interaction is a matter of interpretation, but their combined reality must be a metaphor—and not a facile cliché—of the Old West." The realism of the jail is produced through a "flat . . . interior" while the "American Melodrama Stage" with all of the ironic mythification of the capital letters is produced through "painted drops" and "light changes in the public eye."[15] The realistic and melodramatic settings share one actor playing Vásquez, but his mannerisms and style in the two environments are varied, much in the same way that the settings are contrasted. Through this doubled visual, theatrical performance, the audience receives a much clearer understanding of the influence of genre on the frames through which identity is realized.

In one frame, Vásquez is playing in front of painted scenery that presents a physical two-dimensional realism, though it is simultaneously a three-dimensional perspective scene for those willing to accept the theatrical convention. This illusion, produced through perspective scenery, mirrors the illusion of the melodramatic character. His heightened emotionalism, histrionic flourishes, and grand declarations create a figure who constantly strives for the transcendence of a tragic hero but is held back by the demands and expectations of the genre: the Impresario staging the melodrama never grants him substantial cultural importance. In terms of emotional character, the realistic Vásquez has fewer pretensions toward tragedy and a greater predilection toward pride and vanity.

The action begins on the melodrama stage, in a whorehouse where Vásquez encounters Sheriff Rowland of Los Angeles but manages to pass himself off as another Californio. For Broyles-González these whorehouse scenes create the unnecessary image of a "libertine,"[16] but these moments are equally condemned by Vásquez in the "realistic" portion of the play where he accuses the impresario Samuel Gillette of breaking their production agreement and portraying him as an "ass."[17] Vásquez's presence in the whorehouse is justified because the madam, California Kate, is his gun-running contact, and it is in her presence that he first proposes the possibility of revolution. Speaking to Rowland in the third person, he claims that Vásquez is "planning a series of robberies that's going to terrorize the whole of California." Rowland replies, "He'll have the railroad and the telegraph to contend with. Progress is going to hang the horse thief. . . ."[18] This faith in technological progress as a counter to the "criminal" resistance of the Californio population is symptomatic of the valuation of progress and industrial development that justified the myth of Anglo superiority. In moments such as this, the play carefully comments on the economic and political situation of California circa 1875 while remaining faithful to known facts about Vásquez's life.

Like the historical Vásquez, his manifestations in Valdez's drama are also very invested in self-representation and identity, both in the realistic scenes that frame the melodrama and in the melodrama itself. Recognizing the theatrical qualities of his every activity, the Vásquez of the frame sees his demeanor at the gallows as a crucial representational moment: "Damned if I don't put on a bravura performance . . . when the time comes." Following both reports of his stoicism and the expectations of a melodramatic "hero," Vásquez insists that his exterior presentation will be appropriate and even worthy of praise. But, in fact, it is his very appearance that causes much of the difficulty of representation within the play: "is this noble countenance the twisted visage of a convicted stage robber?" he asks early, a question potentially answered by the claim that "he doesn't seem like such a bad fellow." However, in the mind of Gillette, the impresario responsible for the staging of the melodrama, the audience is "attracted to [his] villainy."[19]

In fact, the contrast between the noble bearing of Vásquez and his criminal representation romanticizes him even within the realist frame. In daguerreotypes he is presented as a gentleman with his beard trimmed, his face calm, composed, and perhaps most important, very light skinned.[20] From the visual semiotics of racialized discourse within the nineteenth century, he was clearly a Californio gentleman, not a "greasy Mexican," a contrast emphasized in the play, though more in class than racial terms. However, to an extent, his whiteness creates an ironic distance from the claim of identity as a bandido. On the frontispiece of the printed play, there is a reproduction of a daguerreotype with the word *Bandido!* above it and his name below. The distance between the stereotypical visual associations of the word *bandido* and the portrait creates a potential jarring sensation that is aided by the visual addition of a specific name at the bottom of the photograph. *Bandido!* as title thus marks a stereotypical social role that is rewritten by both the name and the face.

The visage we see is not "twisted," nor does it fit the melodramatic expectation of an expressionistic visual world in which evil in the soul is marked by ugliness on the body. In fact, even detractors such as Richard Hornby acknowledge Vásquez "was handsome and debonair, and may even have been something of a poet, but his career was that of a cheap crook."[21] Willing to accept a version of romanticized identity, Hornby was unwilling to grant the bandido a role as liberator or even social bandit, bringing his own moral code to bear in his willingness to condemn the man for murder.

However, as the reviewer Hornby correctly points out, the conviction and death of Vásquez were certain because within California legal code, his status as an accessory made him just as guilty as the actual murderers. This legal imagination constructs a group identity in dialectical relationship with the individual identity of the daguerreotype. Granting Vásquez individual significance avoids condemning the play from the very beginning. Refusing to grant him historical significance in the larger social arena insures he exists only as a bandido. As such, this reviewer becomes an exemplar of the dangerous potential of mainstream audience response to the play. Hornby attempts to contain Valdez's wrighting of Vásquez through his unwillingness to allow for either creative license or an alternative history, a strategy that is echoed in the exchanges between Vásquez and the Impresario.

Vásquez's conflict with the Impresario clearly conveys Valdez's perceptions of the inherent dangers and aesthetic expectations of melodrama. In refusing to add scenes Vásquez composed to his melodrama, the Impresario labels them "lies" before he has glanced at them, demonstrating the reductive assumptions of mainstream representation. "Twenty years as a vicious desperado and never a single, solitary slaying? It won't wash, Vásquez. You're [sic] entire career is too full of dubious moral questions. We're talking about melodrama here. What's right is right, what's wrong is wrong. The public will only buy tickets to savor the evil in your soul."[22] By emphasizing a fixed notion of melodramatic morality (or marketability, which is the same thing for the Impresario) combined with a spotlight on evil rather than good, the Impresario seems to be in agreement with Mason's conception of the ethos of the genre.

This speech about the narrative of Vásquez's career and the limits of melodramatic representation produces his only anger within the realistic frame. The anger is not just about Gillette's claims about his life; it is also about the perceived limits of control over its representation. He grabs the Impresario, threatening, "Don't make me prove I'm a murderer, as well, Gillette." Attempting to recuperate and control the reception of this remark on the ears of Sheriff Adams, Vásquez dismisses it as a theatrical gesture: "I hope you weren't deceived by my little melodramatic aside to Gillette? It was just an act." The voice of the law tellingly and predictably replies, "Save your act for the court, Tiburcio."[23] As in *Zoot Suit*, the courtroom becomes a metaphor for the theater, and legal defense is a series of competing performances to control representation.

However, in *Bandido!* there is no courtroom drama, only the presentation of the melodrama and Vásquez's jail commentary. Valdez wrights this situation to explore the practice of melodrama as a mode of (self)representation. In Gillette's mind melodrama is the only way Vásquez's story will be told. At the same time, it makes Vásquez's career as a bandido into a commodity to be purchased by Anglo voyeurs of the exotic and the transgressive, of the "foreign other" who often embodies evil on the melodrama stage. Even more than an attempt at a multicultural revision of the historical myths of the American West, Valdez's speculation on representation speaks to the problems of articulating identity within the politics of the "new ethnicities" as they gained greater prominence and problematic cultural cachet through the 1980s and 1990s. Authenticity rests within the judgmental mind of an audience willing to invest emotionally and financially only in something that fits within a predetermined script. The easiest way to satisfy this audience is stereotypical exaggeration. Thus, as Jorge Huerta argues in his introduction to the collection *Zoot Suit and Other Plays*, the Impresario becomes the real villain of the piece because he continually insists on a normative melodramatic presentation. The photographs and melodrama are Vásquez's attempt to "save" his own life, while the play itself is Valdez's effort to do the same thing.

The melodrama has all of the traditional trappings of the genre but presents the problematic Vásquez as the "hero" of the piece, since the only major Anglo character that could even vie for such a role is Sheriff Adams, who has previously failed to capture him. Aside from Vásquez, we have the tragic woman Rosario, the blind father-in-law, and plenty of minor bandido characters, taken from accounts of Vásquez's life. When we first encounter "the gang," the audience is treated to an education in the trade of the bandido, including lessons in how to command those you are robbing and which accoutrements of the trade are necessary. Careful to justify their behavior ("It's no crime at any time to steal from thieves"), they are clear about the social forces underlying their position. At the same time, they acknowledge that the proper construction of a bandido requires a menacing visage. Discussing the newest recruit in the group, Rita, the camp follower, articulates what it takes: "Now Chávez here, he's going to make a great bandit. It won't take much for this Mexican to look dangerous." Vásquez continues in this vein, telling Teodoro Moreno that he's "a bandido now. Look sloppy and more desperate." Here Vásquez begins the role of stage manager, insisting that they move "to our melodrama. I have the guns. Let me see your get-ups. And I want to see some tough, mean looking hombres." To Gonzalez, he comments that he looks "like a natural born greaser," a comment Gonzalez chooses to take as a compliment.[24] The clear humor of this situation is ironized both by the ease with which these men can be transformed into bandidos, as well as by the occasional linguistic reference to contemporary barrio culture.

In the melodramatic representation of the robbery of Tres Pinos, Abdon Leiva is the guilty party: the man who turned state's evidence against Vásquez after discovering his wife Rosario's adultery. In the court case, Vásquez is accused of at least one murder, but in the melo-drama he is innocent. He claims, "It always hurts the gringo more to lose his money than his life" and that "just the site (*sic*) of Tiburcio Vásquez and his band of cutthroats ought to do the trick."[25] The claim that visual representation is equal to the physical threat of actual bodies plays with the myth-making that underlies Vásquez. Unsurprisingly, this mythic portrait is articulated in the third person, as if he represents a position rather than an individual person.

Going to the house of Andres Pico, a hero from the Battle of San Pascual, a fight more symbolic of the Californio's ability to fight on equal terms with the U.S. invaders than a significant battle in the war,[26] Pico tells him to "save yourself. Or at least save the rest of us the grief and humiliation of watching them hang you." Here, Vásquez proposes his "rebellion that will crack the state of California in two," but Pico advocates caution and negotiation, indicating his belief that Vásquez is "over dramatizing" the situation, ironically articulating the historical counternarrative to Vásquez's revolutionary claims. On Vásquez's last night on earth, Gillette tells him, "Reality and theater don't mix, sir. That's your problem. You're too damned real, like those photographs of your face. If you were less familiar, like that Murrieta fellow, I'd turn your life into a genuine California romance. Your legend needs a little more grandeur."[27] Vásquez promises him grandeur that turns out to be the glorious melodramatic conclusion: a re-creation of the last legal, public execution in the State of California. He even gets the last word, a command to the hangman: "*pronto!*"

Vásquez's real-life conviction and death are as interesting as the play itself and provide the closest thing we have to theater in his real life. The charge to the jury in the case makes clear that regardless of whether Vásquez pulled the trigger at Tres Pinos, he is equally as guilty of murder. Although this collective guilt has eerie recollections of the miscarriage of justice in the Sleepy Lagoon murder trial, California legal code in the nineteenth century did allow such a ruling. Perhaps the strangest thing about Vásquez's execution for a modern reader is that it was a public hanging to which admission was granted by means of nontransferable formal invitation:

> *Pursuant to the statute in such cases, you are hereby*
> *invited to be present at the execution of Tiburcio*
> *Vásquez, at the jail of said county, in San Jose, on*
> *the 19th day of March, A.D., 1875, at 1:30 P.M.*

> J. H. ADAMS, SHERIFF

> *Present at jail entrance.*   *Not transferable.*[28]

Valdez provides an altered version of this invitation at the beginning of the 1994 text, imaginatively transforming the audience into invited witnesses of the execution.

The gradual fading of both capital punishment and public execution was having its effect in California in 1875, for the hanging was held within the jail rather than in the public space of a town square. The fear attached to such public displays of violence was connected to ideas of individual virtue and the possibility of reformation. Public hangings had become sites of carnivalesque behavior rather than solemn reminders of the penalties of transgression. This celebratory practice, combined with the legal authorities' distrust of both the universal nature of reform and the public display of remorse by the criminal, led to the banning of public execution.[29]

Vasquez's command to the hangman, "*pronto*," and the hanging that follows are central to the 1994 Mark Taper production of the play. In this version the events of the play itself are presented as a series of scenes in Vásquez's head in the thirteen seconds between his hanging and death. Scenes are linked by the command "*pronto*," and Vásquez is haunted not only by a vague sense of his own death as his life is replayed but by the Impresario, who functions as a figure of death. In this version, the Impresario exists in a space much closer to the surreal.[30] The difficulties of articulating the complexity of the real Vásquez within the vagaries of historical representation have made Valdez change his play multiple times.

Because of these changes, the six-week run at the Mark Taper Forum in the summer of 1994 was considered the world premiere of the work, although it had been staged in 1981 in San Juan Bautista in an earlier version.[31] The Taper production did extremely well financially but was not well received by reviewers. Part of the appeal for the audience was the lack of meaningful representation of Latinos in other media. During the 1994–95 television season, Latinos represented only "two percent of all characters," and although from 1992 to 1994 "[t]he proportion of Latino characters committing crimes fell dramatically, dropping from 16 percent to 6 percent," that was still one and a half times the number of white characters committing a crime.[32]

Though reviewers recognized the play's historical project and its gestures toward the transformation of the American mythology of the West, most still considered it a critical failure. Rob Eshman attacked its revisionary history as insufficiently aware of the actual heterogeneity of the "Anglo" community.[33] According to Laurie Winer, the play's events "are told in Valdez's signature mix, an almost vaudevillian mélange of song, posturing dialogue that occasionally quiets to a less hyperbolic state, and character as Symbol. It is a form both child-like and naive and one that flirts dangerously with cliché without necessarily elevating or reinventing the familiar." She ends with a critique of Valdez's representation: "It is still a matter of historical debate whether or not Vásquez fired any of the deadly shots at Tres Pinos. That possibility is not acknowledged in the moral universe of 'Bandido!' We are asked to consider Vásquez as a nascent revolutionary fighting the good fight, yet one who never addresses the question of how to have a revolution without killing anybody. This renders Vásquez as not the gentlest, but perhaps the least brilliant, of outlaws."[34]

A slightly more sympathetic criticism of the formal problems of the play was voiced by the musical director of a previous incarnation of the play, Francisco González: "One of the problems with Bandido! is that it never jibed. What you ended up with was a mishmash of ideas that didn't come together. There is so much about stereotyping that the piece becomes a stereotype."[35] Jorge Huerta's sympathetic introduction to the play compares it to an earlier work by El Teatro Campesino, the acto Los Vendidos in which "the playwright turns stereotyping around, making the audience reassess their attitudes about various Chicano and Mexican 'types.' We laugh but also understand that the characteristics exposed are a reflection of Anglo perceptions and, yes, even sometimes our own biases as Chicanos. In both Los Vendidos and Bandido! the playwright is portraying these characters with a clear understanding that they are stereotypes" (italics in original). Huerta recognizes that the very politics of representation are at stake in the play and goes so far as to assert that the Impresario functions as the villain in Valdez's rewriting of the genre: "the conflict is the melodrama itself."[36]

Regardless of the play's failure in the eyes of critics, its figuration of the politics and aesthetics of ethnic representation is important. The failure of the play is not so much a product of a "naive and childlike presentation" but the need of an audience to place such a representation in this category and an inability to recognize the critique of representation built into the very structure of the play. Because Valdez's work is wrighting Vásquez, it has the potential, although not fully realized, to undermine a cherished conceptual framework for ethnicity, the melodramatic.

Historically, the genre of melodrama involved a heightened and declamatory acting style, larger than life, with no attempt to attend to the complexities of conflicting and contradictory emotional states. Instead, the emotional register, like the plot itself, forms clear allegiances and focuses the audience's energy on the hero and the villain, with little or no confusion about which is which. The spectacularity of the stage becomes a means through which cultural dangers are manifest, and the audience is enabled to participate through abuse of the villain and support of the hero. While this definition may be an oversimplification of the theatrical practice, it is not a reduction of the mainstream reception and representation of men of color. Apart from the few leading men in contemporary culture such as movie stars and pop icons whose transgressions are understood as individual actions and therefore fascinating, the fear associated with Latino criminality is attached to an entire ethnic group. Roles are scripted and conventions are hardened, creating representations that support the divisive notion that a difference of ethnicity is a sign of moral difference. Melodramatic discourse about ethnicity echoes the binary reductionism of good and evil in melodrama itself by constituting the ethnic "other" in opposition to mainstream white consciousness.

This discriminatory assumption, embodied in the Impresario, is precisely what Valdez is wrighting. Ironically, his project was attacked for inverting a representational practice that haunts mainstream television, film, and the stage—the reduction of the other into a morally deficient and completely interchangeable character whose two-dimensional role serves a plot function. This type can be quickly read and understood, lacks meaningful psychological depth, and in brief moments of complexity is read as a symbol rather than an individual worthy of being understood. This problematic model is nonetheless the basis for a Reagan-era discourse (*Bandido!* was first developed in the early 1980s) of racial subordination as a result of moral failure. This model displaces rhetorical and physical excess onto the body of the other as a means of constructing an imagined community that defines itself in opposition to this excess. Herman Gray makes a similar argument about bodies of color and criminality represented on television, insisting that the television of the Reagan era helped create fears of an underclass of color as a means of defining whiteness.[37] According to this thinking, an individual's relative lack of success in the marketplace is a reflection of their moral failing, manifest through their failure to work and implicitly suggested to be the product of their ethnic identity.

It is important in this regard to remember that 1994 was a crucial year in the political landscape for Latinos in California. A ballot initiative first labeled Save Our State became Proposition 187, which was supported by then governor Pete Wilson. Intended to restrict public services to undocumented immigrants, Proposition 187 was supported with inflammatory rhetoric about an invasion of Mexicans and Central Americans crossing north into the United States. It passed, in part by constructing the narrative of an underclass threatening the "American" way of life, a script for immigrants that saw them not as valiant and entrepreneurial individuals recognizing the disparity of market forces and doing what was necessary to achieve a living wage (by entering another country at great personal risk and without documentation) but rather as an undifferentiated mass living off the system. According to Rodolfo Acuña's account of the voting, "Middle-class white Americans had spoken; 80 percent of those who voted were white."[38]

Though in the eyes of his critics Valdez distorts history to fit his own political agenda, this critique can be countered on two fronts. First of all, his play demonstrates a close, careful reading of history, and while he is certainly sympathetic to Vásquez, he is not a radical revisionist of the record. Second, while his representation of the white characters may not be psychologically complex, the very genre of melodrama insists on this characterization and Valdez is simply working, in that moment, within the scope of the genre. He uses melodrama for his own ends, and his project never strays too far from the form, demonstrating in the incensed reaction to his work the racist articulations of character that are enabled by the form of melodrama. The irony here is that the two-dimensional types are the traditional white heroes rather than the villains of color. The power of melodrama as an internalized cultural convention distanced from its theatrical roots but retaining the elements of histrionic excess, predictable plot patterns, and a clear moral universe provides basic categories through which mainstream cultural rhetoric constructs models of an ethnic other: (1) a dangerously excessive and attractive figure of difference; (2) a predictable type with scripted behavior and a limited number of publicly visible roles; (3) one trapped in a binary between assimilation and countercultural transgression. While this representational practice is less and less explicit and is highly reductive of individual practice, it continues to haunt the rhetoric of cultural and family values. Admittedly, one could argue that this reductive understanding of characters and people is a necessary means of negotiating a complex cultural environment. However, this argument is countered by the continued representational practice that associates ethnic and racial difference with the disruptive body of the other.

As he does in *Zoot Suit*, Valdez is trying to force the audience to engage self-reflexively. *Bandido!* functions doubly to re-present history and to represent the cultural forces that shape our reception of history. The popular success of the project rests on identification with an idealized melodramatic hero and is enabled by recognition of the tension presented by both the Impresario and the realistic scenes that clarify how much this investment is a fantasy. However, it is not a mere distortion, as some critics would have it, but a self-aware symbolic resistance that potentially recuperates an iconic and ambivalent figure capable of empowering a people. Valdez's employment of melodramatic excess becomes a hybrid form of rascuachi, the Chicano aesthetic. According to Ybarra-Frausto, "to be *rascuachi* is to possess an ebullient spirit of irreverence and insurgency, a carnivalesque topsy-turvy vision where authority and decorum serve as targets for subversion."[39] Such resistance is never simple, and Valdez presents his own awareness of the dangers of his project aesthetically. He chains his melodramatic experiment within a "realistic" jail setting and leaves as the last image of the play the silent body of a dead Vásquez. Unwilling to unrealistically simplify the process of dislodging representation, Valdez will not stop trying.

The very act of performing this play becomes the means to recuperate and reimagine a history from which a community can emerge. Rejecting the easy label of criminal and taking seriously Vásquez's revolutionary potential, Valdez models a strategy of resistance for an audience experiencing a doubled reception: taking pleasure in the melodrama while ideally acknowledging the inversion of a dangerous representational practice that often goes unrecognized. This aesthetic of resistance becomes more important in light of the attitude toward performance in El Teatro Campesino: "'Performance' for the Teatro Campesino was in no way aestheticized into an independent or separate artistic realm. Performance was viewed as part of the material social process of life; as such it always entailed consciousness of community and of one's sense of belonging to and participating in the life of a community."[40] In opposition to this manifestation of resistance culture through embodied practice, one can place the melodrama in its historical role as representing a form of escapist entertainment whose distance from the possible was a part of its charm. In contrast to an aesthetic that carries over to everyday life, melodrama's transformation of everyday life, according to McConachie, occurs in the mutual reconstruction of the audience and theatrical product. Following this logic, in the hope of wrighting a mainstream audience capable of watching his anti-melodrama, Valdez transforms the articulation of ethnicity within the restrictive frame of melodrama.

Stinking Badges: The Everyday Practice of Ethnicity

In *I Don't Have to Show You No Stinking Badges!* Valdez also uses a multilayered theatrical frame to explore ethnicity through the very structure of the play itself. *Badges!* explores the politics of contemporary representation, employing the television situation comedy as a framing device for a Chicano theatrical comedy in which two characters are actors themselves and the protagonist wants to be a director.[41] Here, Valdez deals specifically with the issue of maintaining an authentic identity in the face of stereotypical media representations and the growing visibility of a Chicano middle class socially and economically empowered enough to begin questioning their culpability in the maintenance of these stereotypes. This play functions as a stark reminder of the continued process of criminalized framing and its destructive possibilities in everyday life while wrighting the immediate reality of middle-class Chicano life in California in the mid 1980s.

First performed in February 1986 at the Los Angeles Theatre Center, *Badges!* centers on the emotional and psychological difficulties of Sonny Villa, a young Chicano whose middle-class existence has been fostered by the work his parents have done as "the Silent Bit *King* and *Queen* of Hollywood." A sixteen-year-old Harvard prelaw student in the published text (and a twenty-seven-year-old Harvard law student in the original production), Sonny is going through a fundamental identity crisis—trying to negotiate between being a Harvard student and a cholo in the barrio. Buddy and Connie Villa, his parents, are Sonny's "roots and heritage. They're the reason I went to Harvard, and they're the reason I've returned—to vindicate their silence."[42] Their silence is part and parcel of the very labor that enabled his attendance at Harvard. Each silent role they play, ostensibly solely adding realistic depth, simultaneously sustains the representational stereotypes of Mexican gardeners and maids. Completely aware of the situation in which they are placed, of their role as silent color, Buddy and Connie never stop hoping for better roles but will take what they can get to support their upper-middle-class existence and their children's higher education. Settled into the habits of a relatively conventional middle-aged television couple, they snipe at each other with genuine affection and years of practice.

One of their conflicts emerges because Connie has "a good chance at the part of the madam" in a "Nicholson movie."

> BUDDY: (*Scoffing, spreads his legs into the air.*) Another Mexican whore?
> CONNIE: (*Trying to joke sidles up to him.*) Of course not, she's Costa Rican! Come on, at least I own the house! Buddy, it's a great part. A speaking part. I'd be on location for three weeks.[43]

The excitement of a speaking part leads Connie to audition for a role with on-location responsibilities away from her husband, and although she can joke about the continued limitations placed on her representational possibilities, she is clear about the fact that it is acting. After all, she "wouldn't live in Beverly Hills if they paid [her]. Too many Latina maids at the bus stops."[44] Even so, her own household is a patriarchal space—Buddy critiques her roles and her contributions to the household despite the fact that she is carrying her weight economically. Buddy's reminder about their roles makes her turn serious and retort, "I'm tired of being silent."[45]

The play engages with this silence, the reality of the stereotypical representation of Latinos in television and film, through Sonny's return from Harvard and his goal to transform the entertainment world in order to vindicate his parents and solve his own identity crisis. Sonny's naïve assumption about the feasibility of changing the politics of Hollywood and his presumption that his parents need his vindication add layers of complexity to the comedy of stereotypes enacted in the play itself.

The action occurs in the den of his parents' suburban Los Angeles tract home where Sonny has unexpectedly returned from Harvard. Sonny's abrupt choice to leave Harvard was followed by a cross-country road trip with Anita, a Japanese American dancer whose parents were voluntary evacuees from the West Coast during the internment period of World War II. He plans to come to grips with reality and become the next Woody Allen to "turn this town on its tinsel ear."[46] He wants to change the stereotypes his parents have been forced to portray, disregarding in his idealism the intransigence of the discriminatory structures of representation that kept his parents in the background his entire life. The whole set is framed as a television situation comedy. Initially understated, these elements frame the generic assumptions of this play more visibly as the play progresses.

These elements are a reminder of the conventional assumptions of the audience in broadcast media and film. Meaningful representation of Latinos on prime-time television during the mid and late 1980s was incredibly limited: "In the spring of 1989, 30 network entertainment programs featuring minority characters aired during prime time. A total of 78 minority characters appeared regularly in those shows. . . . Nine are Hispanic . . ."[47] The maids and gardeners that Buddy and Connie play are not reflected in these numbers. Their function is to provide visual representation on prime time that effectively erases their off-camera upper-middle-class careers—Buddy is a restaurant owner and Connie is a real estate agent.

Using situation comedy as his frame allows Valdez to once again work in and against an established genre. In 1986 there were no sitcoms about Latinos on network television, and Valdez's play is a prescient cry from the "decade of the Hispanic" for a more focused and directed series of representational and entertainment possibilities for Latinos. The popularity of the comedic form is understood in part as a result of its invocation of a common denominator, a shared sense of democratic values through appeal to populist sentiment. However, in *Comic Visions* David Marc argues that the situation comedy can be reduced to a series of conventions and writing structures that continually press it toward a centrist political framework devoid of radical critique or transgression. Despite the social commentary of the television comedies of the early and mid 1970s, specifically *All in the Family*, the *Mary Tyler Moore Show*, and *M*A*S*H*, with the advent of shows such as *Happy Days* and associated programming at the end of the 1970s, there was a shift backwards toward a safe nostalgia that echoed the formulaic patriarchal situation comedies of the early and mid 1960s. Though there was a burgeoning African American market, epitomized by *The Cosby Show*, according to Darrell Hamamoto in *Nervous Laughter*, the situation comedy in general became a way of restaging the ideological contradictions of the United States in personal and psychological terms. Although each show allows for some questioning of the ideologies of liberalism, the stage is set for its reformation and return at the close of every episode. Valdez's comedy is thus another investigation of the representational machinery that frames Latinos, limiting and typecasting their possibilities while simultaneously insisting on the arrival of a Latino middle class whose very existence is made visible by their central role on a sitcom.

According to Hamamoto's model, Sonny's angst becomes a way of writing social criticism within the typical U.S. liberal model of an individual as opposed to a structural problem. Rather than initially articulating Sonny's concerns about his parents' situation and his own discomfort at Harvard as products of a structure or system, they are presented as partially the result of adolescent angst in opposition to his parents. Unfortunately, Sonny's adolescent self-indulgence works against his desire to reshape Hollywood in any significant way and allows him the luxury of self-righteous cruelty. When his mother comes home in her maid costume, Sonny comments that she "must be awfully tired of playing Mexican maids."

> CONNIE: (*Archly.*) As Hattie McDaniel used to say: "I'd rather play a maid than be one."
> SONNY: What's the difference? (CONNIE *is a little stunned by* SONNY's *flippant, slightly supercilious manner. She glances at* BUDDY.)
> BUDDY: Don't look at me. I'm just the wetback gardener.[48]

This scene is also a powerful visual moment, because Buddy and Connie return from work in stereotypical television garb, in radical contrast with both their initial "at home" clothes and the more elaborate finery they will adopt later for their visit to the Latino Awards show. The audience is greeted by the familiar image of the Latina maid and "wetback gardener." However, they are actors in costumes both on the stage and in the world of the play, defamiliarizing the representation of these stereotypes. By refusing to recognize his parents' distance from the roles for which they are still dressed, Sonny's comment places him outside even the live theater audience doubling as a sitcom audience. The ease with which he conflates the physical labor of acting with the physical labor of cleaning a house is an additional indication of his upper-middle-class complacency. Connie employs two forms of ironic distance, method of delivery and quotation, to separate herself from the remark and from the role she is playing. Sonny's response, a disgusted literalization that embodies the extreme dangers of representation, compresses acting and identity in a way that causes Buddy himself to feel hostilely thrust into his role as gardener. Sonny's adolescent rebellion allows him only to see the politics of representation that affect everyone except himself. Even more ironically, he places his parents in a subordinated position rather than maintaining the ambivalence between character and actor, the both/and that comes with playing a role on television.

Both his clarity about everyone else and his confusion about himself emerge from the crisis of identity he has undergone at Harvard, triggered by the suicide of his roommate and role model, Monroe James. Playing between the political and the literary, the name of this "good old Anglo Saxon Protestant" recalls both the imperialist arrogance of the Monroe Doctrine and the blue-blooded New England literary tradition of Henry James. Sonny's narrative bridges the two with a performance of the loss of identity grounded in a loss of grammar. Just before witnessing James's suicide, Sonny recounts his own breakdown in language: "MY ENGLISH WAS BREAKING DOWN! Then I couldn't tolerate the space between the words. Finally I got stuck on a hyphen, a lousy hyphen, so I scratched it out. And the HOLE between the two words became an unbridgeable GAP, and I FELL! . . . into a sea of nothingness."[49] The idea of falling into a gap created by the absence of a hyphen resonates in a cultural environment where the very presence of a hyphen in the act of naming groups becomes the site of political contestation. This hyphen is most prominent in the construction *Mexican-American* and the negotiation between two cultural worlds that is implied in this naming practice. Sonny's loss is falling into the space in between, recognizing that staying in the gap might be impossible. The suicide of his roommate suggests that crossing over is not a desirable option.

By scratching out the hyphen, Sonny has removed his own potential identity bridge, or myth thereof, and is left searching for something outside language. That recognition leads him in two interwoven directions, the need for action and the need to control and guard the representation of that action. This combined need leads to his desire to be a director in Hollywood, not merely an actor like his parents; he assumes that the director has control, but he does not realize the limits on this control within the collaborative space of both theater and television. Still, as

Buddy puts it, besides re-creating the episodes of Pancho Villa, "[t]he only other way a Mexican can shoot gringos and get away with it is by becoming a Hollywood director."⁵⁰

Sonny's internalization of the criminal framing of the Chicano manifests this understanding when he becomes a cholo, an up-to-date version of the bandido, after his parents leave to attend the annual Latino actor's banquet. Ironically, he puts on a stereotype at the exact moment his parents are celebrating Latino achievements in Hollywood with other successful actors radically different in appearance from their television "work clothes." The mention of this banquet is both a stab at the complacency of Latino success in Hollywood and a powerful celebration of the presence of Latinos there. The event is also a space for networking and developing contacts, since Sonny's parents are attending it partially to seek additional work, for speaking roles—"The part of a Costa Rican General." As Connie puts it rather pointedly, "Slowly but surely all of these Hollywood stars with brown roots are coming out of the closet."⁵¹

Sonny has also found a way to bring his brown identity to the fore; however, the role he has chosen positions him within an identity crisis manufactured in part by the problematic representation of Chicanos in the mainstream media. As he moves from Harvard prelaw student to cholo homeboy in an attempt to achieve authenticity, he embodies an internalization of the "authenticity" of the stereotypical criminalized Chicano male. The shift is all too easy—he needs only a simple costume change. While changing his shirt and adding a cap, Sonny records, in his movie script, his own conception of the community's rejection of his identity:

> Continuing script and production notes RE: HARVARD HOME-
> BOY MOVIE . . . You're fucking up, homeboy! You're not fool-
> ing anybody, *ese*. You didn't fool nobody in Harvard and
> you ain't fooling jack shit here, *bato*. (SONNY *starts talking
> to himself, as if he is a group of cholos raking him over the
> coals.*) We're the echo from the barrio streets of your mind,
> loco! We know you're middle class; pussy, aye. Harvard
> and all that shit. Well, you're nothing, dude. . . . Get out in
> the streets, and find something real to do, motherfucker.
> Don't just sit there, going out of your fucking mind. OUT
> INTO REALITY! (SONNY *turns off the camera and picks up
> the gun . . .*)⁵²

Sonny's ventriloquism of the imagined values of the street is an articulation not of barrio values but of the distortion of barrio values by the mainstream media. His self-critique is produced not by any external community but by a fictitious one from which he feels displaced because of his middle-class and Ivy League status. In the mid 1980s, cholos who most embodied the visual ideal were often the farthest removed from criminal activity—posture was as important as action. In accusing himself of being middle-class, Sonny shows us his belief that his economic status and education make him a sellout. All that matters to him now is the valorization of the streets, a delusory acceptance of media constructs whose distance from the real identity of Chicanos on the streets should be visible to Sonny more than most people precisely because of his parents' labor as actors in roles and class positions they have never assumed in life.

Sonny's performance of identity is not merely an adolescent fantasy; it disturbingly echoes the real-life performance of a "Harvard Homeboy," Jose Razo.[53] On July 6, 1987, Jose Luis Razo, home on summer break after his sophomore year at Harvard, called the La Habra, California, police department claiming to have information about the murder of Patricia Lopez, a nine-year-old girl from nearby Santa Ana. Although it turned out that Razo did not have any new information about the Lopez case, he did have something to offer the detectives he met with—himself. Razo confessed to the police that he had committed fifteen armed robberies in La Habra and Whittier, California, and Miami, Florida, all while on breaks from Harvard between December 1985 and June 1987. According to La Habra police captain Mike Burch, after discussing the murder case, "we began talking with him about the robberies. Much to our amazement, he began making statements that only the police, the victims, or the robber could have known. We were convinced that he was telling the truth, so we arrested him."[54] When the story went public on July 9, many La Habra residents were as amazed as Captain Burch had been. Razo was a role model: a former altar boy, an active participant in the local Boys Club, and an academic and athletic success. Because of his confession, the question for many people was not whether he was guilty or innocent but why he would have chosen to commit these crimes? Why would a model student who had escaped the barrio choose to throw everything away and become a "common criminal"?

There were many answers, most of them predictable, but even as they emerged, the Razo case continued to elude any form of stereotyped analysis. A "sun child" haunted by the specter of affirmative action and its conservative discontents was one explanatory psychological narrative deployed by "expert" commentators. Provided with tremendous opportunity but burdened with enormous pressure to continue their achievements, successful rising minority students, "sun children," find themselves self-destructing in an equally grand way. Here, criminality becomes defined as a way of defusing pressure. A second psychological explanation advanced by the media was the "imposter syndrome" in which Razo's criminal activities were read as an attempt to get out of a situation in which he felt he did not belong. According to Ken Fineman, "On occasion, they'll engage in behavior that's very risky. One may assume it has to do with their wish to be found out, to be punished for the things they've been getting away with for a long time." However, Fineman was confused by the Razo case because "a kid that has been an achiever all the way through school usually has values consistent with the majority. The values of the criminal element are very different."[55] A medical psychologist, Fineman offers a distinction between the criminal element and the majority, but the problem with his value construction is his inability to perceive that criminality is in fact constructed by that very majority and that regardless of Razo's own values, he was always in danger of being figured as criminal.

For Razo, in fact, it appears that media accounts of Chicano criminal behavior formed an integral part of his ethnic self-identification. One statement made from jail just a day after the first news story broke was offered repeatedly by the media as an explanation: "'At Harvard, I didn't fit,' said the 6-foot, 200-pound Razo. 'I was confused. . . . No one understood me. I'm a 'homeboy' now,' he said, using the Latino term for a neighborhood chum. Then, the scholarship student and football star added in Spanish, 'I don't sell out my own ethnic identity.'"[56] Razo's concern about being a *vendido*, a sellout, is unsurprising, given the importance he attaches to authenticity and belonging. His linguistic code switching exemplifies the translation across boundaries that must be practiced by the media to "understand him," an understanding that demands a recognizable cultural script for his identity verging on pathology, as well as the literal translation of his quotation and the erasure of his Spanish. Razo chooses Spanish here after he claims to be a "homeboy," implicitly arguing for his authenticity through the use of Spanish and through his new role within the criminal justice system.

This assertion of identity fits comfortably within the pattern of Chicano resistance articulated by Mirandé. Similar to the pachuco in its ambivalent relation to the Mexican American and Chicano communities, the cholo figure has not received the same amount of cultural recuperation. A controversial assertion of Chicano masculinity, the cholo was nonetheless, in the mid 1980s, one of the few mass-produced images of Chicano identity. If you were not in a gang, you did not exist as a Chicano within mainstream media. According to Monica Brown's explanation of the subtitle to her book *gang nation*, "The adjective 'delinquent' precedes the term 'citizen' because this sense of Latina/o gang members and perhaps all Latina/o Americans precedes all conceptions of citizenship within mainstream rhetoric. That is, in a way, all urban Latina/o youth carry the mantle of delinquency and danger."[57]

A site of resistance to Anglo culture, cholo also often indicates a gang affiliation. Despite Razo's tattoo and his claims of knowing gang members, however, the police made clear that they had no evidence Razo was involved in a gang. This finding is unsurprising, because individuals most closely associated with the cholo persona during the 1980s were typically peripheral gang members at most and used costume to assert a solidarity not always consistent with a significant level of criminal activity. In this world, the greater visibility one has as a stereotypical gang member, the less likely one is to participate in stereotyped gang behavior, casting into doubt any simple association that might ground such a stereotype.

In talking to Razo's former classmates, newspaper reporters developed a picture of the young man as one who fit in at Harvard even less than other minority students. One of his friends from home claimed "that Razo was angered by the ribbing he got at Harvard about being Mexican-American. In that world, he dressed to flaunt his ethnicity . . . to show 'Joe's not just a Mexican—he's a home boy. He'd walk around campus wearing baggy Levi's, a white shirt and bandanna. They'd just tease him more.'"[58] Two years later, a former Harvard classmate, Ruben Navarrette Jr. wrote, "He seemed to pass through a stage that many scared and alienated young people in elite schools go through—wearing his ethnicity like a badge. Or was it more like a shield? I remember him in the costume of an East L.A. 'homeboy'—the khaki pants, the Pendleton shirt, the bandanna around his head. I remember his tattoos and his homesickness for La Habra. . . . But not every student who sports torn Levi's, or a serape, around Harvard Yard commits armed robbery during summer vacation. There must be more."[59] Though Navarrette's ethnic politics align closely with the position offered by Richard Rodriguez in his early autobiography *Hunger of Memory*, his analysis of Razo's doubled alienation is accurate. Complete with costume and appropriate action, Razo's ethnic "character" is created out of the recognition that he will be read as ethnic from the outside and that his "essential self" is out of his control. He can, however, assert control over the means by which this ethnicity is represented to the world. He can become a cholo, play the myth, and begin to slip outside the boundaries constructed for him. Adopting the costume, the Pendleton and the bandanna, he plays with and against a stereotyped identity by re-placing it on Harvard Yard. This identity in such a location decenters the assumption that criminality is directly associated with a particular style.

This choice to use ethnicity as a "badge" inevitably recalls the title of Valdez's play as well as its source, *The Treasure of the Sierra Madre*. The title of the play comes from a famous exchange between the film characters portrayed by Humphrey Bogart and Alfonso Bedoya that is re-created in the first scene of act 2, with Buddy taking Bedoya's role and Sonny filling in for Bogart. For Buddy, in his big-screen debut as one of the men with Bedoya, "the leader of the *bandidos*" had a greater effect on him than Bogart did. Like Buddy, Bedoya, who for many years characterized a negative Mexican stereotype—greasy and dangerous—on the big screen, had to build his success on playing stereotypical bit parts. Thus when Sonny as Bogart says, "If your (*sic*) the police, where are your badges?" there is legitimacy to Buddy as he delivers Bedoya's answer: "Badges? We ain't got no badges. We don't need no badges. I don't have to show you any stinking [badges]."[60] Though the film goes on to perform a disturbing displacement of murderous responsibility (each time the U.S. characters want to commit murder it is preempted by Mexican violence), both Bogart and Bedoya are here without authorization.

Although Valdez's 1989 published version of the play was changed to reflect his knowledge of the Razo case, including specific references to the "Harvard Homeboy" and the robbery of a fast-food restaurant, as well as the off-stage presence of the police, the ideas about criminalized representation and a Chicano Harvard student were already clearly present in the original 1986 script, including Sonny's desire to dress up as a cholo, his possession of a gun, and a destructive strewing of fast-food garbage around the house. In an ironic synchronicity of art and life, Razo's existential angst was simultaneously being staged by Sonny. While the actual off-stage robbery and police were added, the original production actually had Sonny present Anita with a series of head shots—as a cholo, as a "noble savage" in "brownface," and as Zorro—to illustrate the problematic limits of representation, a scene that disappeared from later versions as Sonny's goal shifted more from acting to directing.[61]

Going through the stage that Fineman argued for, the "imposter syndrome," Sonny Villa repeats Joe Razo's gesture of validating criminal behavior as somehow authentic and legible. Important for the situation-comedy frame, it is his only available script as a TV actor, the only identity he can adopt in this sitcom. He acknowledges this limit, explaining to Anita that to get the only employment available to a Chicano actor, all you need to do is "look dumb, hostile, and potentially violent."[62] In Sonny's understanding of the industry in the 1980s, the only marketable Chicano male is a violent one, and the biggest problem is that he is not wrong. His equivalence of reality and violence and of the middle-class insulation from the reality of the streets is accurate; however, his conception of violence is predicated on an individual liberal logic of extralegal activity involving firearms and theft, rather than the structural violence of poverty from which he is shielded by his class position.

Ironically, even in Sonny's retreat from Harvard he has internalized the notion of the individual liberal subject whose success must be a betrayal of the larger ethnic community, since there is no mainstream conception of advancement apart from individual accomplishment. The limits of Chicano representation become a solvable problem for Sonny through the mechanism of his own individual success and virtuosity. He hopes that as a director, he will be able to radically transform Hollywood representation, but as Valdez himself was finding at the same time in his work as a film director, transforming Hollywood is a difficult task, and the play's sitcom frame acknowledges this reality.

Sonny's attempt to break out into reality begins with his attempts to film his family in the first part of act 2, when he slips between stereotype and character development, but after his parents leave for the "L.A. Latino Actors banquet," perhaps to see María María and Meryl Estripada, his break into reality takes a darker turn. At the end of the first scene Sonny leaves to find reality and returns, in the next scene, after having "robbed the local Crap-in-the-Box," a burger joint. Armed robbery has become his means of achieving contact with reality á la Joe Razo, and to produce such an effect he must be *dressed as a cholo*," since, on the basis of representational conventions, an upper-middle-class Harvard student dressed in conservative clothing would be unable to commit such an act.[63]

Describing the fast-food trash he has just dumped on the floor, Sonny claims "this is all . . . creative garbage . . . and evidence. We're all on trial here, see? In a decidedly precarious pseudo-psycho-juridical conundrum."[64] The trial to which Sonny refers is performed in front of an audience—a jury that does not have legal authority but rather forms the basis for decisions about television programming and the range of acceptable depictions of ethnic identity. From his self-critical monologue during which he ventriloquizes the community of his fictional peers, Sonny seems willing to grant an audience the ability to critique social politics and cultural mores and to serve as the arbiter of authenticity.

With the arrival of the cops, indicated onstage by the sound of sirens and a spotlight shining on the house, Sonny admits to Anita that he has committed robbery, first complaining, "[J]ust because I wear a Pendelton [sic], I'm some kind of burglar! Don't they know I live here?" Recognizing the semiotics of clothing and criminality, Sonny has nonetheless taken away his ability to seriously critique such a practice because he has embraced the same semiotic system. Of course, the cops are right to be there, though Sonny's concern about being in the house offers one more contrast between the domestic living room space and the costume of its inhabitants, echoing the appearance of his parents in their outfits after the afternoon's shoot. Self-reflexively he asks Anita, "Do I seem dangerous to you? Criminally dangerous or merely Hispanic?" Asking for clarification, Anita gets the answer: "I was ACTING! I'm acting—see? No more threatening East L.A. cholo. Check it out. Here's my straight on, neutral shot with an innocuous shit-eating smile all casting directors require? See?"[65]

This metatheatrical moment insists that acting can slip between the real and the theatrical at will, like Tiburcio Vásquez's performance in *Bandido!*; however, this claim is undermined by the aural presence of the cops, who represent the real cultural consequences his actions have produced within the world of the situation comedy. Since the audience never witnesses his criminal act, all they have is Sonny's word for it. In fact, without the police sirens and off-stage voices, the audience might be tempted to see Sonny's claim as male braggadocio; instead, the police actually reaffirm the "reality" of his claim. The presence of law enforcement, or at least the theatrical signs of their off-stage presence, is accompanied by a growing recognition of, and increasing attention to, the trappings of the television studio in which this situation comedy is being filmed.

As the potential drama heightens, the canned laughter begins, and Sonny's character shifts from being dangerous and potentially transgressive to being contained with the liberal centrist space of situation comedy. Reflecting metadramatically, Sonny recognizes that the events of the evening are unfolding as if his entire family is inescapably trapped in a "low-rated situation comedy! (*Looks out at the audience.*) You can almost imagine a studio audience out there . . . sitting, watching, waiting to laugh at this cheap imitation of Anglo life. Superficial innocuous bullshit that has to conceal its humorless emptiness with canned laughter!"[66] This poignant critique is not a moment of high seriousness but the biggest joke of all, as the audience is cued by the canned laughter to recognize that the psychological dissolution of the upper-middle-class family is being refracted into three possible trajectories.

In the first trajectory, the actions of the family become something to be laughed at and with, and the comfortable constraints of the domestic situation comedy protects the "studio audience" from learning anything that will radically upset their cultural viewpoint. As Hamamoto argues, "Although emancipatory democratic values have always informed the situation comedy, the realization of such values in actual practice has been woefully restricted by the commercial system of television."[67] The audience can now recognize that this was a sitcom from the beginning, and with this recognition the stakes of the play may change. However, the self-conscious act of reevaluation is precisely what Valdez intends through his act of wrighting, demanding that the audience recognize their participation in policing the reception of generic conventions. The staging of the entire play as situation comedy then becomes inevitable. Though the television cameras framing the stage are present from the very beginning, Valdez's choice to limit the initial acknowledgment of this frame allows for a moment of dislocation, like the reemergence of Connie and Buddy in their acting garb, when the audience begins to recognize that they have been using an incorrect interpretative lens.

The second possible mode is to recognize Sonny's language as a radical critique of audience expectations and the sitcom form. Through this lens his statement becomes a broad critique of liberal ideology that values individual achievement and plays out societal conflicts within the space of the nuclear family. If this moment exceeds the confines of the sitcom (and of course the theatricality of work that invokes a genre without fulfilling all of its conventions seems to enable this overflow), then we must take seriously Sonny's critique. However, his psychological concern with his own identity position becomes an empty gesture in this world, because creating a personal psychological space for identity does not have a radical effect on commercial media and broadcast representation.

In the third possibility, both individual and communal identities become meaningful and crucial points through which the negotiation of representation can take place. The very real existence of Joe Razo makes Sonny Villa's existential crisis meaningful, even as their individual problems must be understood as preventable through systemic restructuring rather than individual intervention. Sonny's disrespect for his parents comes both from the shame he feels in seeing them as they are seen by a mainstream spectator and from his anger at the mistreatment they have received. Connie's attempt to calm him down by discussing a movie role he has been offered merely revives his derision of his parents' work. In the last moments before a directorial intervention Sonny tells his parents, "You mean I'm finally being convincing? . . . I don't know if I am acting or not anymore . . . Am I being melodramatic? . . . I don't know . . . and I don't care. . . ."[68] This invocation and dismissal of melodrama is particularly resonant given Valdez's understanding of the term in *Bandido!*, but more important, Sonny's increasing confusion enables Valdez to present another layer in this self-reflexive process of wrighting ethnicity.

Feeling displaced and incapable of negotiating the space between acting and being, Sonny decides on an easy resolution, suicide, which would allow him to follow in the footsteps of his Harvard roommate, Monroe James. Before he can make good on his threat, a stagehand takes away his gun and an exchange with the director ensues. Sonny's confrontation with the director is an encounter with himself on video. Loosely echoing the dialogic relationship of Henry Reyna and El Pachuco, Sonny is both actor and director of this sitcom. Here, unfortunately, the two roles are working directly against each other. By making Sonny the director, the play illustrates the complex reality of his dream; though there is a Chicano director, this authoritative voice is potentially the greatest *vendido*, insisting that "WE GOTTA KEEP IT LIGHT, ENTERTAINING, *ESE*."[69] Sonny himself has become divided between two visions of the world, and the only viable agreement is that the legal entanglement must disappear; Sonny the director gives Sonny the actor free rein to transform the end of the play.

This ending is allowed by the need to create a resolution based on generic expectation; the world of the sitcom is full of fantastical endings that maintain the status quo. By veering into fantasy, the ending maintains the possibility of social critique while recognizing that escaping the process of framing is still very much a fiction. In a Chicano science fiction spoof, Sonny prepares to return to Harvard through the gentle offices of a flying saucer in the shape of a giant sombrero, in part echoing Buddy's own gestures at moviemaking at the beginning of the play, when he describes remakes of classic films in a comedic Chicano style. The derivative nature of Sonny's directorial choices and Buddy's plot ideas provides additional commentary on the crisis of representation and the dearth of possibility.

In negotiating the possibilities for an ending, the Director rejects any suggestion that strays outside convention, leaving the "reality" for episodes after the pilot, enlightenment for an "ART FILM," and politics for "AN EDITORIAL." Sonny manages to convince him of the need for a "spectacular ending" because "[w]e can't leave all these high school drop-outs with this downer, man!"[70] As an internal dialogue, between Sonny and his double, it functions like the situation comedy to internalize social politics within the family structure, carrying it to its logical extreme as a solipsistic argument with one's self. The theater sustains the multiplicity that allows the comment about high school dropouts to function as a laugh line, to be an ironic statement about the realities of education for Latinos in the United States, and to reaffirm the presence of middle-class Chicanos who can laugh as a way of asserting their distance from that category.

The stated goal for the new ending is "EMOTIONALLY SATISFYING," followed by the first label of Sonny as "HOMEBOY." If providing emotional satisfaction is a way of asserting authenticity in this alternative situation comedy, then the ending must be read as an explicit alternative to the problematic framing and reception that conflates authenticity and criminal stereotype. However, this epilogue is also "POSITIVELY HILARIOUS," bringing together fantasy, dreams, and a happy ending that gestures back to indigenous roots and forward to science fiction, two concepts that Valdez later unites in his play *Earthquake Sun*. The pleasure of this moment is the pleasure of fantasy, of the happy ending and the restoration of the family and the status quo. However, achieving this "fantastic solution" involves "convincing you that my recent misadventures were only aberrations of my stressed-out over active brain." In Sonny's apology to his parents he tells them, "I'm only sorry I put you through all this melodramatic violence. I just had to come back to the Twilight Zone to find out who I was."[71] The irony here is that his journey is "back to" not "out of" the Twilight Zone, indicating a larger social critique about the American middle class and the situation comedy as Twilight Zones. Hiding behind this extended comedy is the exposure of social fragmentation in which only a fantastic solution can counter the current crisis of representation and displace the power of a hegemonic audience to maintain the unequal distribution of power through the assertion of their learned expectations for ethnic performance. In the original production, the absence of the cops and of the structural difficulty of an actual robbery allowed Sonny's return to articulate a more specific politics of representation; his return to Harvard would allow him to become an entertainment lawyer, to help market films to Latin America, and "to create our own images of America. And they're going to be as real as we are."[72] But with the knowledge of real events and the addition of Razo's experiences, this solution is no longer sufficient.

Reviews of the first production insisted that it was an intelligent comedy attacking both television stereotypes and sitcom morality. At least one reviewer was also aware of the dangers presented by the critique of the rising Latino middle class, the play's ideal audience, in which the cries of Anglo imitation and lack of reality might strike too close to home. Valdez defended the play as a move into a larger sphere, away from specifically Chicano political and cultural concerns, but his move to the mainstream was viewed by some as playing bourgeois politics and selling out to the establishment. Following this argument, despite its parody of a criminalized Chicano identity, we see that the level of critique in the play never successfully transforms the cholo identity into a successful resistance of Anglo commodification. Even more insidiously, the play appears to insist that a Chicano director would not solve the very problems that Sonny hopes to address, instead trapping Sonny as director in a world of commercial concerns that hold precedence over aesthetic judgments. The sitcom setting becomes a closed world in which there are no repercussions, only magical solutions.

However, the play is much more sophisticated than an initial reading of its ending might suggest. At the same time that it acknowledges the overwhelming power of Hollywood representational machinery, it also subverts such representational machinery. However, unlike *Zoot Suit*, in which the controversial figure of El Pachuco is clearly also a symbol of resistance in a racist environment, Sonny's ventures into his own street fantasies and postadolescent *bildungsroman* are clearly acting, and these comments about the theatricality of identity generate the play's power.

In many ways the character of Sonny is both the strength and the weakness of the play. At times trapped in a whining, self-pitying adolescent angst, at times eerily prescient about the politics of Hollywood representation, Sonny is built on several internal contradictions, most of which seem to resist easy reduction to a stereotype, unless it is a self-conscious presentation. As self-reflexive stereotypes, the characters in the play stretch stereotypes to the point of meaninglessness while reaffirming that they are Hollywood productions, just like everything else in the play. In their failure to entertain, stereotypes also reveal their inability to explain. According to a reviewer of the first production, "Robert Beltran's considerable power as a performer almost rescues the complex Sonny from the confusion built into his role. He at least keeps us seriously wondering—and caring—if the young man is psychotic or schizoid or just depressed. But there's no overcoming the basic inconsistencies of his character."[73] The confusion is produced by a character working against audience expectation and dealing with an identity crisis figured within the space of ethnicity. This exploration of personal identity becomes political precisely because of its cultural location. The easy road is to construct the character as a problem to be solved, to fall into the traps of legal ontology that assumes both the "conflation of the possible legal solubility of a problem with the existence of a problem" and "synthetic individualism (a belief that social relations can be understood only as the sum of readily comprehensible individual relations)."[74] These two reading practices epitomize the containment strategies of an Anglo audience working to "normalize" ethnicity.

Though this description is by a drama critic reviewing Valdez's play, the reading seems to hold for the real-life character of Jose Razo as well. The inability to understand Razo's behavior outside a legal discourse that deals with simple binaries (voluntary vs. involuntary) and narratives of proof results in a confusion that parallels the audience response to the character of Sonny. Unlike the multilayered theater in which Sonny plays himself, the newspapers and courtroom that stage the drama of Razo's identity are unwilling to radically alter the script to serve audience demands for a happy ending. No review of the play reports Sonny's threats of violence or criminal activity, preferring instead to focus on his proclaimed desire to be an actor/director. Yet, it is the very playing of cholo identity that allows the social critique within the play to become manifest.

Like Sonny, Razo seemed to be participating in an internalized critique of his own middle-class status and the way in which that status functioned as a betrayal. Although in Razo's case the criticism is never heard except in his admissions of guilt and his feelings of belonging and identification that emerge after his arrest, it manifests itself as the same ventriloquism of the streets that Sonny enacts. In the relatively hostile environment of Harvard Yard, Razo "wore his ethnicity like a badge" to retain his identity in opposition to that which surrounded him without fitting into a readily identifiable authentic stereotype. Because he is not performing an assimilationist rise through the upper middle class, his identity is rejected both by an Anglo culture that does not register the presence of a cholo on the Harvard grounds and a Chicano community that, even if they have sympathy for this performance of identity, feels cultural pressure to place themselves at a distance from it. While support for the cholo identity within the Chicano community might exist, there is no support for such an identity within the Mexican American community at large.

Razo's behavior can actually be read as a conscious rejection and subversion of the majority conception of criminal behavior. James Vigil recounts an anecdote from one of his many interviews in which

> [o]ne young man, 17, vehemently stated that "police start trouble when they come into the barrio." He reflects a commonly held belief among street youths "that the police assume we are doing something wrong when we are just kicking back, maybe getting high or drinking beer, and just partying." Obviously, "getting high and drinking beer" escaped this person's idea of what constitutes an illegal act.[75]

Although Vigil's almost sardonic comment here is out of place with his general tone, this stylistic break gestures toward an unwillingness to recognize the potentially subversive ideal of a well-developed subculture. Despite his extensive presentation of cholo culture, Vigil seems to miss this point—a dominant legal morality steps in. But, if we go back to his reading of cholo language and group identity, he informs us that "[m]any individuals . . . actually shifted their speech pattern to conform to group expectations when the situation warranted. . . . Especially noteworthy is how communication in this manner occurred when outsiders—for example, various law enforcement and criminal justice authorities—were around, much as if the group required a secret code to shield its members from the intrusions of untrustworthy strangers." This behavior parallels the use of "ism" language and Spanish at the end of *Short Eyes* as a means of excluding those in power. Even without the formation of a linguistic subculture though, one can merely dress up as a cholo: "without thinking, talking, feeling, or acting, one can just dress up and appear to be a cholo in the eyes of observers. . . . In effect, it conjures up the image of a group behind you, even if you are not what you represent. There is a certain amount of security created in that pause when an observer has to think about your social ties."[76]

Outside a certain communal structure—kicking back with homeys—cholo wear and behavior are not considered an acceptable or empowering social position. Wearing his ethnicity like a badge in the form of cholo garb, Razo was making a statement about group identification, whether or not it actually existed. However, by placing himself within that group structure from the outside, from Harvard, he created a situation in which his identity is strictly contingent on clothing and linguistic and gestural mannerisms. If he indeed committed the robberies for which he was convicted, then he is able to remove the contingency of his identification. If not, then he is still guilty.

On the basis of a speech, a confession given while affected by PCP, a Harvard student becomes a criminal. The ease with which a mere knowledge of details could script him into a relatively stereotypically constructed identity is disturbing, but the difficulty he encountered in trying to rewrite the script is terrifying. This incident demonstrates both the power of confession as a version of constructing subjectivity and the rigidity with which utterance becomes identity within a legal framework that has only one concept of criminality—that of the minority and the "other." In this case, the legal system is reproducing the very reading practices Valdez is working against. Once a convenient reading is found, transforming such a narrative becomes a near impossibility regardless of what might be viewed as mitigating circumstances.

The alternative seems to be a negotiation with and appropriation of stereotypical discourse and identity at the same time self-consciousness of this gesture produces a form of existential angst. By choosing to act in a way that dialogues with criminalized stereotypes, Jose Razo and Sonny Villa run directly into the inequalities of symbolic exchange and are left with the necessity to resort to fantasy in order to regain control over the ripples of their identity. They cannot become the directors but instead must wright a new space in which their chosen identity can be empowered.

In the case of Razo, his explanations involve narratives that become unreadable to the general public as his defense shifts: first, to argue for an attempt to understand criminality and, second, to protect others.[77] For Sonny Villa, his stage resistance is framed as comedy and his conclusion must be presented within stereotypical comic derivations. The amount of possible control seems limited, but the desire to offer alternative representations remains. Exposing Chicano complicity in the maintenance of pejorative stereotypes, Valdez attempts not only to teach his audience about the performances they can read but also to expose for them the ways they have been taught to read. Making a plea for Chicanos to understand their position not only as objects of an Anglo gaze but also as an audience with its own hermeneutics, Valdez finds himself describing a real event that seems eerily inevitable given the colonizing power of representation.

Although read by some critics in its initial production as confused and scattered, this play and its protagonist in fact offer a powerful critique of representation by forcing the members of the audience to come to terms with their own need to naturalize, synthesize, and frame in ways with which they are intimately familiar. The presence of the TV camera is only one sign of our abdication of responsibility for our interpretive practice. The need to synthesize, to link events, risks the creation of a representational practice in which individual identity and ethnic identity can be understood in only one way. Valdez's theory, his theater, works against this linearity to disempower the rigidity of a frame that functions both aesthetically and juridically. Instead, Valdez transforms the frame into a permeable space on whose boundaries one must play in order to wright ethnicity.

5

Wrighting the Borders in the 1990s

SEDICIO: Our Mexican friends are embarrassed by Tijuana.
MICHAEL: Not real Mexico, they say.
SEDICIO: Does that mean San Diego is not real USA? Think
about it.

. . .

SEDICIO: Let's go before they think we're committing shocking,
immoral acts that will destroy Western Civilization.
MICHAEL: Like sodomy?
SEDICIO: No, immigrating!
—Guillermo Reyes, *Deporting the Divas*

OFFICER: Well, one sure for sure: I don't much see the difference
between Messican and Merican now. Alla you look like
wetbacks to me.
LUPE: Dat ess what we are. *Mojados*. Eliens. Whatefer border
wi cross.
—Octavio Solis, *El Otro*

The art of interpreting the literal border today involves the simultaneous analysis of the theater and its symbolic dimensions
as well as the actual violence. One should not reduce one to the
other, not become so constructivist as not to notice that people
are being killed, not look so closely at the violence as not to notice
its symbolic dimensions. Holding seeming opposites together is
easy to say, but hard to do in practice.
—Renato Rosaldo, "Foreword"

Writing the Real and Metaphorical Border

The U.S.-Mexican border is a site of national, political, and economic contestation that has been used increasingly as a conceptual paradigm for explicating new forms of identity, culture, and information that incorporate the in-between or liminal nature of border space. The contemporary border with Mexico is a result of U.S. aggression during the Mexican-American War and the subsequent territorial division and essentially forced sale of Mexican territory, a historical reality that grounds Rodolfo Acuña's seminal history of Chicano culture, *Occupied America*, and the Chicano claim that "we didn't cross the border, the border crossed us." Despite this history, mainstream culture often assumes that Chicano and Latino identity indicates a history of immigration rather than colonization or conquest. This construction of ethnicity rests on the transformational process of border crossing. On one side of the border, people are read in national terms, while the act of crossing confers on them an identity structured by ethnicity. The tension between the real and the metaphorical implications of this crossing provides a rich space in which to wright ethnicity in the theater.

Theatrical space is important for understanding borders not only because the theater can function as border space but also because the border itself is often understood as a theater. Thinking of the border as a theater provides a site-specific frame for understanding theatricality as a spatial practice and explicating the relationship between space and the framing of ethnicity. Although the border as theater is a metaphor, the political importance of the border helps focus attention on all the activity that takes place at its site, paralleling the semiotic intensity of theatrical space. In the act of crossing, people play out scripted roles, asking and answering questions and behaving within a restricted range of acceptable physical gestures and emotional states. The space of the border demands specific constructions of identity—guest worker, resident, tourist, citizen, and agent. In the context of this paradigm the space of performance, specifically the space of the stage, becomes a physical reflection of the shifting geographies that are possible within a consciously structured intersection of topography and identity.

While theater and identity at the border clearly are connected, the richness and contested nature of this connection emerges from tension between the metaphorical and the material conceptions of this space. Placing theater and the border in dialogue helps shift the increasing conflicts between studies that use the border as metaphor and those that attend to the materiality of the literal border. This dialogue creates new ways of thinking about ethnicity as a border identity. Theater is useful in this regard because it literally takes place, occupying space and often demanding a three-dimensional representation of a place. Borders operate both metaphorically and literally in stage space: the sign systems of theatrical representation are predicated on the establishment and manipulation of conventional frames that function spatially as boundaries. The abstraction of the material stage enables radical spatial transformation; one location can become another and multiple locations can indicate the palimpsest of history materialized on one common ground. The frames that separate the stage from everyday life enable this fungibility.

Theater's physical manifestations of bodies in space help clarify the integrally in-between quality associated with the historical formation of Latino identity while also exposing the limits of this mode of thinking. The conceptual richness of a hybrid identity manifest in the theater becomes not only a question of character but also of formal and aesthetic questions about the logic of the world of the play. Part of the pleasure and power of metatheatricality is the self-conscious creation and disruption of borders and the ways in which theatrical aesthetics are employed to create, police, or disrupt borders. By attending to these frames and foregrounding them metatheatrically, it is possible to catalyze an epiphany and potentially implicate the spectators in their own political and communal identification.

Gloria Anzaldúa's groundbreaking bilingual work of poetic theory *Borderlands/La Frontera* (1987) is paradigmatic for understanding the border as a metaphor for identity. Explicating an identity articulated in and through the border, Anzaldúa's bilingual manifesto argues for the creation of a new subjectivity, a *mestiza* identity whose subject position is entirely within the space of the border. This work germinated a series of critical, metaphorical articulations of border space intended to create a geography for the marginalized whose power rests on the deconstructive potential for rewriting from the margin as a way of shifting the center. A central text in the metaphorical paradigm of the border, Anzaldúa's work has been widely cited, highly influential, and criticized for its essentialism.[1]

The timing of the publication of Anzaldúa's text in 1987 implicitly establishes it as a critical response to substantial changes in legislation that controls commerce and immigration. Since the second half of the 1980s there has been increasing public and legislative outcry for more extensive policing of the U.S. southern border, primarily as a result of legislation that changed the nature of immigration and increased the market interdependence of the United States and Mexico. Nineteen eighty-six, an important year for these changes, included the passage of the Immigration Reform and Control Act (IRCA) and Mexico's entry into the General Agreement on Trades and Tariffs (GATT). The IRCA disrupted the established flow of migration by, on the one hand, offering amnesty to workers who could provide proof of an extended residency and a labor history in the United States and, on the other hand, increasing the restrictions on the number of documented laborers. This explicitly Janus-faced relationship with the Mexican population, accepting workers to provide necessary labor while labeling immigration a threat to national security, is a repetition of the historical moment of the Zoot Suit Riots in 1943 when the Bracero program was simultaneously employing large numbers of Mexicans to help the military, industrial, and agricultural economies of the United States. While this change was occurring in relationship to worker populations, Mexico's entry into GATT helped the integration of North American markets, an integration that increased dramatically with the passage of the North American Free Trade Agreement (NAFTA) in 1994. Both of these agreements opened various markets for goods, facilitating their flow across borders without providing the same ease of transit for labor.[2]

While supporting the amnesty contained in ICRA, President Ronald Reagan also referenced potential terror from the south as a reason for reforms. His call for increasing attention to border security was supported by the claim that "terrorists are just a day's drive away from Harlingen, Texas."[3] While Reagan was referring to Central American leftist revolutionaries, this slippage between revolutionary and terrorist is echoed in the post-9/11 anxiety about the conflation of "illegal" and "terrorist."

As the metaphor of the border proliferated as a paradigmatic concept in the early and mid 1990s, concurrent with the popularization of the critical language of performativity, critics began articulating the creation of new hybrid subjects in a range of cultural spaces marked by significant populations of Latinos. Border subjectivity was no longer present only on the literal border; it also was manifest in cosmopolitan urban spaces such as Los Angeles, where ethnic communities and performances of identity were recognized as processual and transformative of the world around them. Neighborhoods became border spaces whose aesthetics emerged from a creative weaving of cultural threads to fashion new identities, as well as linguistic and cultural practices.

In this paradigmatic model, Nuyorican and Chicano are both border identities based on their spatiality. Nuyorican is based in the colonial displacement from Puerto Rico (a product of labor practices and economics rather than direct forced migration) in which the everyday lives of Puerto Ricans in New York mutually rewrite the space and the people. Chicano identity not only is created in the geographic reality of a shift in national borders, it exists in the spaces between U.S. and Mexican subject positions.

Despite the explanatory power of the border, however, the ease with which it is deployed rhetorically as a description of hyphenated, hybrid, and fragmented identities has created a haunting sense of exhaustion with its metaphorical use.[4] This saturation has led to recognition of the failure of its metaphorical capacity for liberation and rethinking. The paradigm is often too quickly deployed as the frame for an alternative space whose scope is never fully explored and whose material realities are often erased. This lack of exploration has led to a scholarly call for a materialist specificity conceived in direct opposition to the paradigmatic metaphorical and conceptual figuration of the border. Thus, successful deployments of the border as a critical and performance discourse increasingly grant attention to the specific materialities of the border and a growing desire to listen to the actual inhabitants of the literal borderlands in order to understand their lived realities. This attention is crucial, since the critical utopia attached to the border space has had no effect on the global corporations whose productive capacity in the border spaces continues to increase, along with the sustained violence against women in border cities such as Ciudad Juárez, Chihuahua. The creation of highly profitable *maquiladoras*—factories that import their raw materials and machinery duty-free and create goods for export—continues to expand in these border spaces controlled by multilateral (though unequal) trade agreements. This expansion reflects the political power of the global, transnational corporations whose profits they generate. These problematic spaces of capital offer a chilling alternative to the easy deployment of the border as a rhetorical space of resistance.

While the existence of national borders is a lived reality for all of us, the pervasive effects of economic disparity and egregious labor practices in the liminal spaces of *maquiladoras* impact primarily those south of the U.S. border and those attempting to move northward. Popular narratives articulate the border as a meaningful divider whose reality is never fully defined except in terms of its failure to sustain a "legal"

America, implicitly white and English, in the face of "illegals," "criminals" who continue to undermine this possibility by exposing the relative porousness of the border. The primary crime of these "illegals," hyped ceaselessly on conservative talk radio shows, is an attempt to secure employment at a higher wage without first satisfying bureaucratic and governmental regulations. Ironically, the increasingly vitriolic rhetoric against immigration has clarified the fundamental uncertainty attached to claims of the negative economic impact of this population.

There is little willingness to publicly acknowledge the importance of undocumented labor, though surprisingly George W. Bush has begun advocating for streamlined work visas for Mexican laborers. And the film *A Day without a Mexican*, which clearly articulates the U.S. dependence on Mexican labor, actually received a relatively widespread distribution. While national borders are becoming increasingly transparent in terms of commercial trade, the same is not true for human movement. Like the so-called war on drugs directed south from the United States, the "war on people" implies that the generative impulse for the northward flow has nothing to do with consumptive desire north of the Rio Grande. Immigration still is being tied to concerns about international terrorism, a connection that fosters nativist acts of racist reprisal against brown people, whether they are of Middle Eastern descent or Latino. Though Arab Americans are receiving the bulk of this mistreatment, the new threat is troped onto the Mechicano body as well. This visual slippage can be seen in the use of Latino actors to play Middle Eastern terrorists on television, such as Tony Plana's role on season four of the television show *24*.

The legislative equivalent of this nativist sentiment is the December 2005 passage of HR 4437 in the House of Representatives, which was intended to make "unauthorized presence," the official charge for illegal immigration, a criminal offense. In doing so, passage of the bill not only would change a civil offense into a felony but also would have effectively criminalized the act of aiding an undocumented immigrant. Though this bill was not signed into law, the widespread support for such increasing criminalization and policing led to a national proimmigrant movement that manifest itself in public marches and demonstrations. Resolution of the immigration issue is difficult, as there are few verifiable empirical data about the economic impact of undocumented labor in the United States. The rhetoric of security is still a justification for harsh legislative and juridical treatment of undocumented immigrants, and while recent legislative approval for expansion of the physical border fence between the United States and Mexico has been greeted with disgust by progressives in the north, it is viewed as a much more explicit act of militarized violence in the south.

Performing the Border

One of the most thoroughly documented and academically recognizable series of performances of border art is the work of Guillermo Gomez-Peña. In pieces such as *Mexterminator* and *Border Brujo*, Gomez-Peña articulates ethnic identities trapped in the global representational machine. His wide recognition as a performance artist is propelled not only by his invocation of globalization but also his shift from more explicit performance on the border to an increasing acceptance of the border as a paradigm for thinking as well as a material site. His success is also shaped by his willingness and ability to articulate his thinking through a theoretically infused language that engages directly with the scholarship of the border, especially the ethnographic scholarship. Gomez-Peña's success can also be seen as a sign of the academic fascination with the border paradigm as a utopian site of resistance and privileged space for alternative forms of knowledge and identity.

However, as Kirsten Nigro has been careful to articulate, the view looking north is very different from the view looking south. While for the most part U.S. Latino and Chicano artists figure the border as both a material reality and a useful metaphor for understanding identity, the metaphorical elements are rarely present looking north. Instead, the border is seen as a militarized and material reality whose political, economic, and cultural effects are the objects of critique. This is not to say that there is an absence of a sustained critique of the border looking from the north, but there is a need to situate and historicize articulations of the border and moments of resistance.[5]

One powerful example of theater that engages with these material realities looking south is Teatro de la Esperanza's 1976 play *La víctima*. Conceived as an episodic docudrama to elucidate the economic causes of cross-border migration and the emotional toll inflicted by border policing, the play follows the life of Amparo, a woman who crosses the border north as a child with her family because of the violence and displacement of the Mexican revolution. She returns to Mexico during the Great Depression as a result of decreasing labor opportunities and is separated (by the masses of people at the train station) from her eldest son, Samuel, who remains in the United States. Samuel is adopted, grows up, serves in the Korean War, and begins working for the Immigration and Naturalization Service (INS). With the continued economic difficulties in Mexico, Samuel's family eventually returns to the United States, finding work in a factory and participating in the labor movements of the early 1970s.

Samuel, promoted to take charge of immigration raids, is eventually responsible for deporting his own mother and half brother in a graphic exploration of the "*herida abierta*," the "open wound" of the border for a Mechicano population.[6] Samuel capitulates to the economic pressure of his employment despite his daughter's disapproval. Not fully aware of the dehumanization that he has experienced, the play ends with the emotional trauma that his separation and subsequent act of deportation have caused him. His wife, who supports his work because of the economic security it offers, has already reassured him, "She's not your mother," despite the audience's (and Samuel's) knowledge to the contrary.[7] The play presents Samuel as the product of a dehumanizing system, and the horror of the confrontation with his mother is situated within a larger critical analysis of systemic forces. He is a seminal figure for the psychologically conflicted Mexican American border patrol agent who faces the difficult task of deporting his or her own relatives.

This historicized critique of border policy reflects the more explicit political language of the 1970s, but it still retains power as witnessed in a 2006 production at Teatro Visión in San José, California, intended to further the current conversation about immigration politics and policy. Modified in several ways, this production ended with a substantial change: the final theatrical gesture involved Samuel's daughter claiming allegiance with her grandmother and bringing down the back wall of the second act set, the border wall, to bring the deported characters back on stage for a final bow.

This destruction of the literal border fence, a structure that did not exist in 1976, is intended as a gesture of hope in a contemporary milieu in which legislation authorizing an additional seven hundred miles of border fencing passed in 2006. This physical barrier has both a symbolic and a real function in policing the border, and its existence is highly controversial. Concerns about the structure and the realistic possibility of bringing it down are the focus of the 2003 play *Nuevo California* by Bernardo Solano and Allan Havis, supported by Animating Democracy and produced by the San Diego REPertory Theatre. The play is community-based, and the politics and points of view were formulated through a coming-together of community members and artists from both sides of the San Diego-Tijuana border. According to Lynn E. Stern,

> The International Border Fence, a 14-mile metal wall that divides San Diego and its neighboring city Tijuana, served as the project's springboard for cross-border dialogue on critical regional issues and the new play's theme. San Diego REPertory Theatre, together with project partners San Diego Dialogue, Centro Cultural Tijuana, and an ensemble of U.S. and Mexican artists posed a provocative civic question to Mexican and U.S. residents of the border area: "Tear down the fence or fortify it?" Their deliberations and responses gave birth to *Nuevo California*, a multidisciplinary, multilingual theater piece of multiple voices and viewpoints that imagines border life with the fence—and without it.[8]

Although intended to be a binational project, in the end the play was more "U.S.-focused," a reality reflected in the dominance of English as a language of performance.[9] The play imagines dismantling the border fence, but to make this possibility a believable political reality, the work takes on an almost fantastical quality. It is set in 2028, after a massive earthquake has radically altered the geography and politics of California. The reigning pope, a liberal Mexican American, has orchestrated the creation of a new city-state, bringing together San Diego and Tijuana. The project is heavily financed through the oil wealth of the indigenous Kumeyaay.

In *Nuevo California* the border fence becomes a living monument to the suffering that border politics and cultural difference have created; its existence sustains and nurtures the festering sorrows of individual loss. These losses are articulated by individuals as the product of intercultural interaction and become the justification for maintaining the wall. One U.S. woman's home was accidentally burned to the ground by Mexican workers; one Mexican man's sister was raped by U.S. military personnel. Like the recent production of *La víctima*, the play ends with a central figure beginning to tear down the wall despite the assassination of the pope; however, in this play it is an ambivalent gesture, as only one person acts while the others merely watch. As the play ends, she has only begun the process. The character, Sin Fin, whose name means "without end" in Spanish, is a linguistic artist experimenting in the boundaries between languages, creating doublings of Spanish and English, such as "see*veo*."[10] This doubling of the verb to see (*veo* means "I see" in

Spanish) suggests that the possibility of clear and progressive thinking requires a doubled language of seeing, not only the ability to see in both languages but to see in both languages simultaneously. This is an alternative to the code switching between languages and insists on an idea of *both* English and Spanish rather than something in between.

Though the wall is not destroyed, the necessity of freeing the ghosts trapped within the wall by memory and sorrow is made clear. The pope, in his coma after the assassination attempt, takes on the role of various figures of loss (fathers, sons, etc.) and goes to comfort those who have suffered because of the wall. This process of emotional exorcism is a necessary step before the wall can come down, and when he has created the possibility of forgiveness, he moves on into death. His assassin, the Man Standing Still, cannot imagine the possibility of change despite its inevitability. When Rebecca Rowland, the reporter covering the creation of the new city-state announces, "This is Nuevo California" at the very end of the play, her statement offers the possibility of speaking directly to the theater audience in the literal space of Nuevo California—the border city of San Diego.[11] This conflation of the stage and theater space is itself a political statement about the continued existence and maintenance of borders. This political space is thus tinged with tragedy and loss. It calls on the audience to be agents of transformation even as the play itself illustrates the vehement opposition to such change. This complex positioning reflects the increasingly conflicted border issues in the wake of 9/11. The possibility exists for transformation, but the polyphony of cultures, voices, and attitudes makes it difficult to wright.

Wrighting the Border in the 1990s

Slightly different from the two plays discussed above, Latino theater in the 1990s represents the U.S.-Mexican border as a site of crossing and the human interactions and cultural assumptions that haunt this real or perceived act of transgression. This focus on border crossing within the theater is made even more interesting by the rhetorical and spectacular construction of the actual border in highly theatrical and representational terms. During the 1990s, legislative and policing activities were designed less to efficiently and effectively deal with the sustained issue of human migration than to create a sense that something is being done, to reassure the population that the southern border of the United States is being protected. This goal was accomplished, unfortunately, by decreasing the visibility of undocumented human traffic, shifting the flow of migration from highly populated urban centers to increasingly hazardous and remote terrain far from the eyes of the media.[12]

Writing in the 1990s, the central playwrights examined in this chapter are engaging with contemporary cultural understandings of the border, manifest through militarized gestures and the construction of actual fences, as a site that must be closed to prevent economic and political dangers. These dangers are invoked through a racialized and polarized language of opposition, "they are different," as well as tropes of colonization and displacement, "they are taking away our jobs and changing our way of life." In response to these rhetorical and symbolic gestures, these playwrights demonstrate the theatricality of border space to rethink the problematic binary of "us vs. them" established by perceiving ethnicity as present primarily on an immigrant body made into an other by nationalist thinking. This change is accomplished through the use of the border as a site of identity negotiation in multiple registers, as well as explicit representational attention to the practice of policing and the cultural and political status of policing agents, the border patrol or, more colloquially, "*la migra*." These playwrights wright the border using humor; they carry the logic of the border to extremes while not erasing its material dangers, exposing the emptiness and futility of conceptualizing the border as a solid boundary, especially given the increasingly permeable and symbiotic relationship between the United States and Mexico.

Unlike the constructed stereotypes of Gomez-Peña, politicized docudramas, or community-based explorations, the works of these playwrights primarily traffic in the mainstream cultural rhetoric of the border. They are speaking to an audience not necessarily familiar with the complexity of hybrid identities, an audience whose members are invited to engage these identities through the experience of the play. Though often addressing a gentrified middle class rather than recent immigrants, the plays are written in solidarity with the political experiences of recent immigrants. In doing so, these artists wright a border saturated with satiric critique. The cultural force of this representation rests in the sustained conflation of multiple metaphors that in their framing demonstrate the legally and culturally contested nature of the border. This shared act of wrighting, intended to reconfigure the politics and reception of the border, implies a shared political community and a cultural investment in transforming the representational practices of the mainstream media and the average citizen concerned about the constructed (and real) dangers posed by the border.

The theater becomes a particularly powerful site in which to change thinking about borders, because its very liminality as a space that is "not really real" echoes both the celebratory and cautionary tales that accrete around discussions of the border. At the same time, though eminently fungible, the space of theater still provides a form of materiality that can be experienced. The very gesture of staging within the theater serves as an embodied counter to the often disembodied rhetoric invoked to mystify the realities of border crossing and border crossers. Playwrights use the space of the theater itself to help explicate the conceptual disjunctures present in the space of the border. Radically different materialities are geographically contiguous on the border, and the act of walking across a bridge becomes narrated as a movement between worlds, between two radically different productions of space.

Representationally, it is still easy to elide the material realities of border crossing and border living, the transnational economies that foster the violence of everyday life within the borderlands, the real physical dangers of crossing the border, ranging from being shot by militarized border guards to starvation, dehydration, rape, robbery, vehicular homicide, and exposure to toxic waste. Though the following works do not fully explore the material realities of the border, they nonetheless expose the assumptions of the audience that continue to locate the site of poverty, of danger, and of difference as something over there, something Mexican. Pablo Vila provides a sociological account of this imaginative tendency in his exploration of the increasing complexity of Mexican American identity in a cultural space in which the border is materially present (El Paso–Ciudad Juárez). Through interviews, he exposes a logic that permeates a diverse range of communities: "In El Paso, as in other areas of the country, the discourse of ethnicity is pervasive. However, here it combines with a discourse of nationality in a volatile mixture that marks anything that is stigmatized as Mexican. Poverty is named in Spanish in El Paso—and in El Paso, Spanish signifies Mexican. For instance, the poor neighborhoods of the city are known not as neighborhoods, slums, ghettos, or shantytowns but as *colonias.* . . . This is the case irrespective of the language or the ethnicity of the speaker."[13]

As a counter to this equivalence of stigmatization and Mexican it is necessary to think about audience transformation as a step in the construction of a political community achieved through providing the audience a moment of deportation, of distance from their everyday lives. In this moment of reception, cultural work is being done precisely because the nature of borders and the activity of crossing are placed in an alternative and more immediate conceptual framework. As witnesses to transgressive border crossing and the forms of policing that exist on the border, audience members may indeed participate in the supposed transgression or encounter their own individual resistances. While one could argue that this is only metaphorical, part of the power of these plays is their insistence on the literalization of metaphors. This gesture of instantiation, of bringing into being in the theater, parallels the emerging content of ethnicity within the theatrical space itself as something that is a product of the intersection of audience and actor.

Comedy and the Border Agent

In negotiating the border there is often an agent involved, one who is able to facilitate or stymie the act of crossing. Although border crossing is a recognized cultural phenomenon, its manifestation in the mainstream U.S. cultural imaginary is almost always envisioned as the difficulties or dangers of Mexicans and Central Americans moving northward into the United States rather than a constant interchange between countries. Popular accounts primarily provide either a version of the coyote, the not-to-be trusted agent who brings groups without papers north, or the border patrol agent, the gatekeeper and policeman, armed and dangerous.

Culture Clash, the Chicano comedy troupe, has its own version of the complexities of interfacing with border agents in *Bordertown* (1999).[14] Part of a series of site-specific projects they developed in the 1990s, *Bordertown*, like *Nuyorican Stories*, explores the nature of a specific urban geography through a unique culture lens. In this case, the focus is the geographic relationship of San Diego and Tijuana; the gap between these two proximate urban spaces is central to the project. The opening of the play satirizes both the obvious public investment in protecting the militarized border and echoes the parallel treatment on both sides of the border, comically (and perhaps ontologically accurately) presenting the embodiment of the dangerous security and paramilitary presence as closet theatergoers. At the beginning of the first act the playwrights are stopped by a U.S. militiaman who ends the encounter by asking for *Christmas Carol* tickets; the beginning of the second act is an encounter with a Mexican militiaman who ends the conversation with the same request.

The three initial characters, listed as Mexican 1, Mexican 2, and Militia Man, play out the exhaustively repeated scenario of racial profiling that haunts policing practices at the border. The self-appointed protector of the border conflates the visual semiotics of Chicano identity with the absence of U.S. citizenship. As a "volunteer," he represents the ideological power of the desire to control the border as a means of delineating and protecting U.S. identity. This desire has led to a range of highly controversial independent attempts to control the flow of bodies across the border, most recognizably various groups of Minute Men who advocate for a populist conservative and often nativist agenda and encourage individual members to guard national borders.

This volunteer policing and its attendant dangers are sustained culturally because of individual narratives of loss in relationship to border crossing, just like the resistance in *Nuevo California*. The militarization of the border and the restriction of border crossing options as a way of deflecting media attention has shifted the process to less accessible and visible spaces of the border. In these remote locations the human risks are much greater, and at times, the migratory patterns impinge economically on individual farmers and ranchers whose fences are repeatedly cut and whose water supplies are damaged by migrants desperate for water. Ironically, of course, the increased personal loss here (along with the cost placed on local communities and avoided by the federal government for the care of undocumented migrants) is partially a result of a flawed series of attempts to control the theater of the border within a media-saturated political environment. Most of the scholarly explanations of migration patterns are based on classical models that have never been demonstrated in relationship to real migration patterns and especially not to U.S.-Mexican migration patterns. And all of the government legislation enacted from the mid 1980s through the 1990s has merely destabilized and disrupted what was a well-functioning, albeit "illegal," flow of labor north and south.[15]

The metatheatrical irony of this moment of performance is that the two Mexicans are members of Culture Clash doing cultural research for the play the audience is currently witnessing. Rather than recognizing them as legitimate cultural workers, the militia assumes they are transgressive figures, drug runners, coyotes, or undocumented immigrants. Ironically the section ends with an alien presence, echoing the comedic ending of *I Don't Have to Show You No Stinking Badges!*, displacing the real material issue of the border through the invocation of a body completely distanced from the realities of the border itself. This "real" alien tells the audience to "prepare to escape from San Diego and leave behind your personal, cultural, and political borders. Journey with us to the borderless cosmos, where race, creed, and religion does [*sic*] not matter. . . ."[16] Anticipating *Nuevo California*, here the disappearance of borders requires a displacement in either time or space. This displacement is made most politically powerful through the connection with the idea of deportation—of removing an individual from a space for political reasons.

The Militia Man in *Bordertown* echoes the language of personal experience through the story of "Mrs. Westcott," articulating a politics informed by the individual experience of a rancher whose adaptation to the reality of migration is destroyed in the face of increasing numbers. This rhetorical gesture makes the oppositional discourse against immigration more material and complex, personalizing an otherwise abstract opposition. At the same time, Mexican 2 counters this argument with "I have factual border abuse cases of people detained in cells for five days without water. Border Patrol agents abusing and detaining U.S. citizens because they looked Mexican, that was their crime, looking like a Mexican!"[17] This encounter between the Militia Man and the "actors" follows a recognizable script that delineates the space as the border with lights to heighten the aspects of visibility and control. The absence of a "set" for the border reinforces the idea that the border is itself an arbitrary space to be articulated through a series of practiced gestures, an almost theatrical performance that, as Renato Rosaldo reminds us, exists in a state "simultaneously symbolic and material."[18] There is a clear series of answers and questions that must successfully be negotiated at any space of border crossing, and before 9/11 the proper documentation was often superfluous, provided the spoken answers were correct (and correctly accented) and the performance of identity did not lead one to a suspicion of migration as opposed to mere crossing.[19]

The attachment of the border patrolman to a specific regional geography is ironically echoed in John Leguizamo's performance of Pepe Vásquez in his one-man show *Mambo Mouth*. Here we see an undocumented worker attempting to talk himself out of incarceration and deportation in a scene set in New York City, rather than on the U.S.-Mexico border itself. Among a series of rhetorical gambits to get released, Pepe attempts to assert solidarity with the law-enforcement official he is addressing. The monologue, staged in relative darkness with Leguizamo's face partially obscured by the hood of his sweatshirt, is also set "behind bars," as a window of bars functions as the only set. Minimal lighting indirectly delineates the rest of his prison, but it is crucial that he maintains a position that emphasizes the legal separation of the bars during his monologue—a clear framing of the "criminality" of the undocumented immigrant.

Trapped at La Guardia by the promise of some free gifts, Pepe voices the Anglo concerns with border crossing: the fear of the population explosion in the third world, the loss of English as a primary language of communication, and the overuse of welfare and state-supported programs by illegal immigrants. Although admittedly large numbers of Mexicans and Central Americans work *sin papeles* in the United States, they *are* working, and without this work, the economy of the United States might suffer. As Pepe puts it: "Okay, go ahead and send me back. But who's going to clean for you? Because if we all stopped cleaning and said 'adiós,' we'd still be the same people but you'd be dirty! Who's going to pick your chef salads? And who's going to make your guacamole? You need us more than we need you. 'Cause we're here revitalizing the American labor force!"[20]

Clearly aware of the political implications of his identity, Pepe is representative of an entire group of Latino characters emerging from the dramaturgy of the 1980s and 1990s. Aware of the stereotypes he is working against as well as the fantasies projected on him by the powers that be, he succeeds in questioning the hierarchy of power without being represented as somehow beyond such an activity. In this case, Pepe is arrested in one of the notorious busts in which criminals are sent notification through the mail that they are being awarded something or being honored for something. Instead, what they encounter is an INS, FBI, or police sting.

There is no way for Pepe to pass as a legal worker. The individual working without papers is seen as transgressive, not the system that will not allow him to enter legally or the employer who has chosen to pay him. By dint of his "unauthorized presence" the man is already criminalized and transgressive. And, even if he has proper papers, the default assumption (depending on his competency in English) is that he is does not have them. He is illegal by definition, by stereotype, simply by existing. Although in the play he has varied explanations and complaints, including his attempted validation of legal identity through the possession of Mets tickets, he is unsuccessful in winning his freedom. Pepe's final payback is to expose one of the implicit fears that fuels the entire practice of deportation and border patrol, at least along the southern border: "Go ahead and try and keep us back. Because we're going to multiply and multiply (*thrusts hips*) so uncontrollably till we push you so far up, you'll be living in Canada! Oh, scary monsters, huh? You might have to learn a second language. Oh the horror!"[21] This exposure of the roots of the fear that allows for the stringent policing of borders helps wright the possibility of an alternative thinking about the presence of undocumented workers. Pepe, while undocumented, is ironically articulating the fear of the use of Spanish as a public language in English, adding an additional level of irony.

The agent is particularly complex when the figure is a Chicano border patrolman like Samuel, in *La víctima*, one who has cultural (and perhaps even familial ties) to some of the people crossing over. The moment of recognition of one's own culpability in the oppression of those with whom you share an ethnicity functions effectively in forms of solo performance that move in the direction of stand-up comedy. This act of wrighting creates an interpretive pathway for a mainstream audience to follow by playing on their cultural assumptions and then exposing the fallacies of those assumptions. Through solo performance, the very minimal staging heightens the ease with which cultural frames are employed, and the genre itself provides a space for a radical pedagogy masked in comedy—audiences listen to a cultural lecture in a space that deflects any sense of direct culpability even as serious cultural issues are explored.

This figure of potential scorn and ridicule—the bigot who closes the gate in denial of his own ethnic heritage—is played out in Rick Najera's *The Pain of the Macho*. Rather than staging this event as a crisis of individual identity and moral responsibility, Najera presents a radical revision of the border agent that accounts for the social roots of the individual imagination. The comic distance allows for a potentially radical critique of the position of the supposed betrayer. Najera's vision of legalistic policing is a complex critique of the current state of the performance of immigration policy.

Emerging from his work in Latins Anonymous, *Pain of the Macho* is a one-man show dealing with representations of Latino masculinity; it portrays the border patrol agent as only one manifestation of Latino identity. The agent, Bufford Gómez, comes to the border patrol by way of the military. After fighting against "people who look like [him]" in foreign countries, he ends up doing the same thing in the United States, so now he is "fighting an invasion, and there's not been a shot fired."[22] Bufford's recognition that his supposed enemies in fact look like him is brought on by his examination of a Mexican man run over by a car during his attempts to cross over. This epiphany, that the man may have been his own brother, leads to a transformation in his categories of illegal and alien.

> I was enlightened. I made a vow. I decided I ain't hassling people who look like me. It ain't right. . . . But I've got to follow orders. So every time you liberals pass the San Clemente border checkpoint, you can just stop flipping me off under your dashboards, 'cause I'm doing my job to stop the aliens. (*Gets angry.*) Yeah, I'm going to pull over everyone who looks like an alien, but they'll just be any blue-eyed, light-skinned aliens, blonde-haired Aryans. They could be illegal British or illegal Norwegian aliens or illegal Canadian aliens taking hockey jobs from Americans. You can never tell. You've got to be on your guard. . . . If the original Mexican border patrol had pulled over more Anglos, this would have still been Mexico.[23]

Shifting the category "alien" from Mexican to Norwegian, Canadian, and British is intended to produce laughter; however, this laughter emerges precisely because of the discomfort elicited by his claims.

The reconceptualization of identity and ethnicity is at the heart of this process. Patrolling the border is not about policing national origins, even though that is the purported function, but rather about preserving certain forms of racial identity that are implicitly tied up in the notion of "American" identity. The humor of the situation makes clear how culpable the entire culture is in the racialization of the border. The extent to which Bufford's solution appears "absurd" is precisely the degree that both class (he begins pulling over drivers of Saabs and Mercedes) and racial assumptions play in decision-making processes at the border. "Alien" is both a class and a racial category, as are, through transitive properties, both "illegal" and "immigrant." Taking his job seriously, Bufford continues to perform his duty, but he is now going to do so within the letter of the law, not the discriminatory spirit. His concept of identity will be staged in "purely" nationalistic terms, and national identity may be proven through only one mechanism—legal documentation. By constructing Aryans as potential aliens, forcing Anglos to prove themselves as citizens, demanding papers and green cards, he inverts the practice of asking anyone with brown skin who speaks Spanish to prove their identity in multiple ways. Taking seriously the legal implications of his position, Bufford places the law on his side and uses it to preserve the sovereignty of a country, but without making any racial or class assumptions about the source of threats to that sovereignty. Operating in a purely legalistic model, he undercuts the whole concept of the border by showing the myths on which it is based. And, by making the historical claim in regard to Mexican sovereignty, he also comments on the historicity of borders and the specific exclusion of U.S. practices.

A review of the 2005 Broadway performance of *Latinologues*, Najera's evolving portrait of Latinos, seems to counter the presumed political efficacy of this work, on the one hand, while reaffirming its necessity on the other. Charles Isherwood's review of the performance claims that the "characters . . . are neither fresh nor fully realized . . . the men and women of 'Latinologues' are composites of worn, obvious stereotypes."[24] He later remarks, "'Latinologues' has been seen . . . in many American cities with large Latino populations, suggesting that it is serving a real need. As the odd gringo out in the audience, duty compels me to report that the cheerful folks surrounding me did seem to find Mr. Najera's broad-brush portraits of Latino experience endearing. ('Latinologues' is performed in English, but the characters often embroider their monologues with profanities in Spanish)."[25]

These comments are crucial for understanding the possibilities of transformation and the limits of this performance. Isherwood's claim that these characters are outdated is correct in the sense that in some cases they have had a stage life of more than ten years. More important, there has been a sea change in thinking about ethnic representation during this decade, a movement away from exploding stereotypes to representational choices that resist the potential imposition of stereotypes. Still, the most disturbing aspect of this review, besides the lack of professionalism attributed to the show, is Isherwood's dutiful acknowledgement of the enjoyment of his fellow audience. Clearly he is not part of this audience, but even more important, he has to indicate that it is not a language barrier that has isolated him from taking pleasure in this moment and being transformed.

This review is sharply contrasted by Marilyn Stasio's review in *Variety*, where she delineates the contents of Bufford's very different diatribe: "The switch-hitting scribe scores big as Buford Gomez, a Tex-Mex officer with the U.S. Border Patrol who makes the generous gesture of educating the audience about border jumpers. Having established that 'not every single Latino is Mexican,' he goes on to define the ethnic differences in pointed barbs at every Latin American cultural group (presumably) sitting in the audience. 'Puerto Ricans are legal Mexicans.

... Cubans are Mexicans with rafts. ... Dominicans are Mexicans who play baseball really well. ..."[26] Her assumption is that this is a "barb" at a specific audience, but underlying the gesture is Najera's critique of the continued homogenization of Latino heterogeneity into the category of Mexican as the primary sign of undocumented border crossing. Najera wrights this logic by pointing out the ludicrousness of this reduction, and the laughter emerges from the recognition of its continued influence. Still, as an agent, he maintains his function as the one able to direct and shape this discourse around ethnicity for an audience.

Negotiating the Borders with an Agent

The notion of the border patrol agent becomes even more complex in Guillermo Reyes's *Deporting the Divas*, where Michael González, a bisexual Mexican American INS officer, explores the intersections of sexual, cultural, and national identities. In Reyes's play, identity is always potentially transgressive; it becomes not only a cultural construct and a way of negotiating with the world but also a form of aesthetic self-expression. Underlying Michael's concerns about his profession and its implications for his identity are the political, racial, class, and sexual concerns produced by languages in and around the border. According to Reyes, "*Deporting the Divas* is the most political play I have written, but I wasn't trying to promote a specific point of view about gay immigrants. The most important issue for me in *Divas* was that I was going to deal with the duality in this young border-patrolman's mind. He is Mexican-American, bisexual, having an affair with an illegal alien male, and my interest was in how he negotiates this."[27]

At stake in this play is the concept of being defined by borders and the possibility of refusing that form of identification. Beatriz Cortez articulates this "alternative" as "a flowing hybrid identity that makes it possible . . . to simultaneously belong to a variety of spaces of difference and/or to shift from one space to the other."[28] Characters have the capacity to stage themselves, and there is an explicit self-referentiality to the work, both in the introductory framing and in the "text" itself. Women characters are played by male actors, and characters are in some cases very aware of being played by the same actor. The protagonist has an alter ego realized within the dramatic language of film noir, and characters are subjected to the dramaturgical control of other characters' ability to disrupt the linearity of narrative. The combination of these dramaturgical effects makes it difficult to define what a border is, what it means to cross a border, and how this activity might take place.

Reyes attempts to resituate the border agent by adding to the mix the aesthetic self-reflection of various forms of theatricality, especially the diva, itself a palimpsest of gender and sexual identities. The title, *Deporting the Divas*, already makes clear some of these issues. Deporting clarifies that the act of illegal immigration has already occurred and that the mental and physical process is to reinstate a space that may never have existed—one without divas. The replacement of aliens or immigrants with divas is the first explicit link between notions of aesthetic subjectivity and national identity. This connection does more than simply demonstrate the easy occlusion of immigrant and illegal alien—and of "questionable" civic status with other forms of "questionable" civic participation—it changes the relationships of space, performance, and identity. By using the diva as a central concept, Reyes wrights deportation into an alternate political universe where the act is spectacular, visible, and empowering rather than hidden and disempowering.

Michael's negotiations with the borders he polices, imagines, and crosses are staged in epistemological and theatrical terms. Finding himself in a relationship with an "illegal alien," he is forced to a moment of disjuncture, a moment in which he must reevaluate and reexamine the world. Establishing intimacy with an "illegal immigrant" is staged in a space of exchange in which the prize for the other is legitimacy. But, in this case, it is not that simple. In the introduction to *Divas* Marge McCarthy—a cousin of Joseph McCarthy—tries to explain the play to her ladies club that she has brought for the evening: "I think, however, frankly, you ladies would be a lot more intimidated tonight by the immigrant issue. Having a gay son these days is not as tragic as having an immigrant in the family."[29] In an earlier draft manuscript of the play, Marge continued, "I often stay up nights worrying my son Jeremy will come home from Princeton and confess he's an illegal alien. He's hidden this secret all these years, and he knew this about himself when he was ten years old. You ladies would probably ostracize me. . . ."[30]

Marge's "horrible fantasy" of having an illegal alien in the family is expressed in the same language of coming out as the supposed lesser of the two evils, gay identity. Being an illegal alien is the greater tragedy, but this fear is predicated on a series of impossibilities. First and foremost it would require the literal existence of Freud's family romance—Jeremy would indeed have to have been adopted. However, the act of adoption would "legitimate" him, even if he began life as a noncitizen. The other possibility is that Marge herself is not a citizen and gave birth to Jeremy in a foreign country, though this version would indicate the "illegal" status of the entire family.

Of course, there are additional ways of imagining this fantastic problem. In one we have the racial and class implications of such an identity, which are as horrifying to a conservative blue blood as the claim of a particular sexual identity (since the latter does not have any necessary racial or class implications). Perhaps the most fascinating part of Reyes's model is the displacement of biology through the idea that Jeremy's parents should always have known about this identity. And perhaps it is this very impossibility that made Reyes erase this extended parallel from the published text.

In the case of sexual identity, parental denial often deliberately prolongs ignorance. However, in the case of an illegal alien, the possibility of ignorance is only rhetorical; there is not even space for plausible deniability. However, Reyes has added one more curious and crucial twist to this account: Marge McCarthy is played by a man. As he makes very clear in the stage directions, this is not a man in drag but a man playing a woman. Thus, biologically he has created a rupture even while culturally he has not disrupted the nuclear family. By playing with gender Reyes problematizes the lineage claimed by the concerned mother. She never was and cannot be the mother of this child and thus does not have control over his national identity or any essential identity markers. Yet Reyes produces a situation where the fantasy becomes a real possibility at the very moment when there is no longer a biological certainty attached to the role of mother.

The ease with which the paradigm of illegal or immigrant identity can be read within the language of the closet emphasizes a cultural fear about the possibility that group identification and even biological and lineal decisions might be chosen; however, the real choice here lies in the site of revelation. The act of concealment is enforced by a community that does not want to admit its existence, policing it only at the most visible moments, while still condoning the presence of this identity insofar as it is functionally useful. The similarity in logic between the policing of the immigrant body—a body that is interchangeable with the illegal alien—and the gay body points towards a logic employed by hegemonic readers against perceived "transgression." However, the very interchangeability of categories emphasizes the limitations of this mode of perception. Reyes is constantly wrighting this demand for categorization, crossing and recrossing borders. This same sense of border guards preserving forms of gender and sexual behavior is articulated in Cherríe Moraga's play *Hungry Woman*, where a lesbian is forced to discuss the nature of her desire and the only male actor in the play is informed that the border guard forms his "revolutionary conscience," indicating the playwright's metaphorical use of the border in a play in which the political borders of national spaces are based on racial divisions.[31]

Deporting the Divas chronicles the experiences of Michael and his film noir alter ego, a Santa Monica policeman, in their explorations of expanding notions of sexual desire. The objects of this desire, the divas, are constituted as illegal or transgressive because of either their national identity or their representation of gender. However, in both manifestations, the divas construct themselves as not only objects of desire but also actors and subjects responsible for staging themselves. The act of staging becomes constitutive of identity within an interpersonal interaction with Michael or his alter ego. Each of the divas—Miss Fresno, "a Guatemalan of German descent" who can pass as a white woman, Sirena, "an Argentinian tango temptress," Silvano, whose "father owns San Salvador" and who is "just fabulous," and Michael's almost lover Sedicio—represents a rupture in Michael's worldview. These ruptures tear apart a fabric initially rent by his vision of a gay Mexican American wedding, an experience he relives at the beginning of the play.[32]

The location and nature of Michael's epiphany clarify both its cultural specificity and its demonstration of the misunderstood policing gestures directed toward placing borders on sexuality. Thinking he was going to arrest a group of illegal immigrants, Michael instead found a gay wedding with everyone's papers in order. Michael's recollection of this moment presents the process of his own perception: "yes, it was a gay wedding—a Mexican—make that a Mexican-American gay wedding—female priest, multi-layered cake, no-host bar, practical gifts. . . ."[33] Michael's presentation demonstrates a level of cultural awareness that insists he already had a conceptual space for such an event. Humorous though his description is intended to be, his ability to employ this vocabulary is itself important. His concern with the ethnic specificity of the celebration suggests that Michael's sexual empowerment and transformation stems from his recognition of a cultural role model; after this event he is aware of a gay Mexican American culture rather than a generic gay culture, something he clearly already understood.

More important, the space of the wedding itself—the desert, the border, and the assumption about what he was going to find and the distance of this from the thing itself—creates an alternative mental and physical space. The location of this wedding, the border, instantiates the transformation here and serves as the site of his utopian vision at the end of the play. The "spooky, ghostly" divas he encounters arise directly out of a reimagination of the border space as a space of joining and celebration in a symbolic sense.[34] This revelation forces him to recognize the power of identities on the border and to reimagine them within his own life. It also begins his experience of displacing the notion of illegal and how that identity is constructed—a fascination the play enacts over and over again. According to Jorge Huerta, "By taking his audience from reality to fantasy and back again, Reyes mirrors the fractured nature of the gay Latino or Latina experience."[35] Reyes's wrighting in fact moves beyond mirroring to force the audience itself to experience the potential dislocation in this shifting space of desire.

Michael's objects of desire are all people conceived as border crossers in multiple ways, yet they do not conceive of themselves as such. This identity is always a product of someone else's claim or imagination. The diva, as a manifestation of the fabulous, is an embodiment of Tony Kushner's vision of the Theater of the Fabulous:

> Style has a dialectical relationship to physical reality. The body is the Real. Style is Theater. The raw materials are reworked into illusion. For style to be truly fabulous, one must completely triumph over tragedy, age, physical insufficiencies—and just as importantly, one's audiences must be made aware of the degree of transcendence, of triumph; must see both the triumph and that over which the triumph has been made. (In this the magic of the Fabulous is precisely the magic of the theater. The wires show. The illusion is always incomplete, inadequate; the work behind the magic is meant to be appreciated.)[36]

Insofar as the product of style must be reflective of both the historical and material circumstances and the theatrical space produced through concrete manipulations of the stage, identity as performance becomes literalized to the level of explicitly theatrical performance and becomes an act of wrighting. There is a sense of excess and exposure, both of which can produce a boundary-crossing identity. Rather than hiding the movement and transformation, these identities privilege the very act of construction for those who know where to look, and the implication is that the audience is sophisticated enough to recognize and appreciate the constructive and creative process. In this sense, the divas are occupying both sides of the border, but the act of moving from one side to another can never be traced through any mode but the theatrical.

The diva operates in a transcendent space that makes the act of deportation mean something different. Because the political and social act of deportation does not effectively sever the multiple ties of identity that these characters possess, it becomes an opportunity for performance. And since the only form of translation (spatially and aesthetically) must be accomplished within the language of theater, deportation becomes the genesis of theater. The border agent becomes a necessary witness and the catalyst for media representation. In the most pedestrian form this transformation manifests in the world of the play and in the politics of California through the interest invested in the act of deportation itself. The clearest model in the play is Silvano, an HIV-positive immigrant who is in the "Private AIDS Hospice of La Jolla." There will be "only one newscamera" to record the headline story of "'Illegal Aliens with AIDS!: Taxpayers Get Stuck with the Bill.'" Of course, when the audience finally sees Silvano, all of the stereotypes of undocumented immigrants are thrown out the window. Talking to Michael, Silvano tells him, "You thought I was just one of these Indian-looking peasants you're used to deporting, didn't you? You didn't count on me speaking English and Spanish better than you. . . . I could have gotten my papers straightened out by marrying a senator's daughter." This deportation becomes a way for Silvano to save money on airfare—his family could have paid for the ticket. His willingness to be deported is a sign not that he is "demented" but that he is "fabulous."[37]

The deportation in its most literal form in this play is manifest as the exit, or more properly, the finale. And, for these divas, the finale is in fact the most theatrical moment of all. Silvano's exit is the most predictable and least theatrical of these—he leads the way out toward the television cameras. However, in his exchange with Michael just before that, the importance of the finale is clarified and the attention it receives explained. Silvano embraces Michael and is left "feeling good" while Michael is "all shocked."[38] Potentially a metatheatrical moment in which Michael recognizes the actor behind the character as an object of his desire, the significance of this moment can vary based on the choice of character doubling. If Silvano shares identities with Sirena or Miss Fresno, then this sharing becomes a reference to the physical similarities of the actor and the character's ability to see through the other character to the shared actor. But if, as the doubling breakdown suggests, all three are played by different actors, then the familiarity has to do more with being a diva, with a particular style and attitude, than with a physical similitude to either character or actor.

According to Silvano, divas "[deserve] to be deported!" because it is a privilege to enact this moment of theatrical struggle, but, as he explains, there are many possible finales depending on the effect intended. Silvano's exit, while not the most spectacular, is still a mystical event, as Reyes's stage directions clarify: "(*Michael is left alone for a second. He looks around. He touches his face, senses some strange sensation about this room, something unfathomable having just occurred, not knowing what to make of it. But a sensation it was.*)"[39] In a sense, the shift that takes place in these exits is from object to subject, from deportee to operatic performer making a specific choice. This choice, this deliberate action in response to the spectator's gaze, becomes a part of the magic.

Sirena, the most explicit diva of them all, is a character in Michael's fantasy episodes. Michael's alter ego, a Santa Monica police sergeant, is an interesting choice not only because the sergeant is a familiar figure in film noir but, more important, because it allows him to maintain his role as someone enforcing the law without having to address issues of national and ethnic identity in his legal decisions. As an L.A.-area cop he does not have to worry about Sirena's Argentinean background, though he can use it to force her to do his bidding.

It is interesting that Michael's fantasy diva not only has no access to his childhood identity but also is the one most explicitly understood to be a man. Although she is "*not just a camp impersonation of woman-hood, she is womanhood*," it is clear to the sergeant what her "real" gender identity is. However, one of the interesting moments of sexual confusion in the play is that Michael's testosterone-laden fantasy vision of himself can only be attracted to men dressed up as women—to a "glamorous tango transvestite"; he can be attracted only to a man willing to play out the fantasy of what a woman should be. As a police sergeant, he will not cross the boundary and desire a man who is not playing some other role. At the same time, his fantasy will never be consummated. In this fantasy world everyone is creating their own theatrical identity through costumes and props to a much greater extent than in the world Michael knows as a border patrol agent. Unable to accept dismissal in the third person, Sirena's language for love, the

Sergeant insists on his love in the first person, but he cannot penetrate Sirena's love for a dead man made up of artificial parts, a man bound and determined to destroy her. They are brought together initially through the hunt for this never-named man, a "Defangeur" who "kidnaps gay men and tries to turn them straight."[40] Although Sirena parts from the Sergeant in act 1 without grand lighting effects, she returns to give the final song—a representation of her stage performance as a tango singer.

The complexities of Michael's fantasy life make the negotiations in his love with Sedicio almost simple. Meeting in a class titled "Beginning Spanish for Pochos," they eventually develop a relationship limited by a series of rules Sedicio has developed.[41] Michael's initial ambivalence stems from anxiety about the effects of his homosexual desire on his masculinity, but he moves beyond this reluctance into what appears to be a genuine relationship. Despite this progress, Michael continues to find it difficult to traverse borders and boundaries. Still married though separated from his wife, he tries his best to separate spatial, legal, and sexual identities, divisions Sedicio seems to have transcended. In a discussion of the possibility of them living together, Sedicio demonstrates his comfort with the way different identities bleed together:

SEDICIO: There's plenty of Americans living in Rosarito, the whole border is a joke anyway. I mean, look at us.
MICHAEL: The border is still the law. You break it, you pay for it.
SEDICIO: It's more complicated than that, you oughta know, you're bisexual.[42]

Even before this exchange, however, Sedicio and Michael have made it clear between them that relationship dynamics are reflected in narrative control:

SEDICIO: This first person narrative can be very patriarchal and oppressive—
MICHAEL: What's that supposed to mean?
SEDICIO: Share your narrative, Michael.[43]

Sedicio wants a fluid sense of narrative and a communal sense of identity, while Michael still attaches himself to fixed, dominant forms. Although this act of sharing creates potential space to develop a relationship on Sedicio's terms, it also reflects Michael's residual need to rely on the rule of law, or in this case, the rule of narrative. Sharing the narrative creates the possibility that it will slip outside conventional bounded narrative practice (which the play of course does constantly). Although Michael is compromised in the end by his inability to stay with Sedicio except as a "very discrete affair," the play nonetheless provides him the opportunity to stage his own finale, an act of wrighting. As Reyes confirms in the stage directions, "*The Divas will be there for him as he works this all out in his vivid, hopeful imagination.*"[44]

Michael and Bufford's negotiations as agents of the border are acts of wrighting in part because they also have some ability to police the border. Bufford's gesture, to literalize the national construction of borders and erase the class and racial constructions that have been implicitly and explicitly attached to it, allows him to retain a policing function that exposes the very problems of such an activity. Michael's potential transformation into a diva presents the culmination of a three-step shift from his presumed function as gatekeeper, to his real function in the play as an uncomfortable witness and participant in border crossing, to a new subjectivity that insists on the necessity and aesthetic value of border crossing as theater. His metamorphosis both is enabled by and creates a space for identity that privileges the role of witness (a task now performed by the audience) but also changes the agent from one who observes, categorizes, and polices to one who enacts deportation (of the self) in an enabling form. The agents' own confusions and resolutions offer not only a space for the exploration of sexual and ethnic borders; they also invite the audience to participate in a moment of crossing-over. This moment enables a symbiotic interchange—both within core ethnic audiences troubled by the political issues raised by the work and within other audiences less familiar with the specific dynamics in play—asking all of them to consider being deported.

El Otro and the Wrighting of Crossing

Wrighting border crossing as a fabulous act of theater runs the risk of slipping into a metaphorical understanding of reception that ignores the real material conditions of deportation. Eliding these conditions—the degradation, disdain, and danger—potentially simplifies the act of crossing the border. Given the increasing media attention to border crossing, migrants moving northward find themselves using increasingly dangerous methods to cross and choosing more and more hostile terrain. In an ironic reality, contemporary border agents find themselves attempting to catch border crossers in part to preserve their lives, though the structural violence of a militarized border creates this paradox.

This militarized border is illustrated within Octavio Solís's play *El Otro*. The play, which was commissioned by the Thick Description Collective, workshopped in 1997, and premiered in 1998, explores a series of literal and metaphorical border crossings—physical and mental journeys that help elucidate the negotiation of identities in relationship to geopolitical and metaphorical borders. Solis indicates the spaces of his play as "*El Paso, the border, El Otro.*"[45] In this play it appears one must move through the border to reach El Otro. Not marked specifically as Ciudad Juárez, El Paso's Mexican counterpart, El Otro instead appears to be a mythical space where *cuentos*, stories, have become myths played out in transcendental form through the peyote-induced visions of the teenage narrator, Romy. Romy is the daughter of Nina and Anastacio, her mother's lover who was killed by her "father" Lupe. The play traces Romy's realization of her place in this story through a trip to get her birthday present, a trip to El Otro led by Lupe, which is simultaneously a literal, physical journey to various sites and a peyote-induced exploration of history and memory. The other crucial figure on this quest is Ben, Nina's new husband, whom Lupe is convinced is the reincarnation of Anastacio. While Ben has no biological relation to Anastacio, Ben is Romy's stepfather, and Anastacio's voice speaks through the body of the actor playing Ben, creating a material connection between the two theatrically.

Initially, the action is framed by the shade of Anastacio, indicating the play's aesthetic location outside traditional psychological realism. Though some might call this magical realism, that aesthetic is too easily read as a commodified form of Latino cultural production that distances the effects of the play from the audience. To do so runs the risk of undercutting the realism of this different space by making the "other" part of a different materiality and effectively sanitizing the representation by displacing anything uncomfortable or unfamiliar on the other side—*el otro lado*. This act of protective displacement becomes a form of border policing, keeping that which is dangerous outside. Solis anticipates this problematic reception and deconstructs it through the use of El Otro as not simply a reference to *el otro lado*.

Romy introduces the conflict in her role as narrator. Lupe's failure as a father has forced her into such a state of frustration that she wants to die, something she attempts to do by escaping into drugs. She does not want to leave Lupe, but as she says, "when he ever look her in the

eye when except to say goodbye," referencing a history of disappearance and irresponsibility.[46] Her story-telling narrative is grammatically
unpunctuated, reflecting both the reality of her altered state and the
transgressive nature of the journey the characters undergo.

After a series of failed attempts to find Romy's birthday present
that introduce the audience obliquely to other elements of this family
history—the mother of Anastacio working as Lupe's maid and Ross,
a client of Lupe's who has just killed his girlfriend—Lupe, as a kind
of reverse coyote, brings Ben across the Rio Grande. In doing so, he
deliberately gets Ben in trouble with the border patrol on the bank. In
response to Romy's disgusted comments "you ain't no real Mexican"
and "[d]on't go fooling yourself" that arise from his unwillingness to
cross the river, as well as his ignorance of Spanish, Ben exclaims, "I'M
A MEXICAN, GODDAMMIT!"[47] Ironically, this assertion of identity attracts
the attention of a Border Patrol Officer.

In this initial encounter both Romy and Lupe speak only Spanish,
casting Ben in the implicit role of coyote leading this border-crossing ex-
pedition, even though in fact he has never been here before. Their choice
to use Spanish and his inability to do so effectively disempowers Ben in
the eyes of the border guard; he falls into the script of a transgressive
border crosser and cannot change the story without Romy and Lupe's
help. Romy attempts to run, and the audience witnesses the potential
violence of the border articulated in the shouted threat of the Officer:
"¡ALTO! ¡NO SE MUEVA O LE DOY UN BALAZO POR LA CABEZA!" (Stop! Don't
move or I'll put a bullet in your head.)[48] Though he finds peyote and
a pistol, the Officer lets them go because they are crossing over, as he
sees it, to the Mexican side. Lupe convinces him: "To keep us out, dat
ees joor yob. To send us bahck ees de same ting."[49]

Lupe's deliberate use of a mix of stereotypically Mexican-accented
English and Spanglish is indicated textually through dialect writing.
This textual marking heightens the act of wrighting, functioning simultaneously as a parodic and a literal marking of border language, of
border writing, and of border rewriting. In a language stereotypically
assumed to reflect limited education, Lupe demonstrates a complex critique of contemporary thinking about the border. Offering the Officer
a logic that enables him to do his job while not interfering with Lupe's
desire to cross the river, Solis locates the Officer in a space similar to an
audience resisting the possibility of transformation. If to keep someone
out of the United States is the same as sending them back, then what is
erased is whatever was accomplished while they were there—the labor,

the cultural experiences, and encounters. The logic of a militarized border participates in this sense of denial, insisting that crossing over does not have cultural significance (except perhaps negative effects) despite the real importance of Mexican labor to the U.S. economy.

Lupe's most powerful critique of U.S. culture and of the border space is articulated in this parodied language. Lupe tells the Officer, "Joo cahn dress her op in jools an fine closs an put mucho make-op on her fase. Joo can get een bed weeth her an mahke sex weeth her an mahke beleef dat chee ees good an muy linda, but joo canna fool joorsef. Chee ees a rotteen corpse an chee duzznt eefen know joo are der. Cos la *verdad, señor*, ees dat chee ees ded to joo an maybee alwaz has bin."[50] Though Ben may be right to insist that Lupe is talking about his ex-wife and not about the United States as the Officer assumes, the sense of death and decadence combined with a fundamental lack of acknowledgment lends credence to the second reading. If the United States is the rotten corpse of a woman unable to acknowledge the man's presence, the crucial question becomes whether she is dead or whether she is "ded to joo." The latter appears to be a specific response to an individual's needs rather than a generalized lack of acknowledgment. This sense of denial permeates the spaces of the border and moves beyond the immigrant experience when it is echoed in the Officer's complaint about his wife: "I go, Lucille, I'm a barb wire fence with Ray-bans. She just stares back at me like I'm not even there. I hate this damn job."[51] Though the Officer allows them to "go back," crossing to El Otro, this is a geography Ben has never experienced.

In the space of El Otro the characters encounter the embodiment of the story of Anastacio's death, El Charro Negro. He is a clear symbol with a material presence, a tattoo artist who carves the story of Lupe's life on his flesh. According to El Charro Negro, "Dead's a relative term in El Otro. When people die, they become story, and when stories die, they become myths, and dead myths become tattoos. I'm a purgastory thirteen years and half a crime old. Suffice to say I'm what's left of an old myth. And that's what he's gonna be."[52] As a living symbol El Charro Negro places the geography of El Otro outside the lived experience of much of the audience. However, because of the nature of theater, he maintains the same level of materiality as Ben and Lupe, creating a situation where in the space of El Otro, and in the theater, each of them is equally real.

Lupe's goal is to kill Ben as he killed Anastacio and to recover Nina for himself. Ben, however, is in the midst of a different story. Through a growing loyalty to Romy he enacts the return of her father, implicitly suggested to be Anastacio. Though he is not her biological father, he claims this role through action. Responding to Lupe's threats, Ben retorts, in a reclamation of identity that moves from third-person distance to first-person intimacy:

> So Hubby number two grows some balls. Hubby number two feeling like home in *El Otro*. Fuckin' *rio* washed me of my whiteness Fuckin' ticks kissed my welcome back *Agave* thickened my *pinche* tongue and your goddamn bat bruised my brownness on. Bam! Bam! Bam! private first class benjamin cortez that man you think I am he's part of me now his blood and my blood blended but no sir uh-uh I do not die like that I will not be so easily dead I have me a mission that mission is father and father say you are my daughter I promised I would see you home and by God almighty
> I
> Will
> See
> You
> Home.[53]

Ben's transformation into Romy's father and not merely her mother's husband is enabled by his experiences of border crossing and violence, a series of experiences the audience has witnessed. The audience is transformed into spectators of, and witnesses to, the grounds of his transformation. His claim as father offers an important counterdiscourse to the problematic language of machismo, since his responsibility as father emerges concurrently with his brownness—his Mexican or Chicano identity.

Ironically, Ben's assumption of fatherhood and his ethnicity are accompanied by his ignorant rejection of a misconstrued geography:

BEN: Just keep my ass away from Mexico. It's a sick and filthy place fulla twisted people and as close to hell as I ever want to come.
NINA: I'm sorry you feel that way, honey, 'cause this ain't Mexico.
BEN: What?
NINA: We're still in Texas. You swam across the river at the point it heads north and the border goes west by fence.

BEN: Holy Crap! All this whole time I been in the States? Then where the hell is *El Otro* supposed to be?[54]

Though the play never explicitly answers this question except through El Charro Negro's suggestive question to Lupe, "We know where it is, don't we, Lupe?" it is crucial to understand that El Otro is not Mexico.[55] It is on the other side of the Rio Grande on a literal level, *el otro lado*, but that other side is not another country. This deliberate shift in geography, forcing reconsideration by both Ben and the audience, is a crucial aspect of this journey.

Having staged a crossing of the Rio Grande, validated by the presence of a Border Patrol Officer who has indeed lost his compass, there is no reason not to assume that the most transgressive activities of the play were perpetrated in the alternative realism of an El Otro geographically located elsewhere and insulated from a U.S. audience by a border. In this account Lupe becomes a different kind of border agent, and his transgressive criminality provides a seductive narrative to follow across the river. Importantly for this argument, Solis actually played the role of Lupe as "an insidious charmer, a sly trickster whose forthright exterior masks his convoluted and vicious manipulations. His eloquence is a verbal sleight-of-hand, dazzling listeners with poetic eruptions of English, Spanish, and Spanglish."[56] He is perhaps the perfect escort across the border and, as an artist, provides us a map to understand this cartography, since he knows indeed where El Otro is. The danger that Lupe poses is at the heart of the problematic shifts between the literal and the metaphorical, the daily lived reality in a border space and the utopian reclamations of plural and hybrid border *mestizaje*.

Solis wrights this necessary doubling within a new conceptualization of the border, demanding that the audience recognize their presence in a new space to successfully understand *El Otro*. Yet, Lupe's death and his misunderstanding of Ben's role clarify the difficulty of both sustaining any consistent grounded narrative within a border and shifting this representational paradigm. Still, these are further steps in a process, started by Ben's own confusion, that lead to reconceptualizing the practice of exoticizing reading—a practice which assumes that the danger is always on the other side. The audience must come to terms with a new knowledge—that Ben's rejection of Mexico is in fact a statement of complete ignorance. El Otro, while still a mythic space, retains the materiality of its geography squarely within the United States. Thus, the reception practice that assumes that violence and magic are always somewhere else must be rethought. The extent to which this realization functions for Ben and for the audience as a new way of knowing, a wake-up call to a different morning, is impossible to tell, but the very possibility of transformation embodied on the theatrical stage reminds us where we are. The theater as the ultimately transformable space becomes an effective material metaphor for the performance of the border—a space clearly within one geopolitical boundary. As Romy narrates the close of the work, the reconstituted family returns "to their rightful place the house already booming with the hollow music of good morning america."[57]

This enunciation of a return to a hollow media-saturated space indicates the emptiness of an "America" that does not stretch beyond its imaginative borders. Ironically, of course, these imaginative borders do not demand a true geographic shift to have an effect. The very presence of the border, even when it is not literally crossed, becomes a transformational site for the Chicano male coming to grips with the realities of his own complex identity formation. The traditional border enables a hegemonic spectator to adopt a voyeuristic stance that displaces the uncomfortable, the different, the dirty, the unfamiliar, and the foreign safely across a geopolitical boundary. This wrighting of the militarized boundary erases the easy assumption of its ability to frame, contain, and distance uncomfortable cultural difference; instead, the border is exposed as a clearly constructed way of maintaining reductive and destructive categories of identity, reducing the complexity of ethnicity in real and metaphoric terms.

José Rivera's Aesthetics of Wrighting

In José Rivera's essay "36 Assumptions about Writing Plays," number 14 is, "If Realism is as artificial as any other genre, strive to create your own realism. If theatre is a handicraft in which you make one of a kind pieces, then you're in complete control of your fictive universe. What are its physical laws? What's gravity like? What does time do? What are the rules of cause and effect? How do your characters behave in this altered universe?"[1] This piece of advice stems from Rivera's own aesthetic practices, and his initial dictum to "create your own realism" is carefully articulated to avoid invoking two categories: magic realism and surrealism. Writing about his play *Each Day Dies with Sleep* in 1992 he offered the following rejection of the critical discourse surrounding it: "The style of the play attracts many labels. Magical realism, surrealism, expressionism—these are ways to talk about the play, though I find them largely irrelevant. In the play, natural logic has been suspended, re-written as it were."[2] More pointedly, in an interview with David Román, he specifically articulated his concern with the presence of a stereotypical reception practice: "[Magic realism] is the new stereotype which has actually replaced Piñero's heroin addicts with levitating virgins and bleeding crucifixes."[3] The problem exists not with the presence of the images themselves but rather with the expectation on the part of audiences and directors that the existence of such images forms the basis for an "authentic" Latino aesthetic. Elements that do not fit traditional realisms are labeled with various other "isms," and the ease with which they are deployed is symptomatic of a critical tendency to attempt to codify any departure from traditional realism. This model of realism is implicitly understood as a psychological relationship with a passive and noninteractive environment.

Rivera's deliberate attempt to open up the critical discourse around his plays is echoed by a number of other Latino playwrights who either refuse the label of magical realism for their work or insist that only a small portion of their plays fits this category. The issue is not one of semantics but of a critical tendency to impose labels that inappropriately and reductively limit the scope of Latino cultural production. Rivera's attempt to free the reception of his play from preconceived limiting expectations that have already coded the work parallels attempts to view Latino ethnicity as a concept in process rather than a prescriptive category.

The category of magical realism often is employed by people who have limited knowledge of its history and complexity as an aesthetic category, much like the limited and stereotyped definitions of *Latino* that restrict the heterogeneity contained within the term. Ironically, this critical gesture often assumes that the presence of magical realism is a sign of an "authentic" Latino artist and an implicit essential characteristic of Latino identity. This assumption not only limits the possibilities for "authentic" Latino cultural production but also suggests that any image that exceeds the bounds of realism is a natural product of culture rather than a product of intellectual labor. Any deviation from traditional realism is read as a symbolic gesture rather than a political or aesthetic gesture engaged in the process of reshaping our understanding of the world.

A term with multiple genealogies, *magical realism* is often conflated with the fantastic, manifest in an assumption that it creates a space outside the real and outside the normal logic of the dramatic or fictive universe. As Rivera makes clear, however, his plays have their own logic, but that logic is operating in an altered universe where events that might seem improbable, mythical, or dreamlike have the same material status as events audiences more regularly encounter. The key is that everything is happening within the same event horizon; there is no gap between what might be labeled real and what might be labeled magic.

Magical realism is, at its simplest, a description of what occurs in a space whose conditions of existence may be different from those structuring a realist aesthetic and, in more politicized definitions, becomes the only means of articulating particular cultural and political realities. It emerged initially as a descriptive term coined by Franz Roh to discuss the work of new objectivists moving away from the heightened emotional and religious content of German expressionism in painting. Instead, the intent was the focus on the object and the power that an everyday object could possess. The term was picked up by scholars of Latin American literature to talk about various writers in the 1940s, around the same time Alejo Carpentier was crafting his first definition of *"lo real maravilloso,"* the marvelous real, an aesthetic specifically tied to the space of America and to the experience of this geography. *Lo real maravilloso* was placed in opposition to the presumed artificiality of European surrealism. As María-Elena Angulo makes clear, the association with a conflation of these terms and Latin American cultural production is typically attributed to Angel Flores and his 1954 paper "Magical Realism in Spanish American Fiction."[4] Scholars then used this term to describe the aesthetics of the Latin American boom novels of the 1960s. Ironically, Flores's category has been picked up by theatrical audiences fascinated with images from the theater that do not conform to the demands of realism. The representation of pragmatic material Catholicism in the form of bleeding saints and love as a physical act of transformation are signs not of a necessary aesthetic practice but of an artistic and political choice. These images are not magical but an attempt to understand the world as it is and to expand the conceptual possibilities of the perceived and lived. As such, they can be paralleled with the wrighting of ethnicity, but it always must be understood as one form of this practice and not the necessary manifestation of it.

Rivera is interested in a broad range of representation and is increasingly dealing with an extended notion of character in which the environment itself becomes an interactive player in the events of the work. This style can be contrasted with other forms of poetic realism, such as Tennessee Williams's plays, where the set reflects the psychological state of the characters rather than an integrated and symbiotic product. Williams uses the world to suggest the state of the character, while for Rivera, the reduction of set image to character psychology is not so easy. There is a necessary and symbiotic relationship between character and space that extends the thinking of identity beyond the self, pointing not necessarily to community as conventionally understood but to a clearer sense of connection of the individual to a larger social environment.

In a sense, the environment becomes another means of thinking through the formation of community. Rather than environment as a frame for helping to define ethnicity (as is often accomplished sociologically in the link between neighborhood and identity), the environment becomes an interactive manifestation of a connectivity that Rivera is constantly exploring in his work. This connection is present in conceptual terms, but that does not reduce its power within the worlds that

Rivera creates. The power of ethnicity in traditional readings rests on the dangerous but necessary conflation of individual and group identity that runs the risk of reducing the individual to the group. In the theater this reduction is particularly dangerous, because something on the stage is always both itself and a sign of itself, a sign that is often extended beyond the particular example to the larger category. Thus, as is the practice with stereotyping, the individual Latino body becomes a sign for Latino identity as a whole rather than a mere instance of a vaguely defined and heterogeneous group. Rivera's wrighting suggests that a primary focus on character is a potentially limiting way of understanding identity. Instead, his insistence on interconnectivity with the environment suggests the extension of identity beyond the individual as a possible basis for Latino aesthetics that goes beyond a simple definition of representation of a particular cultural practice and language.

Visibility, Community, and the End of *Marisol*

> I think that there are a lot of things in the system that we have now [that are] clearly doing very badly. People live with an absolutely insupportable level of stress. The environment is collapsing. There's much too much homelessness; I mean, any homelessness is too much. There's poverty, there are kids walking around with guns. Everybody is frightened by the world that we've created, so the system is failing us.
>
> —Tony Kushner, *Conversations with Tony Kushner*

> Homelessness can be viewed from the perspective of the individuals who become homeless, or from the perspective of the social conditions that foster homelessness. Most research on homelessness throughout the 1980's focused on describing the homeless and their problems. The result is an emphasis on the personal pathologies and the difficulties of the people who become homeless. . . . But these solutions ignore the changing social conditions that have pushed people with little money, perhaps coupled with some personal vulnerability, into homelessness.
>
> —Martha Burt, *Over the Edge*

The early 1990s seemed to bring a sustained theatrical investment in the apocalyptic and millenarian visions of the end. Like the better documented and more highly profiled *Angels in America*, José Rivera's *Marisol* deals with angels, New York City, and the millennium. In *Marisol*

Rivera wrights a politics of visibility in a literal sense; he calls on the audience to witness the presence of homelessness. In doing so he insists on the recognition of belonging in a larger urban and human community. In this sense, he takes on contemporary critiques that suggest identity politics ignore the structural realities inherent in class differences and interrogates those concerns within the bounds of his play.

Emerging from a profound concern with homelessness, attached both to Rivera's own assimilation and his discovery that one of his uncles died homeless in San Diego, *Marisol* interrogates the madness that emerges from the economic and cultural practices of the 1980s.[5] In talking about his play Rivera suggested, "We need to find new heroes and new myths for our society—the old ones just aren't working. The God we know now is a right-wing, white male, corporate God, in whose world racism, sexism, and political injustice are rampant. As the millennium nears, I am amazed these things are still valid." In reference to a potential convergence between his play and *Angels in America*, he said, "I can't speak for Tony . . . but I have been struck in the last few years by the enormous violence we live through on every level. There's a feeling that people have lost their way, that the basic rules of civilization have been suppressed. The millennium has a big role in that."[6]

Marisol arose out of a cultural awareness that has produced a series of analytical and creative works concerned with the millennium. Yet Rivera's specific way of seeing privileges a different kind of thinking about the space of community. Rivera goes beyond the bourgeois liberalism of Kushner's ostensibly radical play, and though he does not make explicit theoretical references, he concretely marks the presence of global capitalism and issues of class linked to forms of identity. *Marisol* is explicit about the issue of homelessness and raises questions about wealth and class tied to issues of ethnicity to a greater degree, but, most crucially, Rivera reconceives the space of New York City as radically transformative in its reality. As Sandoval-Sánchez reminds us, Rivera is fascinated with home, with the idea of the local, and with the way space itself shapes and forms an identity, thus offering an alternative to Kushner's citation of Benjamin's angel of history as a means of thinking about history and political action at the millennium.[7]

Marisol, instead of focusing on the catalyst for displacement, concentrates on the condition—the difficulties of maintaining identity without a sense of place—by foregrounding issues of class and the space of the Bronx. Though considered dangerous by her coworkers, the South Bronx is still the place Marisol Perez calls home at the beginning of her play. *Marisol*, even in its comedy, does not shirk from radically and graphically articulating a sense of structural violence inherent in the disturbed and transformed New York City environment of the play. Unlike Kushner's play, where the only homeless person is a source of comedy forgotten after she provides directions, *Marisol* is full of pain as neo-Nazi skinheads set homeless bodies on fire.

The play follows Marisol, a Puerto Rican yuppie who has chosen an assimilative path despite her continued residence in the Bronx, through an increasingly disturbing series of encounters with a terrifying New York City environment. Exposed to various threats of random violence, she is initially protected by her guardian angel, an African American *"urban warrior"* woman carrying an Uzi.[8] However, Marisol, along with everyone else, loses this angelic protection because of a new war against God—a war that results in the radical transformation of the urban environment itself. In this world guardian angels speak to their charges only to say good-bye, leaving the poor humans to suffer the violence that emerges from the sick and broken environment. Contemporary violence is emphasized from the very first encounter to the end of the play. Ironically, Kushner's comment in the epigraph at the beginning of this section, issued at least partially in response to a question about the education of artists, presents a picture of the world that Rivera literalizes. Rivera insists on the extremity of the dangers in this environment, dangers he has witnessed, experienced, or read about, with the angel's comment that she has saved Marisol from "one plane crash, one collapsed elevator, one massacre at the hands of a right wing fanatic with an Uzi, and sixty-six-thousand-six-hundred-and-three separate sexual assaults."[9] Although the protection offered by the angel could be read as disempowering Marisol, suggesting her inability to protect herself, it is also read as a darkly humorous recognition of the reality of sexual violence in our culture. This potential victim culture is finally erased by the conclusion of the play, when humanity must join the angelic fight to offer any hope of success.

Rivera's vision of proactive, warlike angels desperate to change a stagnant situation contrasts sharply with Kushner's angels, powerful but static, unable to change the world themselves and completely dependent on the work of humans to do so. Of course, Kushner's angels demand not transformation but the emergence of a passive humanity—precisely the counter of Marisol's angel, who "radiates tremendous heat and light" but has "something tired and lonely about [her]."[10] Unlike the isolated revelation of Kushner's play, *Marisol*'s angels give warning to their charges in a democratic manner, transcendental information is available to all, and the relative position of disempowerment is made explicit in the second act when all of the available space becomes the street. Everyone in the play is now homeless, and there appears to be no possibility for individual escape from this environment.

Marisol begins with a scene of death, reflecting a vision of late-millennium apocalypticism. The Man with Golf Club is a direct threat against Marisol's life, as he threatens to kill her on the subway and is unsuccessful only because of angelic intervention. Ironically, Marisol is killed at the end of the play by a right-wing fanatic with an Uzi, one of the events from which her angel has already protected her. However, the entire play is haunted by the possibility that she in fact died in the incident on the subway, because as she moves through the play, everyone knows that Marisol Perez is dead, killed by a man on the subway with a golf club. As her coworker June puts it at work the next day, "Goddamn vultures are having a field day with this, vast close-ups of Marisol Perez's pummeled face on TV, I mean what's the *point*? There's a prevailing sickness out there, I'm telling you, the Dark Ages are here, Visigoths are climbing the city walls, and I've never felt more like raw food in my life."[11] Everyone is at risk of death as metaphoric consumption; everyone is afraid of becoming dead meat or food. The omnipresence of this metaphor reinforces the integral quality of death and violence in this environment.[12]

Violence emerges directly out of displacement—people hurt and kill because they are in the wrong place and cannot get where they are trying to go. At work, Marisol is again assaulted—this time by a man with an ice cream cone who throws it in her face after she fails to pay him for his role in *Taxi Driver*. This strange form of violence, which Rivera actually witnessed in New York City, is a product of the man's literal misplacement—he is in the wrong office, just as a previous shooting at Marisol's apartment occurred because of a mistaken location. Her friend June is violently assaulted by her own brother Lenny after she kicks him out of the apartment they shared. The violence associated with incidents that involve literal and figurative homelessness functions as a commentary on the implicit violence committed against humanity by the huge increase in homelessness created by Reagonomics in the 1980s.[13]

The entirety of the second act of *Marisol* takes place on the street, a space where "no spoken language works," a space that is "literally unbelievable," a space that suffers from "permanent deniability," according to Lenny. This description clarifies the ease with which the middle class sees past the realities of homelessness and the consequent loss of identity. Marisol learns, as has Lenny, about the reality of this space, a geography that emerges from the angels' move to war: *All the interiors are gone. The entire set now consists of the brick and a huge surreal street that covers the entire stage. . . . On this street, reality has been altered—and this new reality is reflected in the lighting.* This is a space where "Time is crippled. Geography's deformed. You're permanently lost out here!" It is also a space where Marisol's ethnicity becomes more visible in her own language and that of others. She talks of her own displacement and the stripping of her identity: "I lived in the Bronx . . . I commuted light years to this other planet called—Manhattan! I learned new vocabularies . . . wore weird native dress . . . mastered arcane rituals . . . and amputated neat sections of my psyche, my cultural heritage . . . yeah, clean easy amputations . . . with no pain expressed at all—none!—but so much pain kept inside I almost choked on it . . . so far deep inside my Manhattan bosses and Manhattan friends and my broken Bronx consciousness never even suspected. . . ."[14] Marisol's "recitation" comes as a defense against Scar Tissue's claim that she is dead, but this sense of displacement is not the end but the starting point of her movement toward transformation. She realizes that everyone here is looking for something—a way home, missing skin, a friend. Though some of these searches are humorous, each one is crucial within the logic of this world. For example, Scar Tissue's search for skin enables Marisol's own self-reflection, and it is through the erasure of his epidermis as exterior sign of identity (since his name is in fact his condition) that he becomes a visual reinforcement of the violence that is consistently practiced throughout the play. His concern with skin is a corollary to the identity transformation that Marisol has undergone, and his presence suggests a radicalization of environmental effects to the point that the interior of a person is transformed.

Marisol's final determination of identity is one of revolutionary conflict: she will join the angels to fight in the war against heaven. Before she can do so, however, the Woman with Furs stops her, yelling "Traitors! Credit Risks!" and "pumping hundreds of rounds into her" with an Uzi.[15] The Woman with Furs has correctly interpreted Marisol's desire to join the war as a revolutionary act and will do what is necessary to stop it. Lenny and June stay where Marisol's body has fallen, but she appears in a different space *"in her own light"* and gives the final monologue delineating the rebellion's poetic beauty: "then, as if one body, one mind, the innocent of the earth take to the streets with anything they can find—rocks, sticks, screams—and aim their displeasure at the senile sky and fire into the tattered wind on the side of the angels . . . billions of poor, of homeless, of peaceful, of silent, of angry . . . fighting and fighting as no species has ever fought before. Inspired by the earthly noise, the rebels advance! . . . New ideas rip the Heavens. New powers are created. New miracles are signed into law. It's the first day of the new history. . . ."[16] The sense of hope articulated in the play's last words is expressed visually by holding out the golden crown to the audience, along with a bright light directed at them, implicating them in this transition and taking them into *"the wild light of the new millennium."*[17]

Marisol's conclusion is careful to empower the "poor" and "homeless" in a revolutionary and violent act of radical reform. Her death at the hands of the Woman with Furs is a clear act of class warfare, at least in terms of ideological orientation, and if one takes seriously Rivera's argument about the looming danger of homelessness and its ability to destroy, then Marisol must indeed move away from her middle-class assimilated existence to establish solidarity with the poor. Apocalypse is the implied end of a millenarian play, and *Marisol* refigures it as armed combat. In this version of the end there is a certain familiarity, since postmodernism itself is infused with the apocalyptic.[18] Invocation of the millennium and an apocalyptic universe, however, invokes the question of the end of history (or perhaps its rebirth).

Marisol's end not only questions narratives of community and identity; it offers a politics of history that anticipates Jacques Derrida's *Specters of Marx*. The concept of the specter, or the already possibly dead, is prominent in *Marisol*, since she may in fact be dead from the earliest moments of the play. In earlier versions of the text a doppelgänger of Marisol haunted the work. While Rivera eventually eliminated this double, in part because it was too literal, the very spectrality of the live body possibly dead—the reality of the ghost articulated by the Man with Scar Tissue—wrights the possibility of a sustained class critique within a postmodern, apocalyptic space. Though not an explicit Marxist, Rivera is clearly aware of the difficulty and deniability of class dynamics in the United States. In talking to Norma Jenckes about the social concerns in his work, Rivera explained, "Especially in the States, class is determined so much by race and ethnic origin, and country of origin, and when you arrived, and all that kind of thing. It's one of those subjects in America . . . that nobody wants to talk about. It's a 400 pound elephant. It's the thing nobody really wants to talk about—class in America. It's a big part of my make-up."[19]

In this light, it is crucial that Marisol's actual death occurs at the hands of a woman attempting to curry favor with her creditors and reinscribe herself into the normalized world of multinational corporations, of Citibank and TRW. Conflating nationalist and capitalist values, the killer hopes to eliminate a "traitor" and a "credit risk" from the world. Although this semicomedic reference to the power of transnational capital may appear incidental to the text, it is in fact the clearest marker of hegemonic white violence within the play.[20] Thus, the literal specter, the dead Marisol who haunts the end of the play, is produced within the specific violence of capitalism, invoking Derrida's text implicitly at the beginning of the end.

Appropriately for this discussion of theatrical apocalypticism, Derrida's entire text is filled with a series of theatrical metaphors, beginning and ending with the return of the ghost in *Hamlet*. Along the way it passes through moments that point out the theatricality and staging of the commodity, moments where direct references to the work of theater and the theatrical gesture become increasingly visible. In his invocation of the term *"hauntology,"* the notion of performance is already imminent: "'An interpretation that transforms what it interprets' is a definition of the performative as unorthodox with regard to speech act theory as it is with regard to the 11th Thesis on Feuerbach ('The philosophers have only *interpreted* the world in certain ways; the point, however, is to *change* it . . .')."[21] It is not simply enough to interpret, one must, through the act of interpretation, transform the world: wright it. It is not simply enough to suggest a new beginning in a dream; the beginning must be embodied and realized in the moment of its invocation. In this sense, Marisol's spectral reality wrights a different starting point for the closing and opening of history.

Marisol's return is not the only form of spectrality within Rivera's text. Marisol's narrative of revolution is embodied by *"a single homeless person angrily throwing rocks at the sky. The homeless person is joined by Lenny and June."*[22] Crucial to an understanding of this ending is the involvement of the homeless man throwing rocks, a figure marked by his very displacement, unnamed, and yet in the moment of revolutionary transformation, more visible and active than he has been. If the "invisible" reality of homelessness is the most powerful example of the "permanent deniability" of the street, then the argument for the spectrality of the homeless becomes even more necessary. They are people who become invisible, people we see past, yet people who in the end do have an effect.

Rivera's realization that he had an uncle who died homeless was one of the catalytic creative moments for this work. In that autobiographical moment of creation is it possible to see the way a person, in this case Rivera's uncle, returns to history only at the moment of death or loss. Given a callous, corporate Republican culture that understands homelessness not as a structural problem but as an individual pathology, the invisibility of the homeless in life, their existence as living specters, gains poignancy. In this particular argument, Derrida's sense of history as responsibility articulated through an understanding of embodiment itself "disjointed," is paralleled in Rivera's dis-placement of the violent utopian end into a cry for visibility and embodiment, a recognition of those already spectralized in the culture.

Rivera's choice to represent his angels as interdependent beings whose very embodiment is in question (they are visible to the theatrical audience but not always to the characters) places his audience within a unique perceptual space in the theatrical world he has created. Appearances of angels, mediated in the space of dreams and death for the characters, are visible incarnations of a theatrical presence for the audience. In the same way, this phenomenological attention may lead to the possible visibility of those who have been erased—the homeless. Appropriately, in the final assault on heaven the homeless lead the way, because in their haunted space they can see the others that form a core constituency of this "out of joint" space, the distortion created by the violence of life on the street.

In the final chapter of *Politics Out of History*, Wendy Brown argues, "Together, Derrida's and Benjamin's writings on history offer partial strategies for configuring responsible political consciousness and political agency in the unsettling and unsettled time after progress."[23] Kushner and other critics have made clear that *Angels in America* owes a debt to Walter Benjamin's conception of history articulated through his "Theses on the Philosophy of History,"[24] and *Marisol* appears to anticipate *Specters of Marx* as a form of wrighting contemporary culture. If so, the two theatrical works, both fantastic and ultimately utopian, offer complementary responses to the problem of Reagan's 1980s America, achieving in their differences a more comprehensive account of the social crises of the period. For Rivera, death—a death perhaps already inevitably present in the system and only temporarily postponed by angelic intervention—provides the space for wrighting. Rivera's angels are more human, more locally concerned, and willing to fight, and his characters reflect this willingness. He literalizes the concerns of class and globalization within a sustained practice of creating an alternative realism.[25] Within this world can be no return, no reinstatement of history, for he sees, as Derrida argues, that

> No justice—let us not say no law and once again we are not speaking here of laws—seems possible or thinkable without the principle of some *responsibility*, beyond all living present, within that which disjoins the living present, before the ghosts of those who are not yet born or who are already dead, be they victims of wars, political or other kinds of violence, nationalist, racist, colonialist, sexist, or other kinds of exterminations, victims of the oppressions of capitalist imperialism or any of the forms of totalitarianism. Without this *non-contemporaneity with itself of the living present*, without that which secretly unhinges it, without this responsibility and this respect for justice considering those who *are not there*, of those who are no longer or not yet *present and living*, what sense would there be to ask the question "where? "where tomorrow" "whither?"[26]

Derrida's language is an attempt to open up a space for change and transformation, for ethics, and for a future. This vision of generational responsibility comes to fruition within Rivera's staging of the graves of the "angelitos," the street children who die, at times before they even receive their names. Lenny's failed pregnancy, a sign of the collapse of rebirth (and of course a comedic commentary on gender roles and reproduction itself), leads to a staging space of death, marked by changing angels into the Spanish diminutive "angelitos." Here the human embodiment of the angelic function as a form of social responsibility is held for those whom responsibility must be taken—the innocent homeless children displaced and destroyed by the structural violence of our culture. Marisol's listing of these names insures their visibility despite their death.[27]

"Magical" Thinking: Wrighting Love, Theatricality, and Ethnicity

While in *Marisol* Rivera wrights ethnicity within a structure of institutional violence, countering the critiques that suggest identity politics ignores class and economic issues, he also points toward a sense of dematerialized connectivity that helps structure community. In Rivera's dramaturgy, thinking shapes the very nature of the environment. While this idea might be categorized as an expressionist distortion of the environment based on an individual subjective perspective, Rivera's conception of the symbiotic interconnectedness of individual and environment extends into an interactivity in which perception is shaped by conception that in turn shapes the world.

Causality and the premises of realism are still very present in Rivera's dramatic universe, but his realism understands the convention of causality is a sign of this aesthetic; the elements of causality do not need to function in conventionally limited terms as a "mirror" of reality. Ineffable concepts become materialized in poetic titles that shape the realities of the world in which these characters coexist. While Marisol is simply the name of the protagonist of one play, the name is a conflation of sea and sun, and her body becomes the site of a series of transformations. Three more explicitly poetic works, *Cloud Tectonics*, *Each Day Dies with Sleep*, and *References to Salvador Dali Make Me Hot*, all contain metaphorical images that retain power within the text. In each of these poetic works is a complex exploration of the relational dynamics of love as a potentially material connectivity.

The transformational power of the connectivity of love is typically registered either as a psychological phenomenon (an individual in love has the energy and confidence to achieve great things) or as a magical phenomenon that literally changes the world around the person in love (the world appears different to a person in love). The manifestation of this latter model is typically read within Latino cultural production as an instance of magical realism, a problematic and reductive assumption. As an alternative, an act of wrighting, Rivera explores the specific realities of a simultaneously material and ineffable condition. This link parallels the connection that many presume shared ethnicity already provides. While two individuals sharing an ethnicity are connected by that ethnicity, the nature of that connection is rarely precisely articulated and assumptions about the connection lead to impositions and misunderstandings.

Rivera does not approach this question directly; instead he provides poetic meditations on connections between individuals. In exploring relational dynamics, Rivera offers a model of love that literally transforms the world around it, retaining its creativity without allowing it to transcend the world around it. Though love is a space of poetry and transformation, and operates in a manner that exceeds the expectations of psychological realism, this excess implicitly suggests the limits of conceptual models of human connectivity, and ethnicity as a connective tissue. In Rivera's work love becomes a transformational element that wrights the world around it. Being in love and recognizing a connectedness transform not only the individual but also various elements of the symbolic environment; there is a change in the perception of space and the psychic mapping of that space within the reality created. Different from Piñero's recuperation of ethical community in spaces of transgressive difference, Rivera's space becomes much more intimate and potentially claustrophobic as he articulates the transformation of love's effects on a surrounding geography.

Each Day Dies with Sleep (1990) is a powerful exploration of the difficulties of negotiating personal liberation within two structures of social formation—poverty and a repressive family. The internal domestic space becomes the site of repression and conflict instead of outside forces. The protagonist, Nelly, attempts to construct a life for herself through a search for acknowledgment from her father, Augie, caring for him even though he demonstrates little appreciation for her. She tends to his needs in hopes of reshaping a domestic space in which a lack of care and love are manifest in an almost cancerous growth of the house, of children, and of the wild animals kept by them. Nelly's domestic entrapment is embodied in two physical features: she is unable to articulate words at the same speed that her brain processes them, which results in fragmented and occasionally nonlinear language, and she is unable to stand upright, walking on all fours, exposing herself to mistreatment in this animalistic or infantile position of submission. Rivera implicitly manifests the conditions of poverty on the stage as existence in a domestic space haunted by an excess of people who have little or no relationship to one another besides being part of a family. In doing so he charts the effects of this space on an individual, establishing the house as something to be escaped, destroyed, or transformed to insure Nellie's survival.

Here, causality is a function of desire and of the language required to articulate those desires. Nelly can see the future, and yet she does not possess the agency to transform it until she can be desired in a meaningful and direct way by someone else—in this case, Johnny Amengual. Names have power, and Augie's inability (or deliberate choice not) to remember Nelly's name is a part of what maintains his control over her. It appears that she cannot assert a sense of self without the acknowledgment of another person. The source of this acknowledgment shifts from her father to Johnny, a questionable masculine figure already responsible for fathering six of her nieces and nephews with three of her sisters. Still, her relationship with Johnny gives her the strength to stand upright and allows her the geographic mobility to escape the stultifying and destructive space of her home. In his attempt to keep Nelly as a slave, Augie becomes wheelchair-bound after he is struck by a car while chasing her; with this accident, the dominant physicality that controlled the home and, to a limited extent, everyone in it, changes into a sycophantic and pathetic parasite. Augie demands love and respect, practices a selfish ethos of destruction, and manipulates the child whose name he cannot remember into making a sacrifice to keep him happy.

In this play metaphor is literalized: Nelly's inability to stand on her own two feet is real in the beginning of the play, as is her need to establish a connection in order to escape from her father's tyranny. The language of entrapment used to describe conditions of poverty and the homogenizing impositions of patriarchy are manifest onstage not as mere symbols but as constituent parts of the environment. Like the return to visibility articulated in *Marisol*, the characters of *Each Day Dies with Sleep* embody the realities of poverty and the difficulty of class mobility in a space that literalizes the metaphors associated with a lack of human agency and a loss of identity.

Love, here, becomes a literally transformative agent—a connective tissue that grants power and agency. The play follows Johnny and Nelly's move to Los Angeles, always keeping the history of her home potentially visible. Her father's manipulations follow them and drain their relationship, just like Johnny's self-destructive womanizing. The destruction of their relationship is represented onstage by images of blackened oranges. Augie's failure to manipulate Nelly leads to a suggestion of suicide to Johnny, who has lost his sense of self in a disfiguring accident. This shifting of manipulation results in a powerful series of final scenes. In the first, Johnny offers a series of self-deprecating third-person descriptions—"Johnny is reductive," "Johnny is derivative,"—before immolating himself with the gasoline from the burned-out dream of an orange. As he burns, he reverses the rhetorical gesture and speaks positively of Nelly: "Nelly is good. Nelly is clever. Nelly is fierce. Nelly is loyal. Nelly is warm. Nelly is kind. Nelly is . . . Nelly is . . . is . . . is . . . is . . . is. Nelly is." This last series if followed by an image of Nelly running on all fours and at the very end of the play she *"shoots to her feet as if every muscle in her body was electrified. She stands. Blackout."*[28]

This concluding act of liberation—Nelly is once again standing on her own two feet—has a curious relationship to Johnny's assertion of her worth. On the one hand, it is enabled after his death and after his verbal assertions that seem to become less articulate. The final claim, however, is the most powerful gift of all. Rather than searching for a descriptive adjective, Johnny offers to Nelly the simple importance of her existence. It is not *what* she is, but *that* she exists that is important. This is the transformative power of love in its fullest and most complete.

According to Giorgio Agamben, "Love is never directed toward this or that property of the loved one (being blond, being small, being tender, being lame), but neither does it neglect the properties in favor of an insipid generality (universal love): The lover wants the loved one *with all of its predicates*, its being such as it is. . . . The movement Plato describes as erotic anamnesis is the movement that transports the object not toward another thing or place, but towards its own taking-place—toward the Idea."[29] Here Agamben insists that love manifests the total possibility of an individual. Rivera articulates this manifestation within Nelly by clarifying that in the end, it is not the movement of geographic change or even the process of standing on her own two feet early in the play that frees her but a recognition of herself as herself—an identity not predicated on others. Nelly's ability to leave does not free her from the influence of family and potential destruction; rather, it is her full assumption of agency at the close of the play, unfettered by the limitation of a descriptor that provides the energy for her transformation.

This change suggests a different relationship between actor and spectator, transforming the actor and limiting the power of the spectator and the space by the end of the play. This radical change, in which being is enough, runs the risk of being contained by a critical language that sees this transformation as a symbolic gesture rather than a real, physical one. In making it a symbol, the act of wrighting through love becomes merely a sign rather than a true granting of agency to another in their fullness. But it is more than a sign as the actress's body changes at the very end of its visibility, suggesting a transformation that exceeds the play itself. This physical alteration, this electricity, implicitly suggests a model for a connective and symbiotic relationship between spectator and performer—through the ineffable materiality of love.

In *Cloud Tectonics*, Rivera imagines a human body that operates outside time, a woman whose presence exerts a similar transformation on her immediate environment. Her reality, in which time has acquired a different meaning because of its lack of coherence and consistency, is shaped by memory. However, memories are also figured within particular notions of chronological, linear time and are ordered and made sense of within this frame. This sense of time parallels Rivera's fascination with the fungibility of environment and its ability to transform character and create causalities. At one level the play is also making an argument about archetypal mythic figures with inverted gender identities: the woman is Celestina del Sol (of the sun), and the men, Aníbal and Nelson, are de la Luna (of the moon).

These notions of myth and literary history are placed in relationship to a highly metatheatrical conception of the possibilities of linear representation of action on the stage. The events of the play are linear, and time does pass, but the problem is the speed at which it passes. Following Walter Benjamin, Bert States has argued that the clearest introduction of the real into the theatrical is the presence of a working clock on the theatrical stage.[30] The visible passage of clock time forces the audience to come to grips with the idea that they are actively reconstructing time to preserve a notion of realism—that in fact realism is predicated on this very theatrical capacity of stretching and compressing the passage of time. By forcing themselves to forget this process, the audience is able to naturalize theatrical events.

Cloud Tectonics heightens the visibility of this issue by insisting that as Celestina enters the stage space of a home, time stops. The method of this representation becomes a question not only of design but of materializing time in a different way. It is easy enough to stop time by cutting the power to various appliances in a kitchen set: the microwave and perhaps an overhead clock. Analog clocks pose no problem, as their function is predicated on a direct line of power. The problem with a digital clock is that it begins blinking "12:00" rather than stopping in place. While this would not normally be a problem, the play adds the difficulty of Celestina's departure. When she leaves the space, the clocks begin working right where they stopped.

This stage direction becomes a near impossibility, as manual programming is necessary to restart digital devices in the absence of a woman whose aura is literally capable of stopping time. Ironically, the problem exists not within the space of the analog but rather in the space of the digital, marking a specific historical moment of representation. The simplest solution, to project clocks on the backdrop and then to project a different series of clocks at her departure, makes this visual trick possible but only by replacing the clocks with projections or spatially shifting the representation of time itself. This question of environmental representation is at the heart of Rivera's investigations of love and connection.

The description of Celestina at the beginning of the play promotes her ambiguity and the difficulty of figuring her within a consistent narrative: *"She looks exhausted, as if she's been wandering on foot for days. It's impossible to tell her actual age. It's impossible to tell if she's rich or poor. She's very, very pregnant."*[31] The use of "as if" is an attempt to clarify the terms of Celestina's apparent exhaustion—it is the fatigue of someone who has traveled for a time. Yet, the very construction "as if" also implies that this is not what she has been doing, but that she must be represented as such. The legibility of her physical characteristics can be understood only within a narrative that is already comprehensible to both the actress playing the role and the audience attempting to understand it. The "as if" also underscores the impossibility of marking Celestina's physical condition in relation to a passage of time. This detachment from time is not simply a shift into subjective notions of time (or subjunctive grammars). It is not a shift from objective to experiential but rather a complete inability to understand the concept, because it does not exist in her consciousness as a meaningful marker of anything.

In this sense, it could be read as subjective, but to do so seems to prematurely offer the possibility that subjective time somehow "explains" Celestina, something it cannot and should not do. Her appearance is certain only within the realm of the physical, the body. She is exhausted; she is wet; she is pregnant. Everything else becomes "impossible to tell." The identity she projects defeats the perceptive ability of the audience attempting to understand her. This gesture demonstrates the very lack of necessity of such descriptors at the same moment that it makes clear the incessant search for discriminating markers of identity in order to codify it.

In fact, as we learn from Celestina's own account and her attempt to describe Rodrigo Cruz, the man who impregnated her, these are *"details"* that *"might have changed."*[32] The reliance on time-specific identity markers such as appearance, age, social standing, and clothing style is so naturalized that it takes a moment to recognize just how many of these markers change over time. Even the day-to-day practicality of the act of naming can shift as nicknames and diminutions acquire or lose favor. This radical contingency argues for a time-specific identity, a reality that echoes powerfully with the concerns of Latino theater artists in the 1990s. Identity is a product of the time; the joining and separating of identities are a result of specific times and places, and yet there still remains the possibility that identity is not entirely contingent on time.

As Albert Einstein made clear, space and time are actually operative in a continuum, an idea Rivera theatricalizes through the physical staging of the prologue. While Celestina and Aníbal perform their scene in front of microphones, *"Aníbal's house in the Echo Park section of Los Angeles is loaded in. This should take as long as the Prologue takes to perform."* By mapping an imaginary action onto a real one, the actual passage of time in relation to the theatrical passage of time becomes particularly evident. The construction of the house foregrounds the theatrical reality, as does the refusal of the actors to participate in a "pantomime" of "being in a car."[33] Their space does not necessarily mean anything crucial in this world except insofar as Celestina's effect on time seems to have a limited range.

In response to Aníbal's confusion about Celestina's lack of knowledge of the passage of time, the latter responds, "I don't have a watch . . . I don't keep a watch . . . I don't keep 'time.' . . . 'Time' and I don't hang out together!" The notion of time shifts from the more mundane to the strange as she processes the shift from the object marking clock time to the possession of the abstract concept to an anthropomorphic conception of time as something to hang out with. This shift becomes particularly apparent when the "natural" markers for the passage of time disappear. It is not surprising that all of the clocks in Aníbal's house become dysfunctional in the presence of Celestina. What is more disturbing, however, is the idea that her physical cycles do not map onto preconceived paradigms. She has been pregnant for "two years," and her one night in Aníbal's house lasts just as long.[34]

Cloud Tectonics is powered simultaneously by the attempt to understand time and the desire of the three characters. Celestina is on a quest to find the father of her baby, the only man she has ever had sex with. Sex for her is an obsession, although not in the sense that she desires everyone but rather that she desires sex with the right person. In a sense, she is pointing toward the idea of the spiritual and the timeless in the act of physical human connection, one moment where time holds less meaning for everyone. On the other hand, she becomes the object of desire and fantasy for both Aníbal and his brother Nelson. Although their interest is not particularly predatory, they still seem drawn to Celestina. At the same time, they are not necessarily in control of these fantasies, because the construction of fantasy is predicated on the control of subjective time and Celestina's very existence creates a wrinkle in that reality.

The gendered shifting of fantasy also has a particular relationship to memory and the formation of linear narrative sequences. Despite its questioning of time as a thing in and of itself and not merely the projection of a subconscious sensory organ, the play still operates on a version of clock time, both in the sense that it lasts an objectively measurable time and, more importantly, that the events within the play itself take place sequentially. What is uncertain, however, is the physical effect of aging within the various passings of time.

Aníbal's brother Nelson enters soon after Celestina's arrival and is enamored of her in the same way that Aníbal is, willing to become the father of her child and to take her into his life. Of course, Celestina must wait for Nelson because he has to fulfill his military service. She does not necessarily agree to wait for him, though Nelson projects agreement on her. However, when he returns, which for Celestina and Aníbal is the next morning and for Nelson is two years later, he feels betrayed not by their supposed relationship but by their refusal to admit the passage of time. Celestina's continuous pregnancy is assumed by Nelson to be a second one.

Although the second encounter is strained because Nelson thinks Celestina and Aníbal are lying to him, the first encounter is difficult as well, because the brothers have been apart for "six years"; but as Nelson observes, "Time flies, motherfucker!" They are aware of the subjective nature of time and the possibility of it passing faster than they would like to believe. Celestina, however, is the incarnation of this interjection. Her presence suggests not only that time is subjective but that subjectivity itself is constituted through a particular relationship to time. While time clearly shapes identity, the radical implication of this claim is the potentially seamless shift between memory and actuality, between static object and progressing subject, between a history that makes sense and one that is merely an appendage, not a constituent factor. This shift is implicit in Aníbal's claim that his house is from "the Middle Ages," the way Angelenos construe time, demonstrating that ways of reading time place one in history and in a specific spatial identity.[35]

Another way of imagining this shift is the difference between the room that Celestina occupied in Montauk Point, New Jersey, and the space Aníbal occupies in Los Angeles. The first had "no order," and while that is clearly in part a result of her spending an entire life in that room, it also presents the possibility that time itself is just one means of establishing order, whether or not that is a good thing. This possibility becomes a reality when Aníbal opens the door at Nelson's return and the porch is covered with *"hundreds of Sparkletts water bottles."*[36] This law of thermodynamics, the progression from order to chaos that seems to preserve a linearity of time, is countered by the idea of love that has its own logic but that must be renegotiated through changes of times and bodies.

Love is the force that transforms all of the languages of the body, and desire becomes a means of passing through time. For Celestina, Spanish is the language of love, and during an extensive monologue in Spanish she talks about loving Aníbal through his entire life. Unfortunately, this one moment in which she seems to consider the passage of time something worth observing passes by Aníbal, because he has forgotten Spanish. This moment imagines ethnic identity as something constructed through language and always in the past. Since language can be forgotten, a temporal activity, then ethnicity itself is predicated on a sense of temporality.

Yet not everything is simply a memory to be forgotten, for love has the power to transform both the physical body and the environment. In relating the narrative of his relations with women, Aníbal refers to his first sexual experience, with his cousin Eva, as a powerfully altering moment: "It's like . . . the space around my body was permanently curved—or dented—by Eva's heaviness. I wonder if love sometimes does that to you. It alters the physics around you in some way: changing the speed of light and the shape of space and how you experience time."[37] The idea that love becomes a radically transformative force in part explains the attraction both men have for Celestina. In a sense, she becomes the impossible object that forces them to confront their own notion of being in the world, their own sense of temporality and identity. Their identities are formed in relationships, relationships that can safely exist only within a close physical proximity. Otherwise, a different sense of time takes over and the possibility of forgetting emerges. Here, absence does not always increase desire; sometimes it makes it disappear. Yet the very importance of desire seems to privilege a certain form of presence, of being in contact.

In the epilogue, Celestina, who has disappeared after Nelson's return, finds Aníbal forty years later. He has forgotten her, because the two years they spent together lasted only one night for him. Aníbal's memory returns with physical contact—she rubs his feet, and his voice changes to present the narrative of that long past time (if indeed it was so long ago). His narrative transforms into an attempt to understand Celestina, and it is from this moment that the play's title arises. He expounds, "And that trying to understand such a life, and why love matters to it, why a god would need to be loved too, was like trying to understand the anatomy of the wind or the architecture of silence or cloud tectonics. . . . What better way to respond to a miracle than to fall in love with it?"[38] The need for a miracle to love and be loved by seems oxymoronic to Aníbal; the poetic illustrations he chooses describe the anthropomorphic parsing of a natural phenomenon, the spatial examination of an aural phenomenon, and the shifting friction of porous vapor.

What Aníbal does not understand is that being in love involves, in its truest form, separating one's self from time. Thus, one who is separated from time must indeed function through and with love. As inscrutable as his examples appear, they provide an interpretative framework on which to lay stronger memories than the one he had received through the action of the play itself—he is able to recite Celestina's entire speech in Spanish. This time, she echoes him, speaking in English, and the English monolingual audience members learn for the first time (another way of playing with temporality) that Celestina's speech was about wanting to love Aníbal through time and to experience time with him, something impossible for her to do. Although true love for Celestina is literally timeless, her timelessness is broken into discrete segments that intersect only sporadically with the world around her. In wrighting the experience of time in *Cloud Tectonics*, Rivera reimagines the possibilities of connection that shape identity.

In his most explicit dialogue with surrealism, *References to Salvador Dali Make Me Hot*, Rivera not only points to the connective tissue between two people manifest in the materiality of love; he also insists on the intellectual practice of engaging in a sustained way with an aesthetic in the act of wrighting it. In contrast to magical realism, surrealism's initial exploration of dream logic through automatic writing was understood to be an explicit refusal of rational logic as an explanatory paradigm. Within the U.S. cultural imaginary, the figure most closely associated with surrealism is the Spanish painter Salvador Dalí. Most recently controversial because of some questionable financial pandering in the 1980s, Dalí constructed an exuberant and flamboyant alternative persona to introduce himself to the U.S. public in the 1930s and 1940s. To the disgust of André Breton and others in the surrealist movement who had very specific aesthetic and political notions about the function and practice of surrealism, Dalí consistently said that he saw his work as an aesthetic and not a political project, and he eventually turned to classicism and political conservatism. He isolated himself from the revolutionary political aspects of the movement, preferring to understand his contribution as in part a shocking display for the moneyed purveyors of culture who would provide financial support for his work.

Ironically, Dalí himself was initially opposed to the surrealist movement, primarily because of the focus on automatism that ran counter to his mode of interpretation and creation, predicated on a much more active, though equally psychoanalytically grounded practice: paranoiac-critical activity, an idea strongly influenced by Lacan's thesis on paranoia published in the surrealist journal *Minotaure*. Dalí's strongest association with the surrealists, ironically, emerged through their championing of this creative and analytic mode that Dalí defined as a "spontaneous method of irrational knowledge based on the interpretative-critical association of delirious phenomena."[39] In his narcissistic and ego-driven manner, Dalí worked to rewrite the history of surrealism as a movement that culminated in his discovery of paranoiac-critical activity.

Dalí's theorizing tended to remain vague and contradictory enough to leave himself a way out of his theoretical constructs. Whether playfulness or a lack of certainty, his contradictions nonetheless make it more difficult to clearly define the aesthetic project of his paranoiac-critical activity, though certainly among its practical manifestations are his paintings that contain figures with multiple representational possibilities. By exploring the literal and metaphorical references to Dalí in Rivera's play, it becomes possible to illustrate the complex symbiotic relationship between writing and critical practice. Providing a specific Daliesque conception of *References* does not limit it as such. Instead, it demonstrates Rivera's continued and specific investment in the construction of new realisms. In the process of finding a different way to articulate the world, Rivera illustrates the complexity and excess of signification that demands more knowledge, not less. In *References* he manifests a fundamental interconnectivity between language and imagination and between representation and the status of reality through a complex process of theatrical construction.

Much of the critical success of *References* seems to rest on the performance of the poetic language and the willingness of the individual critic to view the play's formal experimentation as a necessary component of the work. Those who see the experimentation as a gratuitous deployment of an aesthetic mode variously and unsurprisingly labeled surrealism, magical realism, or both tend to view the play less sympathetically. The central conflict of the play is a domestic struggle between the soldier husband, Benito, and his wife, Gabriela, on the day of Benito's return from the field.

Though his return is an event they have played out repeatedly in their ten-year relationship, this time it is different. This time they are trying to re-create a familiar routine after a single aberration—Benito's return from the Gulf War. Rather than dealing directly with Benito's return from the war, an event charged with its own sense of urgency, Rivera's play, by dramatizing the subsequent return after a noncombat assignment, explores the ways that the experience of war transforms people and their relationships. Benito reminds Gabriela and the audience that military life creates human beings whose job is to kill and who must do so to successfully complete their work. The transformation in Benito and the impact it has had on Gabriela strengthen her doubts about their relationship and increase the difficulty of reaccommodating him into her life. Played out in four acts and a prologue, the two framing acts, in which all of the dialogue is in italics, explore the world Gabriela experiences in Benito's absence, one in which she has the freedom to engage in lyrical poetic investigations joined by the moon, her cat, and a coyote, all of whom talk, though the coyote never addresses her directly.

The middle acts, in roman type, narrate Benito's initial return and a later conflict that evening. Gabriela feels isolated and alone, and is desperate to reassure herself that Benito is the same man she married, one who would take time to admire the moon, even while being chased by skinheads bent on blood. Benito is troubled by his experiences in the war, especially his choice to order an air strike on a village after the war officially ended, but also frustrated by his inability to understand the needs of his wife, who, he says, insists that "everything's got to be like something else."[40] Though in part Benito is merely expressing his frustration with Gabriela's attempts to communicate her emotional need through description and analogy rather than direct statement, this comment also references one of the basic motifs of Dalí's notion of paranoiac painting: Dalí develops a technique to sustain multiple images in one work, a technique that is occurring in Rivera's play as well.

Dalí's work is referenced in two much more direct ways, however. In the first and most literal, a mention of the title of Dalí's painting *Two Pieces of Bread Expressing the Sentiment of Love* (1940) by the moon in his attempted seduction of Gabriela in act 1 generates Gabriela's response and the title of the play.[41] The painting, a poster of which hangs in Gabriela's bedroom, is an oblique portrait of love, as three fragmented pieces of bread and their crumbs are center stage with a pawn in a desert landscape haunted by two lightly sketched human figures in the distance. The play's form is also Daliesque in that there seem to be two realities operating, one of which may be a dream but both of which sustain their own logic. A contained reading of the play separates the dream space, consisting of the first and fourth acts written in italics, from the other reality. However, the "dreaming" Gabriela refers to her experiences in acts 2 and 3 as a dream, questioning this separation. Rivera is not merely interested in offering an inversion of the conventional expectations of dreams and everyday logic; he lets the two spaces bleed together by allowing the young Chicano neighbor, Martín, to inhabit both spaces. Even more powerfully, the close of the play is a repetition of the initial moments of Benito's homecoming in unmarked "real life," but this time the language of the text and of his action is written in italics.

The permeability between the "real" and the "dream" and the difficulty of separating these two was more present in the original 2000 published text than in the 2003 revision for the publication by Theatre Communications Group.[42] The irony is that in the further development for publication there seems to be an increasing pressure to reduce the complexity of the play in order to limit the polyphony of its representation. While most of the changes are phrasal ones or reordered speeches, three major changes make the play potentially more accessible and more legible within a "traditional" and reductive sense of surrealism (the space of dreams) and magical realism. The first major change is the addition of a prologue that places Gabriela in the backyard and puts her to sleep. Her language in the prologue is taken from act 1 material from the 2000 version, but her act of going to sleep in the backyard makes it much easier to read the presence of the talking moon as a product of Gabriela's dreams. Of course, Rivera leaves a way around this explanation through the deployment of italics in this prologue. It becomes clear that italics are actually a spatial marking: everything in the backyard is in italics, while everything in the house is not.

The second crucial change is the decision to no longer double the moon and Benito. The characters of the cat and the coyote, which function as one possible double for the relationship of Benito and Gabriela, become much more symbolically stable without the doubling of the moon and Benito. By stopping this doubling, Benito has only one appearance in the italicized play: at the very end, when he loosely repeats the entrance that begins act 2; this time, however, it is in the backyard and thus italicized, making it unclear as to whether his two appearances have the same level of materiality. Perhaps the first was indeed a dream, as Gabriela maintains, or perhaps his return is the one Benito plans to enact at his departure at the end of act 3. This second possibility gains force precisely because of the looseness with which the scene is played. As a repetition it cannot maintain the same energy as the initial manifestation of the return. The tension shifts to Gabriela's anxiety about Benito's response to her test—whether Benito noticed the moon this evening. If indeed the genesis and maintenance of her love are predicated on his attention to the moon, then making him into the moon presents one more possibility for him, and the death of the coyote at the hands of the moon makes the relationship between the cat and the coyote less a simple equation with the situation of Gabriela and Benito.[43]

The third change related to this general sense of simplifying the aesthetic practice of the play is the elimination of a number of exchanges between the coyote and the cat. While this streamlining is perhaps demanded by the constraints of time, it nonetheless shifts the focus to the human energy in the play and presents the cat and the coyote more as doubles of Benito and Gabriela than as characters whose individual narratives are important.

Although Rivera's revisions have made the realism more conventional by gesturing toward a more symbolic function for the first and fourth acts, it is more important to acknowledge that this deliberate aesthetic investment on Rivera's part reflects his focus not on form per se but on its symbiotic relationship with human interaction. In the essay on *Each Day Dies with Sleep* referenced earlier, Rivera insists that "true human drama transcends form," and indeed if Rivera's italics indicate a spatial rather than a formal or conceptual marking, one should attempt to think about the Daliesque aesthetics within the space of the domestic conflict itself. Though hostile critics consider the crisis between Benito and Gabriela overlong and trite, their conclusion arises from the ease with which they reduce the conflict to a "mere" question of love. Dalí's presence is not merely in the reflective dream/real structure of the play but also in the characterological construction of Gabriela as a practitioner of paranoiac-critical activity. As Dalí said about his concept of paranoia, "Of a cubist picture one asks: 'What does that represent?' Of a surrealist picture one sees what it represents but one asks: 'What does that mean?' Of a paranoiac picture one asks abundantly: 'What do I see?,' 'What does that represent?,' 'What does that mean?'"[44]

If the title of the play accurately reflects Gabriela's desire, then it is predicated not merely on language but on an invocation of a particular cultural figure and, perhaps, a unique way of being in the world. If indeed references are enough to make her hot, then her desire for Benito might be predicated on an understanding of him as a man capable of helping her to see the moon in the way she interacts with it in the backyard. In fact, this change in perspective is central to the narrative of their first encounter, in which she rescues him from physical abuse stemming from discrimination (he and his buddies are being beaten by skinheads in a bar), but he stops to look at the moon. This aesthetic act in the space of violence and racism becomes the linchpin with which Gabriela attempts to recapture the Benito she knew before the war, a Benito that may be only a memory.

As a last associative gesture, Dalí's book of poems *L'Amour et la mémoire*, published in 1931 and translated as "Love and Memory," has a parenthetical comment or subtitle: "(There are motionless things like bread)." For Rivera's play, this poem forms a potential intersection between the specific choice of Dalí painting, *Two Pieces of Bread Expressing the Sentiment of Love*, and the question of establishing a relationship in which love is predicated on memory, a necessary reality Rivera wrights to its fullest. In doing so he demonstrates the importance of memory for love and identity; a past event must be remembered and always potentially re-creatable to maintain Benito as the man with whom Gabriela fell in love.

Wrighting Community

The centrality of the connection between individuals as a mode of wrighting ethnicity is carried conceptually to the communal level in *Sonnets for an Old Century*. On the surface, *Sonnets* seems to make no explicit reference to theatricality and community. The play is a series of monologues told by strangers after death, and although there are possible intersections—shared interests, related experiences, and a witness and an attacker perhaps speaking of the same event—the play is a series of final statements whose very premise extracts a level of poetic profundity from the language of everyday life. These statements are spoken out into the nothing, although within the space of the theater, the audience members occupy the void that receives these monologues, and they sit and wait for the truth as it emerges from each of the speakers. These personal truths, the sonnets spoken at the end of a century, mark a particular moment. Some of the stories tell of the individual's death, and others of beautiful memories spoken in order to be shared and treasured.

From one point of view a fundamentally undramatic work, in many ways this is the most theatrical of Rivera's works and the one most deeply invested in a notion of community. The language of these speakers forms an ecology of the spirit, and the sonnets contain a pedagogical imperative. This message is the same one that impending death often generates: a regeneration of the possibility of community in the moment of loss. If death is an easy closure from a theatrical point of view, this literally liminal play evacuates that possibility by pausing in the moment of transition and deliberately stating as a part of the activity that the end is merely "a slow fade to black."[45] While the location can be anywhere—though the suggestions Rivera provides are not markers of beauty, transcendence, or distance from the everyday—there is a clear indication that this is the afterlife and that the only way to interface with it is to "stand here and make your statement."[46]

Thinking metatheatrically, this rhetorical performance sets up theater as an ultimate expression of humanity in the space of death. What were originally unnamed characters were given the names of actors as an act of homage, even though the names are never spoken in the text. Each individual speaks what she or he chooses—this is their last opportunity to speak. But in these moments of revelation and in the moments of witnessing these revelations—these moments in the theater—the possible genesis of a community is written. Here no one belongs; they are simply occupying a shared space and a shared experience. The limits of this sharing are articulated within a sense of the nation; the people are diverse and from various parts of the United States, but they are from the United States, which indicates a political and geographic linkage. However, the very diversity of this confessional space means that the possibility of a community is not something articulated or understood by the speakers. Instead, it emerges as an experience of the audience in the moment of witnessing, of listening to the activity onstage, much as community is created through the act of listening in the cigar factory in Nilo Cruz's *Anna in the Tropics*.

The formal structure of the play does not necessarily allow for connectivity between the actors; there is no dialogue, though there are moments that indicate they are clearly listening. The final statement is a list rather than a story, and the end refuses to offer any kind of response to any of the stories. In doing so, Rivera insists that each person can say what they must and these statements must be respected in and of themselves, rather than as a sign of something else. As such, the possibility of community as a being-in-common may be emerging.

Though the easy assumption is that the shared space and experience of limbo would in fact lead to this sense of community for the speakers, the monologues indicate otherwise—suggesting a radical individuality that is always maintained. Rivera's choice to name the characters after actors he respects heightens the theatricality of the drama through a specific reference to a personal and contemporary history of theater. This homage to the voice, body, and name of the actor suggests a serious question about a future progress enabled by the theater itself. If these are indeed sonnets for an old century, then they are intended to acknowledge the millennium passing and suggest in their nostalgia and anger the possibility of a future unknown. As an alternative postmortem revolutionary act to the violence of Marisol at the end of her play, these characters choose to speak. The stories they tell are the poetry of their identity, and those stories may catalyze self-reflection and potential transformation through ritual exposure to death. However, this is the space of the theater and not a funeral. Because the dead speak for themselves, there is a heightened sense that the theater itself provides the transformative energy of the stories—that it is in the act of acting where the speakers come to terms with their own identity and can move on. And in doing so, Rivera wrights the language of theatricality, making the audience witnesses to an act of being.[47] Here, rather than imposing a space of community, Rivera wrights the conditions for its coming-into-being.

Cherríe Moraga and the Wrighting of Community

> Days later, George Bush comes to San Francisco. . . . There is a protest. We, my camarada and I, get off the subway. I can already hear the voices chanting from a distance. We can't make out what they are saying, but they are Latinos and my heart races, seeing so many brown faces. They hold up a banner. The words are still unclear but as I come closer closer to the circle of my people, I am stunned. "¡Viva la paz en Nicaragua!" it states. "¡Viva George Bush! ¡Viva UNO!" And my heart drops. Across the street the "resistance" has congregated—less organized, white, middle-class students. ¿Dónde 'stá mi pueblo?
>
> —Cherríe Moraga, *The Last Generation*

> The objects of desire may be multiple, but the propelling force is the need to transform personal and cultural betrayal into more inclusive forms of community.
>
> —Yvonne Yarbro-Bejarano, *The Wounded Heart*

In her essay "Art in América con Acento," originally presented as a talk written "on the one-week anniversary of the death of the Nicaraguan Revolution" in 1990, Cherríe Moraga expresses frustration with a world in which the revolutionary dreams of the 1960s have disappeared in the face of middle-class integration.[1] Moraga's rhetorical gesture here is not only to critique but also to remind her audience of the fantasy of cultural solidarity that obscures the real heterogeneity of Latino identity. Her account of brown faces in support of George Bush and the politics of U.S. imperialism shifts conventional academic wisdom about people of color in the United States that blithely assumes a democratic, liberal political practice based on a presumed working-class position.

In pointing to an absence, however, Moraga is not capitulating to this reality but rather asking a real question: Where are my people? Her choice of the word *pueblo* is crucial because it denotes both people and space, unlike the more often cited term of unification, *la raza*, used to indicate the people or the race. Thus, her question functions as a cry for both a people and a place absent from the setting of this anecdote, where shared culture, color, and language do not reflect a shared politics. Moraga does not condemn those who have made an oppositional political choice by supporting U.S. imperialism. Instead, she moves forward, searching for her own people, for a group that shares both her political beliefs and cultural position, crucially recognizing that her people need a space in which to manifest themselves. This anecdote points toward her acts of wrighting for the theater that imagine a political community, a *pueblo*, linked by shared values, not imposed expectations.

In her California plays *Heroes and Saints*, *Watsonville*, and *A Circle in the Dirt*, Moraga creates complex, multicultural, and multilingual communities of performance that strive to bring the audience into the performance space. These plays illuminate key contemporary political and cultural issues while charting the labor involved in creating a space in which the articulation of successful resistance becomes possible. Moraga wrights committed dramas that address specific, local issues without reducing the practice of politics to the politics of identity. Addressing the complexity and diversity of Latino and Mexican/Xicana identity, Moraga refuses the easy equation of ethnicity and politics without erasing the specificity and importance of a Mechicano culture.[2] In her fictionalized conceptions of real California spaces, she links the spiritual and the political through a relationship to land that respects the history of the place while offering the possibility of a new understanding of space. Understanding that community emerges out of shared cultural geography as well as literal space, her plays offer the possibility of a transformation into "some place not here," the subtitle of *Watsonville*. By making the land sacred again and by acknowledging the traces of history, Moraga demonstrates a pragmatically utopian conception of transformative theater that wrights the possibility of a new form of inclusive community conscious of its specific historical position within a California landscape shaped by the cultural and political realities of the mid 1990s.

177

These plays parallel Moraga's project to reconceptualize the nation as a space for solidarity and community through rewriting the Chicano cultural nationalist space of Aztlán into a Queer Aztlán. Her project imagines a radically inclusive space under the term *queer*, one intended to "retain our radical naming but expand it to meet a broader and wiser revolution."[3] She continues her investment in raising consciousness and creating a space in which new possibilities for the nation emerge with

> the integration of both the traditional and the revolution-ary, the ancient and the contemporary . . . a new América, where the only "discovery" to be made is the rediscovery of ourselves as members of the global community. Nature will be our teacher, for she alone knows no prejudice. Possibly as we ask men to give up being "men," we must ask humans to give up being "human," or at least give up the human capac-ity for greed. Simply, we must give back to the earth what we take from it. We must submit to a higher "natural" authority, as we invent new ways of making culture, making tribe, to survive and flourish as members of the world community in the next millennium.[4]

The specificity of Moraga's reclamation of this cultural space as an alternative to conservative political developments in mid 1990s Cali-fornia allows her to write in a U.S. cultural space that participated in a backlash against the demographic shift to a majority minority state. This backlash, manifest in legislation such as Proposition 187, clearly demonstrated the disjuncture between ethnic identity and political po-sition. Perhaps because of the Latino support for Proposition 187 that suggests political thinking based on citizenship rather than ethnic iden-tity, Moraga's California plays shift away from the nationalist thinking implied in the recuperation of Aztlán, even a queer one. In doing so, the plays focus on local politics that engage with the specific material reali-ties of a given environment even while pointing to national issues.

For Moraga, theater is ideal for the production of this space because of the fungibility of the stage, the fact that theater literally takes place, and the ability to create a polyphony of conflicting voices on the stage. "In theater I don't have to explain," she said in an interview with Ellie Hernandez. "I can take what are my pressing concerns and what I per-ceive as being *real* issues within our community by simply putting them on stage and let the characters try to play it to each other."[5] In placing these voices in dialogue, allowing the characters themselves to manifest social relationships in a transformable space, she begins the process of creating a place for her people.

Wrighting the Corporeal in *Heroes and Saints*

From her groundbreaking work on the feminist anthology *This Bridge Called My Back: Writing by Radical Women of Color*, Moraga has insisted on the imperative to hear the voices of women of color and to recognize the alternative modalities articulated through their versions of being in the world, as women, as feminists, as radicals. In her essay "La Güera" she reminds her readers, "In this country, lesbianism is a poverty—as is being brown, as is being a woman, as is being just plain poor. The danger lies in ranking the oppression. *The danger lies in failing to acknowledge the specificity of the oppression.* The danger lies in attempting to deal with oppression purely from a theoretical base. Without an emotional, heartfelt grappling with the source of our own oppression, without naming the enemy within ourselves and outside of us, no authentic, non-hierarchical connection among oppressed groups can take place."[6] In this essay and more broadly within her scholarly and artistic work, Moraga consistently stresses the importance of specificity and embodiment. Her concern is to move beyond the problematic hierarchies established even within resistant spaces—the devaluation of Chicana issues in early Chicano nationalism and the invisibility of race and class in 1970s mainstream feminism. Specifically, her insistence on the need for an "authentic, non-hierarchical connection" requires a community established horizontally and inclusively, one that acknowledges the material realities manifest in its bodies and spaces.

The space of the theater enables the possibility of a lived experience of "emotional, heartfelt grappling" manifest in the liminal reality of the stage. Moraga's theatricality makes visible an embodied connection between people that literally brings the community into being on stage as a successful response to an often-disembodied oppression. The conclusions of her plays create communities on the stage that illustrate the political possibility of solidarity and attempt to move this solidarity into the space of the audience.

Heroes and Saints is invested in different manifestations of the body, both super- and supranatural, as well as, like José Rivera's work, materialities that cannot be contained within traditional perceptual frames. By experimenting with different concepts of the body, Moraga offers possibilities for women to imagine their identity outside traditional models. In this play the body is a literal product of its environment, and she asks her audience to take this possibility seriously. The personal is not only the political but also the environmental, emphasizing that identity is also defined within a spatial articulation of community—the *pueblo*.

Moraga's communities are partially constituted in spiritual terms, and the intersection of the spiritual with daily life highlights a pragmatic syncretism that is a direct reflection of the *mestizaje* of Chicana identity. This intersection emerges in the space of the martyr, the saint, and the spiritual investiture of the physical. It is crucial not only to an understanding of Chicana identity but also to an understanding of the theatrical. Of course, the links between theater and spirituality within Western culture go back to the City Dionysia and can be traced through the "reemergence" of theater with the dramatization of the *quem quaeritis* trope in Catholic ritual. In the Americas, this connection is reflected in indigenous dramas such as the *Popul Vuh* and *Rabinal Achí*, as well as the theatricality of religious practice and sacrifice in sixteenth-century Franciscan conversion dramas. Moraga understands the presumed otherworldly quality of the spiritual to be pragmatically alive in everyday life. Bodies achieve meaning through an organic relation to the land itself, which becomes a sacred space in which personal suffering is intertwined with religious iconography. Here, the act of love itself offers the potential for radical transformation; it becomes the generative kernel for inclusion.[7]

Heroes and Saints takes over for the 1990s where the *actos* of El Teatro Campesino left off in the 1970s. Dealing with the continued corrupt and destructive practices of agribusiness, Moraga focuses on the physical and emotional costs. The resulting degradations are responsible not just for poverty but also for loss of life, mutilated and deformed bodies, and constant illness: physical maladies that have psychological effects. These conditions create conflictive relationships between characters and their bodies.[8]

The play is loosely based on actual events in McFarland, California, the site of a cancer cluster whose ravages are symbolized in Cerezita, the central character. Moraga writes that "after viewing the UFW's documentary video *The Wrath of Grapes*, which describes the McFarland situation, an image remained in my mind—a child with no arms or legs, born of a farm worker mother. The mother had been picking in pesticide-sprayed fields while the baby was still in the womb. This child became Cerezita, a character who came to me when I wondered of the child's future as we turn into the next century."[9] Cerezita, the child whose physical appearance is irrevocably marked with the history of worker abuse, is only a head. A product of the pesticides her mother has ingested in the process of working in the fields and living in her community, Cerezita represents the impossibility of normality under these conditions.

Her extreme physical state, unrealizable outside the constraints of the theatrical space, goes beyond the terrifying physicality of destruction represented in the video. A head only, she has mobility and limited control through her "raite," her ride, a mechanized device controlled by her chin that serves the second purpose of concealing the body of the actress. The word *raite* itself reflects one manifestation of Chicana Spanish, the use of an idiomatic U.S. English expression with Spanish spelling and pronunciation. This hybrid word significantly describes her only possibility of mobility, and the positioning of her mobility on the linguistic borderland underscores the alternate geography of Chicana identity.

Always physically a head, at times she assumes a metaphysically transcendent grandeur that insists a fragment of the body is greater than the whole. Comparing her presence to the majesty of the grand stone heads of Olmec antiquity, Moraga invokes both an indigenous heritage and spirituality in insisting that this figure attains "nearly religious proportions."[10] For Moraga, Chicana spirituality can never be divorced from its indigenous, syncretic roots, and she understands fully that *La Virgen de Guadalupe* is Tonantzin, an Aztec goddess, a connection that remains at the heart of the terrestrial, daily, pragmatic, spiritual power of syncretic Mexican Catholicism.

Cerezita forms a nexus for the interrelation of the spiritual and the physical with the discourse of oppression manifest in the economic stranglehold maintained by the large growers. An object of worship in her final manifestation, garbed in the dress of the Virgin, she is from the beginning read as a visible sign of both miracle and sin. The possibility of her public presence becomes a site of contestation between the overprotective mother, who views her daughter's deformity as a sign of personal shame, and the pragmatic manipulations of community activists, who recognize both her miraculous status—the very (im)possibility of her existence—and her potential value as human symbol, as a physical sign of the horrors experienced by the community.

The setting of the written play can be conveyed only metaphorically or iconically on the theatrical stage, creating a heightened focus on the cultural significance of space. Moraga's portrait of a small California Central Valley town suggests powerfully the conflicts between indigenous and corporate notions of land use and production: "The hundreds of miles of soil that surround the lives of Valley dwellers should not be confused with land. What was once land has become dirt. . . . The people that worked the dirt do not call what was once the land their enemy. They remember what land used to be and await its second coming."[11] This metaphoric description, in which suggestion creates a setting that rests firmly within a history, fits well within a conception of Aztlán. Aztlán exists both as a metaphoric space and as a historical real whose boundaries have not been fixed, though more important than physical geography is the possibility of a different and healthier relationship to the land. Referencing indirectly *El Plan Espiritual de Aztlán*, crafted in 1969, Moraga is not emphasizing the nationalist, separatist ideals of the document but rather moving away from the corporatist notions of land ownership toward a healthier reintegration with the land. This argument is also found in ecofeminism, but here she draws on both history and myth, transforming both through wrighting.

Heroes and Saints, consisting of a large number of short, almost cinematic scenes similar to some of Maria Irene Fornes's work in the early 1980s, centers on Cerezita's attempts to gain a public voice, to function as an effective symbol of the bodily oppression brought on by the destructive use of pesticides within the grape fields of the San Joaquin Valley.[12] At the same time it demonstrates a young woman's struggle with a controlling mother figure. Her mother, Dolores (sorrows), recognizes Cerezita's symbolic potential but chooses to envision her as an innocent whose spiritual purity must be protected from the harsh realities of the world outside the Valle (valley) home. The choice of names is crucial, since the family is the valley (the land), and the land is the people, graphically marking the interchangeable concepts at the heart of an integrative notion of a people that exists symbiotically with a space. If, as Lefebvre argues, social space is the product of a specific social and cultural formation, Moraga suggests that space also simultaneously works to create its people.[13]

Dolores's refusal to expose her child stems from her own anxieties. She has internalized her husband's act of abandonment as a sign of her failure, manifest in the physical condition of Cerezita. It is impossible for Dolores to separate her own fears and hurt from the pain inflicted on her by others; she blames herself and takes full responsibility rather than understanding the systemic and environmental roots of her situation. Thus, instead of being an empowering gesture that allows her to move beyond the present circumstances, her acceptance of responsibility traps her in a fight against the wrong enemies. As her *comadre* Amparo tells the leftist priest Father Juan, Dolores believed that Cerezita was a sign of the sins of her husband: "Nobody wants to be a victim, Father. Better to believe that it's the will of God than have to face up to the real sinners. They're purty powerful, those sinners. You start to take them on, pues you could lose. This way, por lo menos, you always get to win in heaven."[14] Dolores's concern with her *virgencita*, Cerezita, effectively silences the political protest of an intelligent mind given no opportunity to do anything but read and think. Cerezita's lack of control over her own mobility (her raite can be disabled by anyone and at that point she can be pushed around) is a direct result of her literal fragmentation.

She is only a head with no body, but this condition alone does not silence her. She recognizes the power of her body as it exists and, more than those who have it, the power inherent in a complete body: the power for sexuality, movement, reproduction, and change. This desire for a body goes back to the iconic significance of the pachuco's body and the "corpo-reality" of Chicano theater. This play is a reflection of and commentary on the work of Valdez, explicitly referencing his character Bellarmino in *The Shrunken Head of Pancho Villa*: Bellarmino's status as a head with no body holds within it the revolutionary potential of Pancho Villa, but the character is unable to act at the conclusion of the play because he needs assistance to inhabit a body.[15] Moraga's Cerezita is not a simple sign of a dematerialized intellectualism necessary to analyze the socioeconomic realities of the plight of Chicano farm workers; she represents the violence done to Chicana bodies. She also functions as a sign of desire for a body; desirable and full of desire, she becomes a central focus for the conflicted priest figure, Juan.

The two parts of Cerezita that have the greatest mobility are her hair and her tongue, and both serve as sites of not only sensual perception but also potential sexual practice. She is constantly shaking her head to feel the contact between her hair and face, one of the few ways her body can touch itself. In her flirtatious conversations with Juan she remarks, "I . . . sometimes just spin my head around so I can feel it brush past my cheeks" like the sensual veils of the Arab women.[16] This moment is sensual but also a sign of autonomy: the freedom to move without anyone's help and to experience sexual pleasure without another person. Insisting on her differently-abled status in which "tongue and teeth and chin had to do the job of your hands," Cerezita brings the flirtatious conversation to a more physical level expressed through language.[17]

The alternated definitions of *tongue* (spoken by both Juan and Cerezita) form a verbal riposte in which definitions point toward metaphoric possibilities. *Tongue* moves from the physical object to "the power of communication through speech," "language," "the charismatic gift of ecstatic speech," and then variants such as "to give tongue" through the verb forms and finally to "tongue tied—disinclined or," as Cerezita adds, "unable to speak freely."[18] Starting from the physical object scientifically invoked, the exchange moves on to the general space of communication. It becomes culturally specific with the idea of language—communication occurs within a specific social space that determines its boundaries (a reality brought to heart in the linguistic blending of the play). The list of definitions also invokes two possibilities at war in Cerezita and in the play: the Pentecostalist transformation, through spiritual possession, that empowers one to speak in a language not of this world and the physical, sexual acts that Cerezita is capable of performing: French-kissing (and fellatio). The exchange concludes with the possibility that all of this can be trapped, stopped, and contained by individual choice or external voices. With this admission of fragility and contingency, the scene enacts this very danger of silence by coming to an end.[19]

The flirtation with Juan is made clearer when it is revealed that he has "the eyes of a man" and that his motivation for entering the priesthood in the first place was to run away from the physicality of his body.[20] Juan is attracted to Cerezita because she shares his intellectual sympathies and her lack of a body poses no threat to his anxious relationship to bodies. However, in another sense, the body of the actress hidden within the raite enacts the same open secret as the priestly robes he could wear and the collar he insists on maintaining in parts of the play—hiding something that everyone knows exists. Here, sexuality is on display by the act of withholding, yet for Cerezita this version of obedience to "higher" laws parallels a submission to the manipulations of the growers, to the ones responsible for all of the suffering in her community. In reaction to the death around her, she sees the possibility of life, of rebirth coming through physical sexuality.[21]

The inability to speak for her people, to function as a public rather than a private symbol, is the central obsession for Cerezita. Only her mother's refusal prevents her from functioning as a public figure. Although everyone knows her status, she functions as a second kind of open secret within the community. Seen only through the window in a manner that hides the absence of a body, Cerezita visually reflects the internalization of guilt Dolores sustains by containing her in the home. By believing the public display of Cerezita is sinful, Dolores plays into the dominant mentality that sees the site of criminality in this valley space not as the death of the young children of the campesinos but as the moment in which their death becomes publicly represented. By crucifying the children, the community makes visible the violence, memorializes them, and literalizes the sacrificial claims of Christianity. Contrasted with this visibility is the absent husband's unwillingness or inability to deal with all of the public attention directed to his fragmented child, a child who could be read as the failure of his own seed if the socioeconomic and environmental factors are not understood clearly. If shame and guilt are allowed to triumph, the result is a destructive silence and a failure of rebirth.

Cerezita's brother, Mario, represents a different image of damaged physicality; a strong, intelligent man, he leaves the family because Dolores cannot deal with his homosexuality, which she condemns as a sin. His problem exists in his relationship to sex, not the particular inclination he practices. He needs the release of sex, a release that he feels echoes "the laying on of hands"; he believes in its ability to heal, "that whatever [he] had crippled or bent up inside" could be cured by sex.[22] Mario's substitution of sexuality without any greater goal is a dangerous emptiness, because his sexuality is not practiced openly but is necessarily deceptive and therefore evolves into relationships that are removed from social and communal significance. His HIV-positive status is not a cry for monogamy, nor even responsibility, but rather an embodiment of the dangers of silence and internalization that fragment the community. In this sense Mario follows in the footsteps of his mother, even as he pretends to himself that he is moving on and escaping.

The anatomy lessons Mario shares with Cerezita exemplify the contested nature of his bodily representation. On the one hand he demonstrates a Western scientific approach to physiology, but this view is tempered by his story of the Mayan body. According to Mario, the Mayan body operates within a theological indigenous language that escapes the vocabulary of the dominant. This spiritual language provides the space in which his sexuality is alive, healthy, and meaningful. Such wrighting locates bodily health within a palimpsest of history that recognizes the power of indigenous identity to mark an alternative relationship to the environment. While this relationship verges on an essentialized romanticization of indigenous identity, the implication is that Mario's story provides a different space for understanding personal identity and points toward the implications of structural violence beyond this valley: "The city's no different. Raza's dying everywhere. Doesn't matter if it's crack or . . . pesticides, AIDS, it's all the same shit."[23]

The play begins with a silent image of the crucifixion of a dead child, an act considered criminal, but this vision merely clarifies that the act of murder is not illegal in the world the play condemns. Rather, the recognition and representation of this previously hidden act is something that must be legislated and constrained as a way of concealing the real violence. The crucifixion is an attempt to make visible the deaths of the children, to prevent them from being forgotten, and to remind everyone of the cause of their death. These crucifixions mirror the crosses of the grapevines: "the trunk of each of the plants is a little gnarled body of Christ writhing in agony."[24] Cerezita insists that each victim is a martyr and should not be forgotten, extending her remembrance to the housekeeper and her daughter murdered along with the Jesuit priests in El Salvador. Ironically, with this memory, Juan masturbates against the side of her raite, making the satisfaction of desire his own and not a shared event. His desire is satiated by a solipsistic notion of silent martyrdom that parallels his own false rejection of the body, a vision that is condemned regardless of where it is manifest. For Moraga and Cerezita, Juan's unwillingness to cross the line and fight for the rights of his flock must be abandoned, because the contingency of representation and the vagaries of history make being in the wrong place at the wrong time a moment of forgetting, exemplified by the housekeeper and her daughter. Initially unable to get past the solitary nature of his masturbatory act, which is in fact a betrayal of the community and not merely self-indulgence in violation of his vows, Juan's guilt drives him to abandon the public act of resistance embodied in the postmortem crucifixion of Evelina, the infant daughter of Cerezita's sister Yolanda.

Juan's priestly status becomes a way of surrendering bodily responsibility to a higher power. He is concerned about infidelity to his vows: "I'm a priest, Cere. I'm not free. My body's not my own." But as the other characters in the play understand clearly, Juan's vocational call was also an attempt to distance himself from his own body, and his claims of responsibility are in fact a disavowal of it. He became "a man of the cloth" because of "the priest's body asleep underneath that cloth, the heavy weight of it tranquilizing him."[25] His fear of a living body, awake and feeling, brings him to the moment of transgression—an act enabled by the fact that the person he attempts to experience sexually is *not* a body. In part, Cerezita is a reflection of his own narcissistic desire to be able to love without a body. Though Juan is running away from himself, what keeps him in the town of McLaughlin, a fictionalized space sonorously proximate to McFarland, is the possibility of being a hero or saint, both of which offer a potentially transformative relationship to the body.

Juan's fears and desires stymie the potential of his transformation but also allow Cerezita a moment to speak clearly about her own role.

> It wasn't your body I wanted. It was mine. All I wanted was for you to make love to me like I had a body because, the fact is, I don't. I was denied one. But for a few minutes, a few minutes before you started *thinking*, I felt myself full of fine flesh filled to the bones in my toes. . . . And I'm sick of all this goddamn dying. If I had your arms and legs, if I had your dick for chrissake, you know what I'd do? I'd burn this motherless town down and all the poisoned fields around it. I'd give healthy babies to each and every childless woman who wanted one and I'd even stick around to watch those babies grow up! . . . You're a waste of a body.[26]

Cerezita's castigation erases any pretensions that membership in the clergy is somehow a justification for spiritual escapism. She recognizes that in Juan's case, unselfish desire has the ability to produce a body; he must separate himself from the constraints of his priestly vows in order to provide the social justice this community needs. Acknowledging the physicality of martyrdom, she insists that Juan's ethical dilemma is a refusal of his corporeal responsibilities. As a healthy body, he has the ability to reproduce healthy bodies; and more than that, Juan has a responsibility to the community: to ensure its continuance as a community and not just as a group of individuals.

Part of the threat to community comes from the assertion that the site of struggle is an individual body rather than a communal one; because of this misperception, the possibility of resistance becomes diffused in the face of the anonymous, corporate technology of agribusiness. Though everyone knows the source of the children's deaths, it remains invisible in the play. However, it is not inaudible; disembodied, it speaks through the noise of the helicopters patrolling the fields, the sound of gunfire, and the night spraying of pesticides and other chemicals. Resisting this enemy is difficult, as Yolanda demonstrates through her futile shouting into the sky. Dolores has already had her own moment of cursing the sky, telling the crop duster to "just drop a bomb, cabrones! It'd be faster that way!"[27] Her cry reflects both the omnipresence of violence and its invisibility in this space.

Yolanda vehemently insists to her mother about Evelina, "I gotta find her killer. Put a face to him, a name, track him down and make him suffer. I want to kill him, 'amá. I want to kill some . . . goddamn body!"[28] By breaking apart her last word with an expletive, Yolanda changes somebody into some body—it is the body that matters here. The corporate culture, the growers, and pesticides that are actually responsible have the possibility of escape; ironically, enemies that are manifest through structural inequities—poverty and differential access to representation—may escape revenge because they do not provide a body to take revenge upon. Like her mother, Yolanda runs the risk of redirecting the guilt from the invisible corporate evil of agribusiness to the function of her own body, and the only means she can see to resolve the situation is to kill a body. In doing so she risks making death a product of internal failures rather than external forces, internalizing the cause of death within the bodies on the stage. Yolanda makes this risk clear when she speculates that her womb is poisoned, that she caused the cancer that killed her daughter. Moraga acknowledges this dangerous possibility, which replicates the general practice of blaming an individual for circumstances beyond her or his control, thus disguising structural problems as individual ones.

In her combination of prose and poetry titled *The Last Generation*, published the year after the first staging of *Heroes and Saints*, Moraga has two accounts that map strongly onto the need of the fragmented feminine body to assert strength in opposition to the masculine forces that deny this body. In her retelling of an Aztec myth in the section "La Fuerza Femenina," Moraga recounts the story of the children of Coatlicue, Coyolxauhqui, her daughter and Huitzilpotchli, God of War:

> When her daughter . . . learns that her mother is about to give birth . . . she conspires to kill Coatlicue rather than submit to a world where War would become God. Huitzilpotchli is warned . . . and vows to defend his mother. At the moment of birth, he murders Coyolxauhqui, cutting off her head and dismembering her body. . . . In my own art, I am writing that wound. That moment when brother is born and sister mutilated by his envy. . . . I pray to the daughter, La Hija Rebelde. She who has been banished, the mutilated sister who transforms herself into the moon. She is la fuerza feminina,

our attempt to pick up the fragments of our dismembered womanhood and reconstitute ourselves. . . . the same faithfulness drives me to write: the search for Coyolxauhqui amid all the disfigured female characters and the broken men who surround them in my plays and poems.[29]

Cerezita's physical mutilation, her "dismemberment," is the visual sign of her mother's own emotional dismemberment. Dolores is destroyed not by her son but by a husband who abandoned her because she saw his sins reflected in Cerezita. His absence makes it easier for her to blame herself for Cerezita's physical state. Thus, her need to immobilize Cerezita, to hide her away from the world and silence her public voice, is partially a product of male absence and reflects this potential silencing of female creativity and social action.

But the absent father is not the only broken male within the play. Juan's failure, his fear, his broken quality prevents the first enactment of the postmortem martyrdom of Evelina. Cerezita wants the corpse crucified on the grape vines to make the environmental violence visible, and she will not allow Juan's failure of courage to prevent this action. She will not allow a personal fear about reproduction and desire to prevent the restaging of violence on the world stage, will not allow guilt to continue the practice of silence. So Cerezita transforms into *La Virgen de Guadalupe* with the aid of the children, taking within her body the sign of a *milagro*, a miracle. She sacrifices her hair and stops speaking in order to visually embody the saint Dolores has always assumed her to be.

By becoming complicit with Dolores's representational fantasy, Cerezita writes herself as a public figure, as a shared vision. In this costuming, this moment of embodying a vision, caused by a transformation witnessed by the audience, Dolores sees "un milagro en nuestra propia casa."[30] Occurring in the "half-darkness" between scenes, this change enables the audience to witness an event that is both part of the theater and a "true miracle" for Dolores. Role-playing and costume become the means of a transformation not only for an individual but also for the community, as the miracle enables Cerezita's public voice.[31]

Cerezita's altered appearance does not produce the same response from her sister Yolanda, who sees her mother prostrate and praying in front of her sister and asks Dolores, "[W]hat did you do to her?"[32] Yolanda is afraid that Cerezita has been sanctified from outside rather than inside, that she has not chosen but has been drafted, and that the sacrifice of her hair, her only site of sensuality and sexuality must be the result of her mother's displaced desires. But Yolanda's question is meaningless, because it is Cerezita's determination that results in this changed appearance, miraculous or pragmatic. And in this play Moraga suggests that miracles and practicalities are the same thing; what matters is the site, the medium, and the meaning of any act of representation. Cerezita's determination and knowledge of how to stop the dying, the poisoning of the land that is destroying her people, forces her mother to allow her to be seen. This visibility both provides her a voice and makes her a symbol.

The miracle echoes Kushner's description of the Theatre of the Fabulous, in which the mechanics of transformation are always exposed to the public. In this model theater becomes the means to counter the invisible but sometimes audible cause of death. The fact that a community can be formed around Cerezita as a constructed symbol places neither the community nor the construction of such a symbol in question. Instead, it makes a claim for wrighting in the theater: altering expectations to bring about social action through a theatrical gesture. The staging of Cerezita as the *Virgen* becomes her means of entering into public space. It engenders unified communal support for an act of resistance to the use of pesticides. It clarifies the effect of pesticides on the very youngest members of the community, who like the "angelitos" in Rivera's *Marisol*, must be made visible. The theatricality of this miracle makes it a part of everyday experience in the same way that the crosses and the crucifixion are viewed as performing cultural work beyond the walls of the church. In a sense Moraga shifts the theoretical anxiety about representation and presence, consubstantiation and transubstantiation, which are at the heart of the Christian ambivalence toward theater as a form, into a demonstration of a miracle's theatricality as a practical and efficient means of organizing communal resistance in a public space.

The importance of the material staging of this resistance is also demonstrated in Moraga's refusal to grant the forces of oppression and repression any visibility. They can only be heard, which helps suggest their systemic reality, but she makes the choice not to provide them any stage space. While this absence provides the audience members the chance to specify the figure of oppression for themselves, it also highlights the power of representing something visually on the stage, implying that Cerezita's miracle is empowering precisely because it is staged.

Cerezita's appearance at the public funeral interrupts the prayer (ironically a response calling for eternal life), and Juan repeats the words of her sister, "[W]hat have they done to you," his concern manifest in her transformation from one symbol to another.[33] Although as the Virgin of Guadalupe she becomes the sign of indigenous and syncretic feminized Catholicism and thus a popular sign of resistance, her own personal characteristics have potentially been subsumed. After this reading, her public persona is made possible only through the displacement of her wounded self, and she becomes the ventriloquized voice of another saint, not of herself. However, this reading neglects the incredible theatricality of her miraculous lived existence on the stage, the absence of a body that continually evokes the violence of pesticides on her individually and on the community as a whole.

Cerezita's final act, the offstage crucifixion of Evelina's corpse, makes her a martyr and demonstrates the communal power of resistance that emerges from an individual gesture. Rather than visually foregrounding the individual act and removing the disturbing power of the violent response through stylized or video enactment, Moraga's choice to place the action offstage allows for the onstage construction of community. The community emerges in the moment of the individual act of resistance, a stage gesture that is repeated explicitly in *A Circle in the Dirt* and to some extent in *Watsonville* as well.

Cerezita's public speech that precedes her action articulates the symbiotic relationship between the community and the land: her internal wound contains the people; individual wounds are a part of the communal reality. The community on stage—and potentially the community in the audience—becomes the people of the wound, of her fragmentation. Cerezita leaves the stage, her intent to show the corpse of a child to the world as a sign of sacrifice for the sins of others. This moment of representation of that which should not be seen threatens the corporate culture, the state apparatus. The representation must be destroyed, and her death comes in the attempt to wright others as she has wrought herself—as a sign and a body capable of rhetorical and literal resistance in public space. By establishing public status as life-threatening, the play insists on the complexities of Chicana political identity at the very moment in which individuals are given voice.

The movement of the play—from the first scene, with the young children in *calavera* masks setting up a crucifix whose body, hidden by the night, is set onstage opposite the silent, gazing figure of Cerezita, to the final moments in which an offstage crucifixion leads to murder in broad daylight—is from silence to noise, from stasis to action, from dark to light. Cerezita, watching in the dark as a passive spectator, becomes a visible actor whose sacrifice inspires not another round of protest but a burning of the fields led by Mario who has returned. Mario's return, a sign of strength in a diseased body unable to bear the weight of his own family, presents an inspiring moment of leadership in which a broken man has been recovered. With the offstage death of Cerezita, the Virgin, El Pueblo is left with its own sense of responsibility. The final image "is the crackling of fire as a sharp red-orange glow spreads over the vineyard and Valle home. The lights slowly fade to black."[34]

This burning strikes a chord when one remembers that this play was first fully staged less than a month before the Los Angeles Rebellion. This gesture at the end, though, is not utopian but eminently pragmatic in that rather than attack the body, the system must be confronted; to transform agribusiness the land must be transformed into a space of rebirth. The final burning is a reclamation of the land back from the dirt, the freeing of all the martyred Mechicanos symbolized by the twisted bodies of the grapevines. It is an act of catharsis that both purifies and sacrifices the fields; it is an attempt to free the poisoned overworked dirt and end the sacrifice of the children whose deaths are the cost of cultivating this ground.

The blessing that Juan gives the community before they leave for the fields is directed not only to the *pueblo* on stage but also to the audience in the theater, to "all those witnessing the play."[35] This moment of witnessing guarantees the social visibility of these deaths at the very moment of their stage invisibility. The inexorable push toward martyrdom recognized by the witnesses in the theater ensures that Cerezita, the Salvadoran housekeeper and her daughter, and other martyrs of everyday life, will not be forgotten, that the forces of death will be fought and that the living will not hide but burn the fields. Moraga places herself within a specific history in which heroes and saints can emerge from everyday life. To be in this world is to risk being honorably sacrificed for the community. The creation of a saint, a spiritual figure willing to fight pragmatically for social justice, restores a community fractured by the destructive forces of capitalism attempting to maintain the invisible status of death.

Pragmatic Spirituality and the Geography of Community

Watsonville, which premiered at Brava Theater Center in 1996, takes up the story of *Heroes and Saints*, shifting the geography from a fictional California town to a real California town articulated in fictional terms. *Watsonville* is also a celebration of the potential transformation of a landscape. The subtitle of this work indicates that it is about "some place not here," suggesting that what is being represented is an alternative space, one that does not yet exist or does not exist here. Wrighting this new place requires the establishment of structures to sustain a place that supports broadly inclusive community.

A sequel, *Watsonville* also functions on its own to explore the effects of four specific historical events juxtaposed to create a "perfect storm" of activism, spirituality, and political resistance. It expands the scope of Moraga's inquiry from a domestic space in one California city and the emergence of an individual public voice of resistance to an epic scope linked to one unique space. The play compresses several California events from the 1980s and 1990s to document the interplay of cultural forces and resistance in the creation of inclusive community. The first event is the 1985–1987 Watsonville cannery strike in which Latina women took center stage. The event is widely studied in contemporary labor history and is the subject of a documentary film because of the determination and success of the workers. According to many reports there was not a single scab among a group of a thousand united workers.[36] The second event was the 1989 Loma Prieta earthquake that devastated several Central Valley communities, including Watsonville. In *Watsonville* this event is a sign of the forces of nature rebelling against the current situation and a call to reestablish a healthy relationship to the land. The third event is the passage of Proposition 187 in 1994 under the auspices of the then governor of California, Pete Wilson. In the play, the bill is a piece of national legislation created by a Hispanic Republican U.S. senator from Florida, ironically anticipating the current national focus on immigration. Moraga's final event is the 1992 appearance of an image of the Virgin of Guadalupe in the bark of an oak tree, first witnessed by one of the women who led the strike. In the play the image is first perceived by Dolores, Cerezita's mother from *Heroes and Saints*.

Watsonville extends the process of mobilizing cultural and religious symbols in the support of political activism, placing spirituality at the center of pragmatic politics. The play takes as its center a traditional and pragmatic spirituality deployable on earth to support its adherents. In this play Dolores's faith is more explicitly articulated in both indigenous and Catholic terms.[37] Her evolution further reinforces the idea that the transformation of her daughter into a saint enabled political action. However, it also demonstrates that an insistence on the political efficacy of spirituality in no way diminishes it as a source of personal strength and solace. This paradox is demonstrated by both the efficacy of Dolores's personal faith in the apparition of the Virgin and by the partial castigation of Juan, now an ex-priest disillusioned with Catholic bureaucracy and working as a labor organizer, for his complete rejection of the church as an inefficient means of achieving social change.

While Moraga is in no way arguing for the reempowerment of the fundamentally conservative institutional church, she does suggest through Juan that the church could provide cultural and political support for a grassroots spirituality. This popular spirituality would value the support of the institutional church, but the absence of this support in no way mitigates the power and possibilities of popular spirituality manifest in the image of the Virgin in the oak tree. This spirituality parallels the practices of Catholic liberation theology in which the idea of the meek inheriting the earth is not so much something that will happen eventually but something that should be worked toward in daily life. This theology provides a license for priests to work for the political and social empowerment of the poor, often called a "preferential option for the poor," and many practitioners eventually left the church to pursue more radical forms of social action. This move toward radicalism is referenced implicitly through the conversation between Juan, Dolores, and the Monsignor. As an ex-priest and labor organizer, Juan is translating Dolores's vision for the Monsignor, who refuses to grant it miracle status. As part of his refusal of Juan's request for the church to validate this vision in *Watsonville*, the Monsignor suggests, "Tell it to your ex-Jesuit compañeros."[38]

Rather than separating religion and politics with the failed revolutionary act of Cerezita's sainthood (martyrdom and decapitation, as is revealed graphically in this play), Moraga continues the logic of offering a public voice of action articulated through faith. However, this time the presence of the Virgin is less unequivocally catalytic toward social action. Ironically, Monsignor Mendez's skepticism regarding the validity of the appearance of the Virgin is heightened by Dolores's belief in Cerezita's sanctity. The question of Cerezita's sanctity is a problem of knowledge that an audience familiar with both plays is asked to engage. Asserting that her transformation was spiritual makes the path to public resistance one staged in spiritual terms as the grounding space for political action. However, what *Watsonville* reminds us even more firmly and explicitly is that the Virgin of Guadalupe is not merely a figure of the institutional Catholic church but also the embodiment of the syncretic association with Tonantzin, the Nahuatl goddess.

To heighten the focus on the transformational power of spirituality, Moraga frames the entire geography of the stage space within the sacred oak grove in which the image of the Virgin first appeared. It is important for the reclaiming and production of space operative in this play that "all the action . . . is housed within the circle of a grove of aging oaks."[39] The power of the oak tree as the natural altar in which this worship can occur offers a vision of the interrelationship between the indigenous peoples and the land, reflected in a spiritual practice connected to the materiality of the lived environment. In contrast, the very idea of a universal Catholic church is implicitly predicated on a dematerialized and homogenous spiritual geography.

As with *Heroes*, the land itself is a part of the conflict and the space of the environment is a necessary participant. One of the changes, besides the passage of time, is the absence of two of the central figures of the first play, Cerezita and Mario. While in this play, Mario's death is only a flicker about the reality of HIV/AIDS, Cerezita's shadow haunts the play through Dolores's constant invocations. Dolores sees an apparition of her daughter in Susana, a physician's assistant who helps the striking women. Also returning is Amparo, Dolores's *comadre*, who is joined by Lucha (struggle or fight), an undocumented worker helping to lead the cannery strike.

The importance of place is crucial to the cultural and political education in this play. Here the oppressive politics are not just the results of disembodied agribusiness but are made visible through masculine hierarchies embodied by Dolores's husband, Don Arturo; Chente, a shop steward negotiating with the corporation; and Monsignor Mendez. Crucially, a single Latino actor portrays these patriarchal figures of domestic space, business, and religion. This choice clarifies that the conflicts of power are not simply divided into ethnic categories, Chicana and Anglo, and suggests differences between ethical and political stances within an ethnic group. In this way Moraga suggests a new form of inclusive community that enables her to move beyond the liberal investment in equating ethnicity and politics. She wrights this community by first recognizing a liberationist politics of diversity represented accurately through individuals of color and then calling for affiliation through a shared geography and politics, rather than assuming preexisting affiliations based on an essential conception of ethnic identity.

One of the critiques of *Watsonville* is that it attempts to deal with too many issues, fragmenting it in a way that limits artistic coherence.[40]

However, this supposed failure of coherence is in fact an invocation of an alternative cultural literacy and the lack of an existing audience knowledgeable of these interlaced events. Moraga makes this argument in her essay "Sour Grapes: The Art of Anger in America." Written in 1996 at the time of *Watsonville*'s premiere, Moraga provides a journal entry from "The Morning After": "*I only remember the performance. What was on a different night too long, last night captured all our attention, our minds & hearts—those of us so hungry to see our lives, our people reflected. I felt vindicated. Yes, I believe that is the word: 'vindicated.' 'You see. Ya ves,' I want to say to all those who doubt us, our complexity, render us invisible. 'We exist . . . y más.' The reviews tomorrow, no doubt, will say they saw something else. But, I must remember the work. I am getting closer, I hope, to some profound portrait of who we are as a people. That's all that really matters: the writing.*"[41]

This response acknowledges the power of visibility and of staging a people, and pushes forward to insist on the complexity of Latino identity. It is also an ethical call to create an audience able to recognize the political coherence and epic power of her multilayered political texts. Moraga's project is to write the potential conditions for a creative community, a generative community, one capable of wrighting itself. While the use value of a community is neither irrelevant nor unimportant, the generation of knowledge, of conceptual work, and of alternative forms of political action and organizing are not often imagined as a part of this efficacy. Moraga calls for the recognition of history and environment as not only tangible forces in the construction of the individual but actual contemporary players whose energy must be addressed within the universe of the play.

Watsonville begins with the voice of Dolores speaking a prayer in Spanish and then shifts to an ingenious expository scene structured as a translated letter written to Cerezita on the *Dia de los Muertos*, the Day of the Dead. This act of translation tells of the loss of Cerezita and Mario while also addressing the current labor difficulties. This structure allows Moraga to establish the strong presence of Spanish in this primarily Mexican immigrant community without alienating an English monolingual audience. However, even in this Spanish-dominant space, Moraga is constructing an inclusive fiction, for she reminds us in the introduction to the play, "The majority of the immigrant population in the real town of Watsonville speaks a beautiful fluent Spanish. . . . An occasional English word enters the conversation only when there is no exact Spanish equivalent. Spanish is the private and public voice of this Mexican community, its voice of prayer, of passion, and of protest. To have that voice truly resonate in the play, at least 70% of the dialogue should have been written in Spanish. So, in many ways, even the language of *Watsonville* is a fiction. . . . My hope is that this balancing act between the two languages ensures both cultural authenticity and accessibility to a new (more broadly-defined) American audience."[42] This broader sense of America extends beyond the inclusion of various U.S. populations into a larger continental conception of the Americas by the end of the play.

As part of this process of inclusion, the play narrates the increasing political participation and activism of the women of Watsonville during the strike as a counter to reactionary patriarchal figures. Don Arturo is a traditional figure of domestic patriarchy threatened by women's independence. As the union negotiator Chente is more invested in his own needs than in helping the workers. Monsignor Mendez, of course, is afraid of placing the power and support of the church behind any potentially political action. However, there are two masculine figures that escape this potential label—Juan and JoJo, Lucha's son.

JoJo's political and social development and Juan's support of both the striking women and Dolores's belief in the miraculous appearance of the Virgin provide alternatives to patriarchal oppression. In creating these characters Moraga clarifies that while much of the oppression rests in patriarchy, the play is about both gender conflict and politics more broadly. JoJo's education as an artist and as a cultural worker occurs through the crafting of a rap song in support of the striking workers. He begins with compositional difficulties, but over the course of the play he completes a song that calls the "raza" to "rise up."[43] Supporting his mother and the striking women, JoJo demonstrates the emergence of a progressive politics in a new generation.

One strand of transformation is the coming together of Lucha and Susana. Lucha frees herself from her dependence on men and recognizes her own power for self-transformation. She successfully resists Chente's attempts to establish an intimate relationship with her, including the threats he bases on her undocumented status. Chente represents a pragmatic capitulation to the status quo of politics that is unacceptable in this place. He agrees to a strike settlement that does not include the undocumented workers, and although he believes he has negotiated successfully, the strikers are unwilling to acknowledge a distinction between undocumented and documented labor, calling on the farm workers to support them in their protest. The solidarity that emerges from the legislative attempt to split the Mechicano community into documented and undocumented workers more forcibly indicates the ways that borders have been established to police the generosity of community. In this play geography is politics, and thus the call to spirituality is not a rejection of the *pueblo* constituted as either the people or the place.

Lucha's struggle to maintain her own identity and practice her own sense of politics despite her undocumented status is central to creating a place "not here." Though never articulated in the play, the putative conservative narrative that the undocumented worker is at the center of labor concerns in the United States heightens the irony of her position. Lucha is not only an active worker and a good mother; she is an entrepreneur who participates in the free market. She demonstrates the innovation and drive that are so often praised within the capitalist mainstream by making and selling tamales to raise extra money, creating a commodity desired and consumed by wealthy white customers.

The use of an *acto* as a play within the larger theatrical production places *Watsonville* even closer to the original political ideals of Chicano theater than *Heroes and Saints*. The *acto* reflects the lived experience of the cannery workers, including the managerial demands for increased productivity without concern for adequate worker protection or care for injured workers. The Huelguistas, the strikers, watch as they stage a play using characters of a Veterana (veteran), an Obrera (worker), "the Forelady," and Mrs. Oprimida (Mrs. Oppressed). Adopting the theatrical aesthetics of the *acto* as a play within a play, Moraga powerfully invokes the living presence of this agitprop theater, reminding the contemporary audience of its political and aesthetic power. In doing so she illustrates the power of theater as a means of education and social change that reflects metatheatrically on the larger play. As the two workers educate the newest laborer, Mrs. Oprimida, on her tasks, she is injured; instead of offering support, the forelady, who caused the injury by demanding increased speed, does little or nothing to resolve the situation. As the Veterana tells her cursing coworker, "¡Eh, obrera! Don't 'agonize.' Organize!"[44] This advice clarifies that only a community working together can resolve the situation.

The clear understanding that resistance and political action take place in highly theatrical ways recalls *El Movimiento*, though in a broader, more inclusive understanding of its political aims. *Watsonville* allows the audience community an opportunity to participate in the process of liberation by becoming reformed scabs who support the strike, refusing to work. This moment of solidarity catalyzes a violent retaliation when the owners recognize the real economic threat of solidarity and try to shut down the possibility for resistance. This moment occurs in the first scene of act 2 when a busload of scabs drives up. This event is marked aurally by dialogue and sound effects.

> [*Sound of bus door swinging open.* LUCHA *walks down the center aisle of the audience, as the center aisle of the bus. She passes out fliers about the strike and the anti-immigration bill.*][45]

Crossing into the space of the audience has several effects, including the literal inclusion of the audience within the play's space. While this move is not unique, doing so at the midpoint rather than the conclusion offers the audience an opportunity to become more personally engaged with the second act. There is also an opportunity for local education, because in addition to fliers referencing the play's issues, Moraga explicitly suggests, "Actual fliers regarding a current local cause affecting Latino/people of color workers can be used here."[46] She is flexible but still retains the importance of class, labor, and racial positioning for the educational function of this moment.

Because of their presumed position, being seated on the bus, the audience members become a group of potential scabs. Brought into the action of the play as laborers willing and eager to take on the work of a cannery, they are displaced from a putative sense of middle-class comfort into a position within the bilingual Latino working class. While one could argue that all of these claims are based on an explicit framing that may not do the political work associated with it—that the audience may in fact not be fully cognizant of the cultural and political implications of their condition as scabs—Moraga masterfully ensures that the audience will actively support the strike by refusing to participate as scabs, counting on the assumed passivity of an audience too startled by a crossing of the proscenium arch to become directly involved in the action. This conventional passivity is transformed into an act of resistance, and thus Moraga creates a utopian theatrical space in which conventional nonaction becomes concrete support for radical action.

The power of this gesture and the implications for the transformation of the theatrical space and the world into an arena in which the conventional gesture in fact is radical and liberatory is heightened by the next event. After Lucha's exhortation the audience witnesses the following:

[*Lucha watches as we hear the sound of a bus door closing and the bus pulling away. A smile comes over her face as the strikers all cheer and wave "Adios." Suddenly there is the sound of a tear gas bomb being tossed and exploding. Smoke fills the air. Screams and the muffled voice of the police trying to disperse the crowd.*

[*In the darkness, brutal sounds of a physical assault are heard: heavy blows to a body with fists and sticks, grunts of pain, the distorted voices of young males, shouting obsenities (sic). They are full of rage and violence. Police sirens interrupt the beating. The stage becomes a maze of spinning red and blue police lights.*][47]

While the scene shifts to Dolores addressing *la Virgen* in the oak grove, what the violent oppression here demonstrates is the real threat manifest by an act of solidarity. Instead of a celebratory moment, Moraga offers a violent one, displacing the easy dismissal of the political significance of the audience's refusal to work. Instead, she provides the audience the possibility of recognizing that this space of radical "nonaction" is the most threatening to the corporate interests. In a classic gesture of Moraga's theatricality, the most violent moment of the play presents the forces of oppression as lights and sounds rather than in a limited physicality.[48] It is important, however, that this violence is staged not at the close of the play but in the first scene of the second act. While Dolores's plea to the Virgin for the health of JoJo offers one response to this violence, it leaves the audience with the important question that Moraga is posing in this scene: How do we get to "some place not here," a place now clearly defined as one in which conventional nonaction is in fact radical action?

There are some parallels between this geography and the theorizing of community, especially Giorgio Agamben's *The Coming Community*. In this text, translated into English by Michael Hardt and resonating powerfully with Hardt and Negri's later work *Empire*, Agamben talks about Tiananmen Square as an example of a radical community: "What could be the politics of whatever singularity, that is of a being whose community is mediated not by any condition of belonging (being red, being Italian, being Communist) nor by the simple absence of conditions . . . but by belonging itself?"[49] For Agamben, the difference between belonging and "belonging to" is that belonging prevents a sense of alliance that places the community in the service of the state, in either support of or resistance to it. "Belonging to" becomes a means through which affiliation offers the state an anchor to answer the needs of a community in a way that does not necessarily address the realities of an alternative space, a place not here. "Belonging" becomes a more flexible way of understanding connections, one that is much less easily co-opted by those in power. The sense of belonging ironically emerges from a lack of clarity regarding the specific political connections in a broader movement of solidarity. In this case, belonging emerges from a shared sense of oppression rather than a specific political platform. Though this belonging is always on the verge of shifting into a specific attachment to the causes of the strikers and a resistance to the problematic legislation, Moraga suggests a political community beyond these local causes, offering the possibility of maintaining a sense of belonging and not merely belonging to.

Moraga's utopian shift in the play is negotiated through the framing of the oak grove that shifts the entire action of the play into a *tierra sagrada*, a sacred land. One response to the violence is a series of women's voices chanting the names of indigenous deities in Nahuatl, reclaiming the space for syncretism and spirituality attached to a sense of place, of land. There is a hint of the violence of the earth, of the earthquake that ends act 2, emerging from these same voices. This new space, however, is a conceptual shift, not necessarily a geographical one, for as Dolores reminds her listeners, "[W]e belong here as much as el gringo. Plant yourself here dice ella. Like that holy tree, tan fuerte, tan viejo, tan sagrado, ustedes tienen raíces that spread all the way to México. (*Pause*) Esta ley no vale nada. . . . Seguimos siendo americanos whether we got papeles or not. This land is the same land as México. Todo es América y la Virgen de Guadalupe es la Emperatríz de América, una América unida."[50] This speech is given to the Mechicano population saved from the earthquake by their act of political solidarity in a religious pilgrimage to the image of *la Virgen*.

This reclamation of the land is an American gesture in the continental rather than the national sense, demanding a radical expansion of the concepts of nation and community. If place is also people, as Moraga reminds her audience with the term *pueblo*, then the place America and the people America can become one in this place not here. While much of this exhortation is in Spanish and presumably understandable primarily to a Mechicano audience because of both the language and the invocation of *la Virgen*, Moraga is nonetheless striving in this moment for a thinking of community beyond this place.

Moraga's final gesture in the play, an epilogue after the earthquake, places the salvation of the Mechicano population, spared by their pilgrimage, squarely in the hands of a miraculous politics. Moraga's insistence on the utopian possibility here allows her to stage the creation of a community of resistance. By the end of the play the space she desires, a return in order to move forward, becomes visible on the stage as a site of power. Juan, who had left the priesthood to become a union organizer, returns to God through "awe so profound, the earth shook open to embrace us."[51] Susana and Lucha articulate their sense of themselves as a couple, and Susana speaks the final words. Susana's body, where Dolores had previously seen a vision of her daughter, becomes in this moment Cerezita's as well, through a spiritual and material connection between bodies, a coming together the play wrights in its closing moments.

The power of spirituality, of the miracle that may not be a miracle, is once again invoked at the close of the play, when solidarity is finally achieved and the individuals in struggle are willing to make a fully principled stand for what they believe. In her conclusion Moraga offers a geography of this community, of this place not here, arguing not for a movement to another place but for one that makes this place somewhere else. She recognizes the utopian quality of her creation, indicating in her introduction to the collection of *Watsonville* and *A Circle in the Dirt* "they are not exactly documentaries because they refuse to end with the bitter facts. . . . These plays are written instead in the spirit of what remains possible in a pueblo in spite of gentrification and globalization. These plays are acts of faith in a people; they are the 'some place not here.'"[52]

The transformation of Watsonville into "some place not here" is a conscious artistic attempt to understand utopia not as a destination but as a creative process, a wrighting of an alternative possibility for existence through performance. In thinking about performative utopias Jill Dolan suggests,

> I'm interested in the material conditions of theater production and reception that evoke the sense that it's even possible to imagine a utopia, that boundless "no place" where the social scourges that currently plague us—from poverty, hunger, cancer, HIV/AIDS, inadequate health care, racial and gender discrimination, hatred of lesbians, gay men, bisexuals and transgendered people, the grossly unequal distribution of wealth and resources globally, religious intolerance, xenophobia expressed in anti-immigrant legislation, lack of access

for the disabled, pay inequity, and of course a host of others—might be ameliorated, cured, redressed, solved, never to haunt us again. I have faith in the possibility that we can imagine such a place, even though I know that we can only imagine it, that we'll never achieve it in our lifetimes.[53]

Dolan's cry for such a production is clearly anticipated by Moraga's sense of the possibilities of theatrical wrighting. While for Dolan the fleeting moments of performance are a potential site of transformation and the primary motivation that brings an audience back to the theater, Moraga goes further in insisting that the creation of these spaces is necessary for the creation of a *pueblo*. She wants these spaces to exist beyond the theater, to become more than a feeling, to bring into being a place for her people.

Radical Inclusion: Wrighting a *Circle in the Dirt*

The sense of spiritual utopia attached to both place and the possibility of community formation is given a different materiality in Moraga's *Circle in the Dirt: El Pueblo de East Palo Alto*. Created in 1994 with the help of theater students at Stanford University and the community of East Palo Alto (EPA), *Circle* gives voice to a community at a moment when complex local histories are being erased by homogenous corporate progress. The play offers a different way of thinking through the notion of belonging in its glimpse of a fragmented community that shares a geography and a history. *Circle* was one of two one-act plays commissioned as a part of "Dreams of a City: The East Palo Alto Project," which was started by the Committee on Black Performing Arts at Stanford University, along with residents of East Palo Alto.[54] Both Moraga and Charles OyamO Gordon, an African American playwright, received commissions to write new works to creatively document and celebrate the history of EPA.

Part of the motivation for this project was to counter the negative media attention that EPA received in 1992 for having the highest per capita murder rate in the country. Project organizers, however, did not intend simply to provide an alternative representational voice separate from the mainstream media. Instead they wanted to document a community that worked together to reduce the rate of violence in a story that would not draw widespread media attention. Their hope was that the city's unique cultural history could be preserved rather than erased by the visibility of violence and the calls for renewal.[55] Like the body of Sonny Villa or Tiburcio Vásquez, the legibility of criminality became the overriding narrative scripting reception of the city. In this case, however, the subject was not an individual but an entire community articulated, even more clearly than *Watsonville*, as a complex and ethnically diverse space.

As in *Watsonville*, the center of *Circle* is the relationship between *el pueblo* and *la tierra*, the people and the land. This relationship, a crucial element of a Chicano identity that acknowledges its indigenous roots, is here broadened to include the palimpsest of history that has created community in this rapidly transforming urban space. Moraga creates an inclusive view of the diversity of the populations of EPA (Japanese American, Vietnamese American, Chicano, and African American) to stage the possibility of community through identification with an existing urban space under the threat of erasure. Her perspective on community allows the inhabitants to voice interethnic concerns while ultimately offering the possibility of new growth.

The relationship between spirituality and geography within the Chicano community is manifest in *Circle* in a specific and localized urban space that echoes the cultural logic embodied by the concept of Aztlán as a cultural geography. Moraga's vision was distilled from a series of interviews conducted by students under the auspices of the Committee on Black Performing Arts at Stanford University, as well as video footage also used to construct a documentary. Moraga recognizes the movement of history within this geography but refuses the tendency toward a developmental teleology grounded on the idea of progress and "urban renewal" as necessarily productive forces. Her alternative is to show the history of the land and its people, giving her audience visual and linguistic access to the stories of the land. She does this not to create a romantic nostalgia for a different and more sacred relationship to space but to establish more resonance between the people and the land, articulating a symbiosis often utopically appropriated by new age philosophy and environmentalists. While both spirituality and respect for the land are integral parts of this relationship, too often the relationship between history, community, and space is neglected. A community exists within particular temporal and spatial configurations, and the shifting of either of these elements, as well as a change in the human composition of the community, will produce a potentially radical change.

The question of history, of temporality, is vexed within the site of performance, because on the one hand there is the recuperation of indigenous presences, an excavation of the palimpsest of cultural in-habitants that have spent time in this particular location. On the other hand, the temporality of the stage space tends toward the symbolic and the transcendent rather than the real and the historical. The notion of space becomes troubled by performance, as a recuperation of the history of EPA as a series of memories is moved from the immediacy of the actual urban space in one community-based performance to the slightly removed materiality of a Stanford University stage. In this shift there is a dual call for an instantiation of an actual community through the deployment of a site-specific piece and a simultaneous expansion of the concept of site-specific where localized political concerns become the means through which sites are recuperated.

Moraga is clearly aware that her practice is a fiction in the broadest sense of the word, since she crafted the language and structure of the piece from found materials, but nevertheless brought her own personal artistic investments into the work. However, the play's fictionality de-tracts neither from the amount of labor involved in the documentary process nor from the political resonance of her theatrical work. And it offers the possibility of articulating a sense of community beyond the very fractures initially represented on the stage. In reflecting the lived diversity of EPA, Moraga creates a work with a more diverse character list than any of her other pieces. At the same time, the specific mate-riality of the creative circumstances makes this choice a product of a community-based thinking and an acknowledgment of the available actors. Yet the clear political and aesthetic connections between this piece and her other work clarify how close all of her work is to the political ideals of community-based theater, even when it is crafted by an individual playwright. Of course this relationship is not surprising for a Chicana play, for as Valdez said in his "Notes on Chicano The-ater," "If the raza will not come to the theatre, then the theatre must go to the raza."[56] And as Harry Elam and Kim Fowler note in their essay "Dreams of a City," Moraga adjusted her script in response to concerns that emerged from community forums where the work in progress was presented and even developed a new character to make use of acting resources in the community.[57]

The play is divided into five scenes with four different stage spaces, along with multimedia projections that present images of people, the ancestors of the space itself. The idea that the ancestors of EPA are shared begins a way of thinking about connection that extends beyond the model of biological lineage, allowing the threads of history and geography to link people. The sharing of history across typical lines of demarcation suggests the limits of such divisions even as the play demonstrates the difficulties of crossing them. This sense of connection offers the possibility that what it really intended by the idea of ethnicity is not a shared culture so much as a shared sensibility that arises from an attitude and relationship to space. If this is the case, then the implicitly assumed connection between ethnicity and community that is too often employed makes sense. Yet in theatrical terms this would be seen as an aesthetic of performance, a theatricality that imbues the total environment.

Circle is a story of the space itself and as such adopts the necessary voices of individuals' memories, nostalgia, and present-day stories to provide a polyphonic view of this urban space facing the problem of "renewal" in its supposedly kindler and gentler form in the 1990s. Through the figure of the Professor, a retired African American history professor; Chuy, a Chicano in his early twenties; and Reginald, an African American in his forties, the audience is provided a sense of the political and cultural history of EPA. More African American in the 1960s, EPA was understood as a space of revolution even before the development of the Vietnamese and then the Mexican American communities. Charting a cultural history of the diversity of the space, the play does not shy away from presenting a strong sense of community through the characters' willingness to discuss, learn, and remember. At the same time, it recognizes that the very presence of this community is predicated on a range of conflicting and paradoxical perceptions.

The first scene takes place in a Buddhist temple, and the three characters there are Japanese American, Vietnamese American, and Mexican American. While for Señora Talamantes the altar and celebration remind her of the *Dia de los Muertos*, it is in fact the New Year within the Asian community. At first offering a glimpse of cultural syncretism and familiar practices across cultural gaps, the scene ends with Señora Talamantes feeling misunderstood and out of place even as all three characters recognize their shared geography and loss of history.

The spaces of the play—a temple, a school, an apartment complex, and a garden—are all public areas that indicate the life of the community outside the confines of an individual dwelling, as might be provided by a typical American domestic drama. The youngest Anglo American character, Stephanie, an evangelical missionary who works with the women from the apartment complex, puts it this way: "I miss Coolie already. All the women were so open to us church workers. They'd invite us in and make us part of the family . . . eating enchiladas . . . planning the feast days . . . It was like everyone just sort of transplanted a village from México. Maybe that sounds strange, but it's a warmth, a sense of community that well, we Americans lack, I think, in our own lives."[58] Stephanie's sense of nostalgia verges on the utopian, and her implicit definition of Americans as being without community places Mexicans outside the definition of "American" in a problematic though oft-encountered formulation. Her voice also offers the strongest critique of spousal violence and the patriarchal dominance of the Mexican household, as well as the presence of immoral and illegal activities such as prostitution, drug dealing, and gang violence. This paradoxical nostalgia that wishes for the maintenance of this community even in the face of the reality of its flaws is at the heart of Moraga's project in this play.

Circle is an act of resistance and of a recuperation of the indigenous memory of the spaces of California. The play brings together a range of issues in an attempt to provide the imaginative space to remember and to grow a community. By setting up a richly textured environment, Moraga establishes not a dialogic but a polyphonic space where the daily lived realities and histories are never erased, but neither are the greater issues of the displacement and dismantling of a community. Each individual story functions less as a through line on its own and more as a way of forcing the audience to reconceptualize the practice of art and politics.

While it is clear that this play alone cannot capture the history of EPA, it nonetheless provides a way of thinking and performing the politics of space, of offering a logic of hope while simultaneously making what might seem mere spirituality into an everyday lived force of politics. It is not by chance that the play begins in the space of a temple, a sacred space, where time is undergoing a change, a rebirth in the form of a New Year. While this space does not in and of itself generate agency, the celebration of the ancestors of a place rather than of an individual people shifts the terms of memory from unproductive nostalgia to a powerful force in the development of a relationship with space. While in a sense the play is a process of mourning the memories that have been lost, such as the community school project that gave students access to an Afrocentric curriculum from kindergarten to college, the very invocation of a transformation enables the beginning of a conversation about recuperation that culminates with the emergence of La Capitana.[59]

La Capitana is a "mission Indian," a *mestiza* elder of the Muwekma and one of the "Most Likely Descendants" of those who participated in the sale of their tribal land in the area.[60] She is called into being by two forces when the Professor draws a circle in the dirt and places within it various forms of native corn. It is important that she is real and not a symbol or fantastical figure. Thus she reflects the materiality of spiritual practice that allows for the blending of progressive social commentary symbiotically tied to individual and communal spirituality, a new sense of history and a new sense of community. In part recalling the famous relationship of Ishi and the University of California, La Capitana speaks of her experience with Stanford University as someone who is presented with the archeological findings of her ancestors' bones, and she begins the laborious process of bringing those bones back to the earth.[61]

In a gesture of solidarity that brings together issues emerging from Moraga's work in *Heroes*, La Capitana escorts Reginald, a young HIV-positive African American, out into the fields and beyond into death. In the process, however, the two interrupt, at least for a day, the destructive forces tearing down the abandoned high school and the Coolie apartment complex to make way for commercial development intended to provide a tax base. They pick oranges and bury bones, activities that reflect both the continued fertility of the land and the human history echoing though buried in this space, their gesture of resistance becoming a space in which the entire *pueblo* of EPA merges into a coherent whole. This coherence is exemplified theatrically by the emergence of all of the characters, gathered in a relatively small group and facing the same direction. Perhaps only temporarily successful (and in the material history of the real place, ultimately unsuccessful, at least in terms of stopping the "development" that is taking place), the gesture nonetheless provides the space for an alternative imaginary of what is to come.

Importantly, this act of resistance, like Cerezita's rush into the fields at the end of *Heroes and Saints*, is offstage and unseen. The power of the moment rests in the sound of the incursion being resisted. In this case it is the sound of bulldozers and other implements of large-scale destruction and construction. Moraga uses sound, eminently theatrical, to displace and disembody the oppositional forces, not stooping to give them space on the projection screens that had previously presented the ancestors of the *pueblo*.

By staging works that articulate in detail the real diversity of local communities, clarifying their special organization through multiple stage locations while simultaneously offering a limited utopia that is itself material, Moraga offers community as a necessary presence in everyday life. Community becomes a means of staging politics and embodying the problems of contemporary identity practices. The real community created by the performance of theater becomes more than a space for personal agency and the performance of identity, as many critics have understood multicultural theater practices; instead, it becomes a crucial site of wrighting: a space for creating knowledge about people and places and for excavating the memories that enable the resistance that sustains them.

In creating an inclusive mode of political community, Moraga provides a version of wrighting that extends the symbiosis between environment and individual explored by Rivera. Even as she acknowledges the framing of identity offered by audiences whose knowledge of ethnicity is shaped by stereotypes and borders, she begins, as do all of the playwrights here, the process of thinking beyond this frame, creating new models in the process of correcting old ones. In doing so, she wrights ethnicity.

Notes
Bibliography
Index

Notes

1. Introduction: Writing, Righting, and Wrighting Ethnicity

1. Adam Kidron quoted and paraphrased in David Montgomery, "An Anthem's Discordant Notes," *Washington Post*, April 28, 2006.

2. Romero, "Introduction," xiv.

3. Hornor, *Hispanic Americans*, xiv. The exact language is repeated in the 2005 edition.

4. Oboler, *Ethnic Labels*.

5. See Oboler for a more extensive description of the diversity of labels employed in specific contexts.

6. Jenkins, "Ethnicity Etcetera," 87. He takes this last idea from Wolf, "Perilous Ideas."

7. Banks, *Ethnicity*, 7, 6, 186.

8. For a broader discussion of Leguizamo's one-man shows, see Chirico, "Laughter."

9. Leguizamo, *Mambo Mouth*, 103.

10. Leguizamo, *Mambo Mouth*, 112, 113, 106.

11. Leguizamo, *Mambo Mouth*, 102, 116, 106, 119.

12. See Geertz, "Blurred Genres."

13. Burns, *Theatricality*, 37–38.

14. Goffman, *Frame Analysis*.

15. Du Bois, *Souls*, 45.

16. In her essay "Theatricality and Civil Society," Davis offers a revised definition of theatricality that suggests, like Banks's definition of ethnicity, it is present in both the eye and the emotional state of the beholder. Built into Davis's definition is a self-reflexivity that creates a critical distance caused by an emotional response, the absence of sympathy within an act of conscious spectatorship. In *How the World Became a Stage*, William Egginton proposes to remove the slipperiness of the term *subjectivity* by

replacing it with *theatricality*, which he argues reflects a new conceptual-ization of space. According to Egginton, the shift from medieval to early modern theater is enabled by the emergence of a relationship with an ab-stract spectator's gaze. This definition continues to focus on this dynamic interplay between observer and event or object, but in this case the actor is manifesting behavior as a result of the assumed presence of an observer. According to Timothy Murray in the introduction to *Mimesis, Masochism and Mime*, the collection reveals "the political role played by theatricality in situating the subject in the desire of the Other and thereby accentuating the Otherness, the unresolved alterity, of spectacle and its heterocosmic impulses" (20).

17. This could be extended to any other self-conscious, ethnically marked theatrical practice.

18. Valdez and Teatro Campesino, *Luis Valdez—Early Works.*

19. In *The Past as Present* Harry Elam Jr. uses a similar construction, (w)righting, to explain August Wilson's use of history: "Wilson (w)rights history through performative rites that pull the action out of time and even ritualize time in order to change the power and potentialities of the now. This process of (w)righting history necessarily critiques how history is constituted and what history means" (3).

20. Du Bois, "Krigwa," 134.

21. Valdez, "Notes," and Geigomah, "New American Indian Theater."

22. See Elam, *Taking.*

23. Seller, *Ethnic Theatre.*

24. Bigsby, *Modern American Drama*, especially chapter 10.

25. See Moraga and Anzaldúa, *This Bridge.*

26. See Anzaldúa, *Borderlands/La Frontera.* Anzaldúa's powerfully innovative thinking has received a series of critiques for its essentialism.

27. Valdez, "Notes," 6.

28. Sandoval-Sánchez, *José Can You See?*, 118. Marrero's essay "From El Teatro Campesino to the Gay 1990s" provides a different cultural his-tory that sees the primary energy of transformation in the 1990s emerging from artists who explicitly deal with sexuality.

29. This cultural nationalism is grounded, for Chicanos, in the idea of Aztlán, a place from which the Mexica left on a journey culminating in the founding of Tenochtitlan (Mexico City). For Mexicans, Aztlán is in northern Mexico; for Chicanos, it is the U.S. Southwest. See Anaya and Lomelí, *Aztlán.*

30. See chapter 3.

31. Arrizón and Manzor, *Latinas*, 13–17.

32. For a good overview of changes in Chicano theater in the 1980s see Huerta, "Professionalizing Teatro."

33. See Svich, "Arrival."

34. Rossini, "Pleasure."

35. Huerta's seminal work *Chicano Theater* and Nicolás Kanellos's *Mexican American Theatre: Legacy and Reality* are some of the important early books. Other work on ethnicity was invested in an excavation of the taxonomy and influence of an ethnic "type" rather than a conceptual engagement with the framework of ethnicity itself.

36. Lee, *Performing Asian*, 5, 26.

37. This argument is similar to that of José Muñoz in *Disidentifications* with regard to queer performance art. However, here the importance of the theater as a genre and as production space is central.

38. Latins Anonymous, *Plays*, 12.

39. Latins Anonymous, *Plays*, 40, 39.

40. Latins Anonymous, *Plays*, 40, 42.

2. Miguel Piñero's Theatricality: Fear, Respect, and Community

1. Melendez, *We Took the Streets*, 105. See pp.88–111 for a detailed account of the history. See also Gandy, "Between Borinquen and the *Barrio*," and Joseph P. Fried, "East Harlem Youths Explain Garbage-Dumping Demonstration," *New York Times*, August 19, 1969.

2. See Gandy, "Between Borinquen and the *Barrio*, 743 ff.

3. Guzman quoted in Baver, "Puerto Rican Politics," 49; Baver, "Puerto Rican Politics," 50.

4. Hernández, *Puerto Rican*, 116.

5. Algarín quoted in Hernández, *Puerto Rican*, 40.

6. The Web site of the Nuyorican Poets Café uses this phrase in its historical account. Clearly, there is some confusion about what constitutes the founding of the café.

7. *Short Eyes* premiered in January 1974 at the Riverside Church; Joe Papp brought it to the Beaumont Theater in June 1974. Winner of the 1973–74 New York Drama Critics Circle citation for best American play, it was filmed in 1977. Piñero's heyday was in the 1970s, but the 2001 release of Leon Ichaso's film biography *Piñero* has regenerated interest in his work.

8. For a detailed account of The Family, see Hart, "The Family."

9. The other major event that shaped Puerto Rican theater in New York was the Puerto Rican Traveling Theatre's 1966 bilingual production of René Marqués's play *La Carreta* (The Ox-Cart), the first important piece of theater to relate the experience of Puerto Ricans in New York. Antush provides a history of this event in the introduction to *Nuestro New York*. Marqués was not articulating a Nuyorican ideal; the antimodern

stance of his play charts the destruction of the central *jíbaro* (peasant) character on his essentially forced labor migration from rural Puerto Rico to San Juan, and then to New York City.

10. Certainly there are important works by Piñero not directly tied to a Nuyorican aesthetic, such as *Midnight Moon at the Greasy Spoon* and *Eulogy for a Small-Time Thief,* but they share a realism that celebrates the emotional richness of the everyday.

11. For a trenchant critique of the New York critics' bias, see Mills, "Seeing Ethnicity."

12. Ailey, *Revelations,* 138–39.

13. Griffith, "Foreword," ix.

14. Culture Clash, *Culture Clash in Americca,* 73.

15. Culture Clash, *Culture Clash in Americca,* 83.

16. Piñero, *Outrageous,* 37, 47, 151.

17. Rosen defines total institution, using the work of Erving Goffman, in the introduction of *Plays of Impasse,* pp. 9ff.

18. Robert Wahls, "Pinero: Prison, Parole & a Prize," *Sunday News,* June 2, 1974, quoted in Mills, "Seeing Ethnicity," 43.

19. Piñero, *Short Eyes,* 7.

20. Piñero, *Short Eyes,* 11, 20.

21. Piñero, *Short Eyes,* 26.

22. Hanson, "*Short Eyes*: Ethnic Identity," addresses these structures of identity.

23. Piñero, *Short Eyes,* 125–26.

24. Piñero, *Short Eyes,* 88.

25. Piñero, *Short Eyes,* 90.

26. Hanson, "*Short Eyes*: Ethnic Identity," 60.

27. Piñero, *Short Eyes,* 126.

28. Alarcón McKesson, "Interview."

29. Piñero, *Short Eyes,* 38. Clark's use of the word *rehearse* indicates reflection and a clear sense of managing his performance to avoid detection.

30. Piñero, *Short Eyes,* 42, 44, 46.

31. Piñero, *Short Eyes,* 35, 44.

32. Piñero, *Short Eyes,* 49.

33. Piñero, *Short Eyes,* 38.

34. Piñero, *Short Eyes,* 70.

35. Piñero, *Short Eyes,* 99.

36. Piñero, *Short Eyes,* 120.

37. Piñero, *Short Eyes,* 40.

38. Piñero, *Short Eyes,* 112.

39. Piñero, *Short Eyes*, 110. Ism language is "a black version of pig Latin" (125).

40. Piñero, *Short Eyes*, 121.

41. Sevcenko, "Loisaida," 293. It is not incidental that the name came into being through poetry and, more important, a play, *El Don Quixote de Loisaida*, the playwrights insisting, according to Sevcenko, that "Loisaida . . . communicated action as well as urban space. Only those people who took action were considered residents of the space" (301).

42. Piñero, *Bodega*, 8.

43. de Certeau, *Practice*, 130.

44. Ramírez, *What It Means*, 67.

45. Lauria, "'Respeto,'" 55. Although these accounts are of interactions on the island, the same question emerges in accounts of the underground economies of metropolitan New York City. See Figueroa, *Survival*, especially pp. 25–33.

46. Piñero, *Sun*, 15. A second published edition, in Kanellos and Huerta, *Nuevos Pasos*, has more complete stage directions.

47. Piñero, *Sun*, 27.

48. Piñero, *Sun*, 30.

49. Piñero, *Sun*, 32–33.

50. Piñero, *Sun*, 26. A *bodega* is a small neighborhood store.

51. Piñero, *Sun*, 26.

52. Piñero, *Sun*, 17.

53. Piñero, *Sun*, 40.

54. Piñero, *Sun*, 45.

55. Piñero, *Sun*, 26

56. Piñero, *Sun*, in Kanellos and Huerta, *Nuevos Pasos*, 173–74.

57. Piñero, *Sun*, 6.

58. Piñero, *Sun*, 45.

3. El Pachuco: Myth, Theatricality, and Ambivalent Community

1. Huerta, *Chicano Drama*, 6.

2. The two most important book-length accounts of El Teatro Campesino are Harry Elam Jr., *Taking It to the Streets*, which compares the ensemble's work to that of the Black Repertory Theater, and Yolanda Broyles-González, *El Teatro Campesino*, an excellent history that rewrites the traditional narrative, which places Valdez as the sole artistic voice of El Teatro Campesino. Aspects of her account have been questioned by some Teatro veterans.

3. Valdez and El Teatro Campesino, *Luis Valdez—Early Works*, 12.

4. See Broyles-González, as well as "The First Chicano Actor" in Burciaga, for more elaborate accounts of the individual contributions.

5. Valdez and El Teatro Campesino, *Luiz Valdez—Early Works*, 168–99.

6. For a full accounting of these various forms, see Huerta's introductions to Valdez's works.

7. Valdez, "Notes," 8.

8. See, for example, Parédez, *El Popul Vuh*.

9. Valdez, "Notes," 6.

10. Elam, *Taking*, 50.

11. Saldívar, *Chicano Narrative*, 7.

12. In discussing a production of Eduardo Gallardo's *Simpson Street*, John Antush talks about an older lady discretely going onstage to move a suitcase farther under a bed to help the protagonist. This gesture marks a real concern with the social power of realism in representation. It's not that an audience can't tell the difference between reality and theater but that they more cogently understand the social power of representation in everyday life given a heightened sense of (in)visibility. For Antush this moment becomes a sign that "[a] theatre of the people and for the people had certainly arrived in New York, and one did not have to be Hispanic to enjoy it" (Gallardo, *Simpson Street*, 4).

13. Two important sources on these events are Pagán, *Murder at the Sleepy Lagoon*, and Mazón, *Zoot Suit Riots*.

14. Barker, *Pachuco*, 13.

15. Barker, *Pachuco*, 21.

16. Barker, *Pachuco*, 34, 33.

17. Barker, *Pachuco*, 33.

18. Paz, *Labyrinth*, 15. Many Mexicans use the term *norteamericano* to refer to persons from the United States.

19. Paz, *Labyrinth*, 16.

20. Paz, *Labyrinth*, 16–17.

21. The essays are produced out of a consciousness manifest during a trip to the United States in which Paz's own position as outsider has drawn self-reflexive attention to his own national subjectivity.

22. Paz, *Labyrinth*, 16–17.

23. Huerta uses the term *Mechicano* in *Chicano Theater* as an inclusive label for people of Mexican heritage. He takes the term from Alurista.

24. In the three plays in these two chapters, Valdez is heavily invested in male protagonists, though he has moved in a very different direction in the recent play *Mummified Deer*.

25. Luis Valdez, "Once Again Meet the Zoot Suiters," *Los Angeles Times*, August 13, 1978.

26. Richard Vasquez, "'Zoot Suit' Image Raises Chicano Consciousness," *Los Angeles Times*, April 22, 1979.

27. The newspaper as furniture and other stage elements were added for the play's production in the Mark Taper Forum main season. For an impressively thorough account of the multiple stagings of the play and film, see Broyles-González, 177–214.

28. Valdez, *Zoot Suit*, 25.

29. Comment by Oliver Mayer, April 4, 2005.

30. Leyvas was the leader of the defendants, according to Alice Greenfield McGrath and the Sleepy Lagoon Defense Committee (Pagán, 204–8).

31. Huerta has commented that while the film is about Henry, the play is clearly El Pachuco's, though Broyles-González suggests that his role in the theater emerged through the multiple revisions (182).

32. Valdez, *Zoot Suit*, 29, 30.

33. This is particularly fascinating, since "none of the male actors in the company wished at first to play the roles of the *Pachucos*. It certainly opens up the question about the supposed masculinism of the Zoot Suiters at the time and about the volatility of their transgressive spectacle of race, class, and also, gender identity" (Sanchez-Tranquilino and Tagg, 569). Broyles-González's recognition of the agency of Socorro Valdez in the construction of the popular Pachuco character Huesos in *El Fin del Mundo* further suggests that gender politics are crucial in unpacking the problematic complexities of this figure.

34. Babcock, "Looking for a Third Space," 223.

35. Sanchez-Tranquilino and Tagg, 561.

36. de Certeau, 130.

37. See chapter 2.

38. Yarbro-Bejarano with Ybarra-Frausto, "'*Zoot Suit* mania.'"

39. Huerta, introduction to Valdez, *Zoot Suit*, 15.

40. Valdez, *Zoot Suit*, 51.

41. Valdez, *Zoot Suit*, 81.

42. Valdez, *Zoot Suit*, 26.

43. Broyles-González, 123.

44. Pizzato, "Brechtian and Aztec Violence," 57. See also Booth, "Dramatic Aspects," especially 425.

45. Richard Eder, "Theater: *Zoot Suit*, Chicano Music-Drama," *New York Times*, March 26, 1979, C13.

46. Jameson, *Brecht*, 89–130.

47. Most recently this potential has been manifest in a desire to articulate the complexity of Latino life in the United States through Olmos's PBS miniseries and accompanying book, *Americanos: Latino Life in the United States*.

48. Broyles-González, 182.

49. See "Edward Olmos—Biography"

50. "Edward Olmos—Biography."

51. Eder, "Theater: *Zoot Suit*."

52. Gutiérrez-Jones, *Rethinking the Borderlands*, 48.

53. Valdez, *Zoot Suit*, 46.

54. Valdez, *Zoot Suit*, 46.

55. Valdez, *Zoot Suit*, 53.

56. Valdez, *Zoot Suit*, 40.

57. Valdez, *Zoot Suit*, 62.

4. Bandidos to Badges: Criminality and the Genre of Ethnicity

1. Mirandé, *Gringo Justice*, 25–26.

2. Valdez, *Zoot Suit*, 97.

3. McConachie takes the concept of "theatrical formation" from Tony Bennett's notion of a "reading formation." McConachie, *Melodramatic Formations*, ix, xii.

4. Mason, *Melodrama*, 16, 18–19.

5. Brooks, *Melodramatic Imagination*, 200, 203.

6. Althusser, *For Marx*, 143.

7. Monroy, *Thrown*, 163.

8. Monroy, Thrown, 165, 201.

9. Monroy, *Thrown*, 211.

10. Monroy, *Thrown*, 211.

11. Burciaga, *Drink Cultura*, 124–25.

12. Beers's reprinted account forms the majority of Greenwood, *California Outlaw*.

13. Monroy, *Thrown*, 215.

14. Broyles-González, 231.

15. Valdez, *Zoot Suit*, 101.

16. Broyles-González, 231.

17. Valdez, *Zoot Suit*, 109.

18. Valdez, *Zoot Suit*, 105.

19. Valdez, *Zoot Suit*, 107, 104, 108, 109.

20. Thanks to Maria Herrera-Sobek, who pointed out the visual semiotics presented by the Taper production poster. Two nineteenth-century

descriptions found in Greenwood support this representation. Sheriff Adams notes that Vásquez's complexion was "light for a Spaniard," and Ben Truman says "he looked little like a man who could create a reign of terror" (15).

21. Hornby, "Review: Bandido!," 176–77.

22. Valdez, *Zoot Suit*, 110.

23. Valdez, *Zoot Suit*, 110, 111.

24. Valdez, *Zoot Suit*, 112, 113, 114, 114, 114.

25. Valdez, *Zoot Suit*, 116.

26. Monroy, *Thrown among Strangers*, 179–80.

27. Valdez, *Zoot Suit*, 137, 138, 150.

28. Beers quoted in Greenwood, *California Outlaw*, 290.

29. Masur, *Rites*, 108–9.

30. See *Bandido!* production notebook from 1994 in the El Teatro Campesino archives, San Juan Bautista, California.

31. The text of this play has been constantly revised. A study of the various versions might reflect Valdez's shifting political and personal investments in Vasquéz. The play was also performed at the San Diego REPertory Theatre in 1999.

32. Center for Media and Public Affairs, *Don't Blink*, 1,2.

33. Rob Eshman, "Counterpunch: *Bandido!* Steals Truth of Early L.A.," *Los Angeles Times*, July 18, 1994.

34. Laurie Winer, "Theatre Review; Once upon a Time in Old California; Luis Valdez's '*Bandido!*' Deconstructs the Myth of 19th Century Legend Tiburcio Vasquez, Playing Up the Tale's Melodramatic Elements," *Los Angeles Times*, June 10, 1994.

35. Quoted in Broyles-González, *Teatro Campesino*, 232. Among other things, Broyles-González is concerned with the misrepresentation of nineteenth-century California history. She attributes this misrepresentation to a desire to appease an Anglo audience to enable mainstream success.

36. Huerta, "Introduction" in *Zoot Sui*, 16, 18. Huerta's role as introducer places him in a position to celebrate rather than criticize the text.

37. Gray, *Watching Race*.

38. Acuña, *Anything but Mexican*, 160.

39. Quoted in Broyles-González, *Teatro Campesino*, 50. According to Ybarra-Frausto, "Rasquachismo is brash and hybrid, sending shudders through the ranks of the elite, who seek solace in less exuberant, more muted, and purer traditions. In an environment always on the edge of coming apart (the car, the job, the toilet), things are held together with spit, grit, and movidas. Movidas are the coping strategies you use to gain time,

to make options, to retain hope. Rasquachismo is a compendium of all the movidas deployed in immediate, day-to-day living" (Broyles-González, *Teatro Campesino*, 49).

40. Broyles-González, *Teatro Campesino*, 87.

41. In the original production the protagonist wanted to be an actor; subsequent productions shifted his focus toward directing.

42. Valdez, *Zoot Suit*, 183. *Villa* refers back to Pancho Villa, the Mexican revolutionary who received significant attention from the U.S. media. This historical figure is also referenced in Valdez's first play, *The Shrunken Head of Pancho Villa*.

43. Valdez, *Zoot Suit*, 163.

44. Valdez, *Zoot Suit*, 162.

45. Valdez, *Zoot Suit*, 165.

46. Valdez, *Zoot Suit*, 184. This desire to be Woody Allen was even more visible in the Jupiter Theater production of the play, although much of that material was eventually eliminated from the published script.

47. Steenland, *Unequal Picture*, 12.

48. Valdez, *Zoot Suit*, 174.

49. Valdez, *Zoot Suit*, 207, 208.

50. Valdez, *Zoot Suit*, 188.

51. Valdez, *Zoot Suit*, 188, 203.

52. Valdez, *Zoot Suit*, 196.

53. Alicia Arrizón acknowledges this connection in her *Ambiente* review.

54. Lonn Johnston and LaMont Jones Jr., "Harvard Student Tied to 'Ski-Mask' Robberies: The Youth Who Had It All Wanted More, Police Say," *Los Angeles Times*, July 9, 1987.

55. Fineman quoted in Lynn Smith, "Experts Say Razo Fits Pattern of Self-Destructive 'Sun Children,'" *Los Angeles Times*, July 12, 1987.

56. Louis Sahagun, "Stole to Help Family Accused Robber Says," *Los Angeles Times*, July 11, 1987.

57. Monica Brown, *gang nation*, xxiii. She goes on: "Latina/o urban gang members are asserting an alternative citizenship in a counternation, one that fulfills fundamental needs not accorded by the state, one that provides a sense of economic security (most often through delinquent behavior), one that establishes its own moral and juridical authority with a history tied to territory, and one that provides a sense of communal identity, belonging."

58. Bob Schwartz, "Contrast in Life Styles: From La Habra to Harvard; Worlds away at Harvard the Razo Tale Is Hard to Figure," *Los Angeles Times*, July 12, 1987.

59. Ruben Navarrette Jr. "Harvard Homeboy: A Chicano on the Fast Track Now Heads for Prison," *Los Angeles Times*, August 5, 1989.

60. Valdez, *Zoot Suit*, 193, 194.

61. See *Badges!* production notebook, Los Angeles Theater Center (LATC), 1987. Script, p. 50. Teatro Campesino Archives, San Juan Bautista, CA. Prop photos of these eight-by-ten head shots are in the archives.

62. Valdez, *Zoot Suit*, 199.

63. Valdez, *Zoot Suit*, 171, 198, 196.

64. Valdez, *Zoot Suit*, 198.

65. All quotes from Valdez, *Zoot Suit*, 198. Ironically, this moment was also in the original script but was used in relationship to his display of his head shots.

66. Valdez, *Zoot Suit*, 199.

67. Hamamoto, *Nervous*, 2.

68. Valdez, *Zoot Suit*, 209.

69. Valdez, *Zoot Suit*, 209.

70. Valdez, *Zoot Suit*, 210.

71. Valdez, *Zoot Suit*, 212.

72. *Badges!* script, p.84, from LATC production notebook.

73. Sylvie Drake, "Stage Review: 'Badges' Punctuates the Hyphenated Life," *Los Angeles Times*, February 7, 1986.

74. Kelman, *Guide*, 269, quoted in Gutiérrez-Jones, *Rethinking the Borderlands*, 13.

75. Vigil, *Barrio Gangs*, 143.

76. Vigil, *Barrio Gangs*, 119, 112.

77. Razo was convicted of only six of ten armed robberies but was sentenced to ten years and four months in prison for his crimes. After serving his time he was arrested in connection with a domestic disturbance, was deported to Mexico, and then was arrested again, this time for violating his deportation agreement. See Mike Anton, "Mexican Ivy League Robber Is Back in U.S. and Back in Jail," *Los Angeles Times*, May 4, 2002.

5. Wrighting the Borders in the 1990s

1. See Arrizón, *Queering Mestizaje*, for one recent scholarly recuperation of Anzaldúa.

2. See Massey, Durand, and Malone, *Beyond Smoke*.

3. Dunn, *Militarization*, 3.

4. In part the term *exhaustion* is intended to invoke the language of Moreiras's *The Exhaustion of Difference*.

5. Nigro, "Theatre on the Border."

6. Anzaldúa, *Borderlands/La Frontera*, 25.

7. Teatro de la Esperanza, *La víctima*, in Huerta, *Necessary Theater*, 364.

8. Stern, "Nuevo California," 1.

9. Stern, "Nuevo California," 19.

10. Solano and Havis, *Nuevo California*, 52.

11. Solano and Havis, *Nuevo California*, 69.

12. See Massey et al, *Beyond Smoke*.

13. Vila, "Polysemy," 111.

14. *Bordertown* was developed for the San Diego REPertory Theatre, the same institution that helped sponsor and premiered *Nuevo California*. Kondo, "Re(V)isions," discusses this play in detail.

15. See Massey et. al., *Beyond Smoke*.

16. Culture Clash, *Culture Clash in Americca*, 18.

17. Culture Clash, *Culture Clash in Americca*, 15.

18. Rosaldo, "Foreword," 1039.

19. Brady, *Extinct Lands,* Chapter 2.

20. Leguizamo, *Mambo Mouth*, 78.

21. Leguizamo, *Mambo Mouth*, 78.

22. Najera, *Pain*, 40, 41.

23. Najera, *Pain*, 42–43.

24. Charles Isherwood, "Skewering the Strengths and Stereotypes of Latino Life," *New York Times*, October 14, 2005.

25. Isherwood, "Skewering."

26. Marilyn Stasio, "Latinologues," *Variety*, October 14, 2005.

27. Lockhart, "Living between Worlds," 118.

28. Cortez, "Hybrid Identities," 138.

29. Reyes, *Deporting*, 116.

30. Reyes, manuscript of *Deporting the Divas* (1996).

31. Moraga, *Hungry Woman*, 78.

32. Reyes, *Deporting*, 122, 139, 169, 169.

33. Reyes, *Deporting*, 117.

34. Reyes, *Deporting*, 118.

35. Huerta, *Chicano Drama*, 178. See also Woodyard, "Rompiendo."

36. Kushner, "Theatre of the Fabulous," vii.

37. Reyes, *Deporting*, 118, 119, 169.

38. Reyes, *Deporting*, 170.

39. Reyes, *Deporting*, 171, 172.

40. Reyes, *Deporting*, 143, 146, 149, 144.

41. Reyes, *Deporting*, 126.

42. Reyes, *Deporting*, 160.

43. Reyes, *Deporting*, 131.

44. Reyes, *Deporting*, 185, 187.

45. Solis, *Plays*, 136.

46. Solis, *Plays*, 139

47. Solis, *Plays*, 153.

48. Solis, *Plays*, 154. Translation mine.

49. Solis, *Plays*, 155.

50. Solis, *Plays*, 155.

51. Solis, *Plays*, 155.

52. Solis, *Plays*, 175.

53. Solis, *Plays*, 189.

54. Solis, *Plays*, 191.

55. Solis, *Plays*, 191.

56. Robert Hurwitt, "Eerie, Comic, Poetic, Solis' 'El Otro' Makes Subtle Segues between Levels," *San Francisco Examiner*, July 28, 1998, http://sfgate.com/cgi-bin/article.cgi?file=/examiner/archive/1998/07/28/STYLE15103.dtl.

57. Solis, *Plays*, 192.

6. José Rivera's Aesthetics of Wrighting

1. Rivera, *References*, 253.

2. Rivera, "Poverty," 165–66.

3. Román, "Interview,"6, quoted in Sandoval-Sanchez, *José Can You See?*, 108.

4. Angulo, *Magic Realism*, 5. See also Menton; Faris, especially chapter 1; and Zamora and Faris.

5. See Vit Wagner, "Marisol's Angel a Rebellious, Pagan Creation: Playwright Says It Was 'Worst Luck' That Play Should Open in the Same Season as *Angels in America*," *Toronto Star*, January 11, 1997; Hatcher, *Art and Craft of Playwriting*, 197; and Jenckes, "Interview with Jose Rivera."

6. Karen Fricker, "Another Playwright Confronts an Angel and the Apocalypse," *New York Times*, May 16, 1993.

7. The angel of history is a part of Walter Benjamin's "Theses on the Philosophy of History" in his *Illuminations*.

8. Rivera, *Marisol*, 6.

9. Rivera, *Marisol*, 15.

10. Rivera, *Marisol*, 5–6.

11. Rivera, *Marisol*, 20.

12. Rivera recognizes that violence has an aesthetic quality and has stated his preference for more poetic representations in Savran, *Playwright's Voice*, 182.

13. Homeless people who have not been involved in any form of institutionalization (for mental illness or drug addiction) "are more likely than other groups to be nonwhite (63 percent), female (26 percent), young (mean age of thirty-five), and never married (62 percent)" (Burt, *Over the Edge*, 25). These statistics actually describe Marisol's demographic categorization. For a description of urban transformation vis-à-vis Ed Koch, see Westgate, "Toward a Rhetoric."

14. Rivera, *Marisol*, 15, 41, 47, 48–49.

15. Rivera, *Marisol*, 66.

16. Rivera, *Marisol*, 68.

17. Rivera, *Marisol*, 68.

18. See, for example, Garner, "*Angels*."

19. Jenckes, "Interview," 29.

20. In a previous moment the Woman with Furs refers to Marisol as a "brown piece of shit" (Rivera, *Marisol*, 46). This conflation of capitalism and racism fits in well with Rivera's understanding of class in American culture.

21. Derrida, *Specters*, 51.

22. Rivera, *Marisol*, 68.

23. Wendy Brown, *Politics*, 144.

24. See, for example, Savran's "Dangerous Materialism."

25. See Rossini, "*Marisol*."

26. Derrida, xix.

27. Rivera, *Marisol*, 62.

28. Rivera, *Marisol*, 129, 130.

29. Agamben, *Coming Community*, 2.

30. States, *Great Reckonings*, 30. This is in part taken from Benjamin's essay "The Work of Art in the Age of Mechanical Reproduction" in *Illuminations*.

31. Rivera, *Marisol*, 137.

32. Rivera, *Marisol*, 140.

33. Rivera, *Marisol*, 138.

34. Rivera, *Marisol*, 139, 154.

35. Rivera, *Marisol*, 155, 144.

36. Rivera, *Marisol*, 169.

37. Rivera, *Marisol*, 166.

38. Rivera, *Marisol*, 183.

39. Finkelstein, *Collected Writings*, 267.

40. Rivera, *References*, 43.

41. Some sources have a comma between the two phrases, "Two Pieces of Bread" and "Expressing the Sentiment of Love," and this might be critical; however, Rivera's description does not have this comma.

42. The 2000 edition is in *Latino Plays from South Coast Repertory*.

43. One reviewer of a production without the doubling read the moon as a representation of Dalí himself.

44. Etherington-Smith, *Dali*, 287.

45. Rivera, *References*, 249.

46. Rivera, *References*, 173.

47. This theme interestingly echoes in Nilo Cruz's *Lorca in a Green Dress*, whose protagonist is Lorca after his death.

7. Cherríe Moraga and the Wrighting of Community

1. Moraga, *Last Generation*, 52.

2. Some writers use the spelling Xicana to further connect Chicana identity to Nahuatl, the lingua franca of the Mexica or Aztecs, and an indigenous language still widely spoken in Mexico and Guatemala.

3. Moraga, *Last Generation*, 150.

4. Moraga, *Last Generation*, 174. Moraga's play *Hungry Woman* is the most literal embodiment of the space of Queer Aztlán as "a kind of metaphysical border region between Gringolandia (U.S.A.) and Aztlán (Mechicano country)" set in "a future [she] imagine[s] based on a history at the turn of the century that never happened" (6).

5. Arrizón and Manzor, *Latinas*, 195.

6. Moraga, "La Güera," in Moraga and Anzaldúa, *This Bridge*, 29. Italics in original.

7. Yarbro-Bejarano uses Cornel West's conception of joy as a way of understanding the construction of community in this space. Joy becomes a means of coming together in solidarity that is greater than the individual experience of pleasure; it explains the genesis for the public resistance of burning the fields at the end of the play. See Yarbro-Bejarano, *Wounded Heart*, 65.

8. Huerta's *Chicano Drama* and Yarbro-Bejarano's *Wounded Heart* have powerful readings of this work.

9. Moraga, *Heroes*, 89.

10. Moraga, *Heroes*, 90.

11. Moraga, *Heroes*, 91.

12. The similarity to Fornes is not surprising, given her influence on many young Hispanic playwrights during the 1980s through her INTAR workshops. Moraga was in residence at INTAR in 1985 (Yarbro-Bejarano, *Wounded Heart*, 28). Also see Huerta, "Moraga's *Heroes*."

13. See Lefebvre, *Production of Space*.

14. Moraga, *Heroes*, 136.

15. Yarbro-Bejarano, *Wounded Heart*, 73, 79. See also Worthen, "Staging América."

16. Moraga, *Heroes*. 107.

17. Moraga, *Heroes*, 108.

18. Moraga, *Heroes*, 108–9.

19. In a similar reading, Yarbro-Bejarano sees this as "the multiple dimensions of their relationship, a cluster of potential roles for Cere in the play, and the limitations and conflicts that hamper their ability to act and speak" (*Wounded Heart*, 71) but does not argue for a sense of progression.

20. Moraga, *Heroes*, 100.

21. Huerta's reading of the scene focuses on the transgression of representing the sexuality of a priest in a Chicano play but also points out the "blending [of] sexual tension, energy and release with political action" (*Chicano Drama*, 121).

22. Moraga, *Heroes*, 141.

23. Moraga, *Heroes*, 141.

24. Moraga, *Heroes*, 134.

25. Moraga, *Heroes*, 144, 115.

26. Moraga, *Heroes*, 144.

27. Moraga, *Heroes*, 126.

28. Moraga, *Heroes*, 132.

29. Moraga, *Last*, 73–76.

30. Moraga, *Heroes*, 145.

31. According to Huerta, "audience members are given a clear objective: take action from the Miracle" (*Chicano Drama*, 71).

32. Moraga, *Heroes*, 145.

33. Moraga, *Heroes*, 148.

34. Moraga, *Heroes*, 149.

35. Moraga, *Heroes*, 149.

36. For one account see Castillo, *Massacre*, chapter 2.

37. Yarbro-Bejarano charts this articulation of faith throughout Moraga's plays *Shadow of a Man* and *Giving Up the Ghost*, though in those two plays the religious symbolism stays at the level of imagery.

38. Moraga, *Watsonville*, 73.

39. Moraga, *Watsonville*, 6.

40. See Huerta, *Chicano Drama*, 159 note 37.

41. Moraga, *Loving*, 160.

42. Moraga, *Watsonville*, 4.

43. Moraga, *Watsonville*, 89.

44. Moraga, *Watsonville*, 19.

45. Moraga, *Watsonville*, 51.

46. Moraga, *Watsonville*, 51.

47. Moraga, *Watsonville*, 51.

48. Moraga repeats this gesture at the close of both *Heroes and Saints* and *Circle in the Dirt*.

49. Agamben, *Coming Community*, 85.

50. Moraga, *Watsonville*, 98. [we belong here as much as the gringo. Plant yourself here she said. Like that holy tree, so strong, so old, so sacred, you all have roots that spread all the way to Mexico. (*Pause*) This law means nothing. . . . We are all Americans whether we got papers or not. This land is the same land as Mexico. All of this is America, and the Virgin of Guadalupe is the Empress of America, a united America.]

51. Moraga, *Watsonville*, 103.

52. Moraga, *Watsonville*, viii.

53. Dolan, *Utopia*, 37.

54. See http://www.stanford.edu/group/CBPA/EPADream.html for more background.

55. Elam and Fowler, "Dreams."

56. Valdez, "Notes," 10.

57. Elam and Fowler, "Dreams," 206.

58. Moraga, *Watsonville*, 154.

59. See the documentary video *Dreams of a City: The East Palo Alto Project*, produced by the Committee on Black Performing Arts at Stanford University.

60. Moraga, *Watsonville*, 158, 159.

61. Ishi was an indigenous person "discovered" by University of California researchers and used as an anthropological research subject.

Bibliography

Acuña, Rodolfo F. *Anything but Mexican: Chicanos in Contemporary Los Angeles*. New York: Verso, 1996.

———. *Occupied America: A History of Chicanos*. New York: Harper, 1988.

Agamben, Giorgio. *The Coming Community*. Translated by Michael Hardt. Minneapolis: University of Minnesota Press, 1993.

Algarín, Miguel, and Miguel Piñero, eds. *Nuyorican Poetry: An Anthology of Words and Feelings*. New York: Morrow, 1975.

Ailey, Alvin. *Revelations: The Autobiography of Alvin Ailey*. With A. Peter Bailey. New York: Birch Lane Press, 1995.

Alarcón McKesson, Norma. "An Interview with Miguel Piñero." *Revista Chicana-Riqueña*, 2, no. 4 (1974): 55–57.

Althusser, Louis. *For Marx*. Translated by Ben Brewster. New York: Vintage Books, 1970.

Anaya, Rudolfo A., and Francisco Lomelí, eds. *Aztlán: Essays on the Chicano Homeland*. Albuquerque: Academia/El Norte Press, 1989.

Angulo, María-Elena. *Magic Realism: Social Context and Discourse*. New York: Garland, 1995.

Antush, John V., ed. *Nuestro New York: An Anthology of Puerto Rican Plays*. New York: Mentor, 1994.

Anzaldúa, Gloria. *Borderlands/La Frontera: The New Mestiza*. 2nd ed. San Francisco: Aunt Lute Books, 1999.

Arrizón, Alicia. *Latina Performance: Traversing the Stage*. Bloomington: Indiana University Press, 1999.

———. *Queering Mestizaje: Transculturation and Performance*. Ann Arbor: University of Michigan Press, 2006.

———. "Theatre Review: *I Don't Have to Show You No Stinkin' Badges*." In *Ambiente: Chicano/Latino Arts and Culture in San Francisco*, 11–12. San Francisco: Galeria De La Raza/Studio 24, 1990.

Arrizón, Alicia, and Lillian Manzor, eds. *Latinas on Stage*. Berkeley: Third Woman Press, 2000.

Babcock, Granger. "Looking for a Third Space: El Pachuco and Chicano Nationalism in Luis Valdez's *Zoot Suit*." In *Staging Difference: Cultural Pluralism in American Theatre and Drama*, edited by Mauc Maufort. New York: Peter Lang, 1995.

Banks, Marcus. *Ethnicity: Anthropological Constructions*. New York: Routledge, 1996.

Barker, George Carpenter. *Pachuco: An American-Spanish Argot and Its Social Functions in Tucson, Arizona*. 1950. Reprint, Tucson: University of Arizona Press, 1958.

Baver, Sherrie. "Puerto Rican Politics in New York City: The Post–World War II Period." In *Puerto Rican Politics in Urban America*, edited by James Jannings and Monte Rivera. Westport, CT: Greenwood Press, 1984.

Benjamin, Walter. *Illuminations*. Edited by Hannah Arendt. Translated by Harry Zohn. New York: Schocken Books, 1969.

Bigsby, C. W. E. *Modern American Drama, 1945–2000*. Cambridge: Cambridge University Press, 2000.

Booth, Willard C. "Dramatic Aspects of Aztec Rituals." *Educational Theatre Journal* 18, no. 4 (Dec. 1966): 421–28.

Brady, Mary Pat. *Extinct Lands, Temporal Geographies: Chicana Literature and the Urgency of Space*. Durham: Duke University Press, 2002.

Brooks, Peter. *The Melodramatic Imagination: Balzac, Henry James, Melodrama, and the Mode of Excess*. New Haven: Yale University Press, 1976.

Brown, Monica. *gang nation: Delinquent Citizens in Puerto Rican, Chicano, and Chicana Narratives*. Minneapolis: University of Minnesota Press, 2002.

Brown, Wendy. *Politics Out of History*. Princeton: Princeton University Press, 2001.

Broyles-González, Yolanda. *El Teatro Campesino: Theater in the Chicano Movement*. Austin: University of Texas Press, 1994.

Burciaga, José Antonio. *Drink Cultura*. Santa Barbara, CA: Joshua Odell Editions, 1993.

Burns, Elizabeth. *Theatricality: A Study of Convention in the Theatre and in Social Life*. London: Longman, 1972.

Burt, Martha R. *Over the Edge: The Growth of Homelessness in the 1980's*. New York: Russell Sage Foundation, 1992.

Butler, Judith. *Bodies That Matter: On the Discursive Limits of "Sex."* New York: Routledge, 1993.

Castillo, Ana. *Massacre of the Dreamers: Essays on Xicanisma*. Albuquerque: University of New Mexico Press, 1994.

Center for Media and Public Affairs. *Don't Blink: Hispanics in Television Entertainment*. Prepared by S. Robert Lichter and Daniel R. Amundson. Washington, DC: National Council of La Raza, 1996.

Chirico, Miriam M. "Laughter and Ethnicity in John Leguizamo's One-Man Worlds." *Latin American Theatre Review*, Fall 2002, 29–50.

Cortez, Beatriz. "Hybrid Identities and Dislocated Consciousness: *Deporting the Divas* by Guillermo Reyes." In *Chicano/Latino Homoerotic Identities*, edited by David William Foster. New York: Garland, 1999.

Culture Clash. *Culture Clash in Americca: Four Plays*. New York: Theatre Communications Group, 2003.

Davis, Tracy C. "Theatricality and Civil Society." In *Theatricality*, edited by Tracy C. Davis and Thomas Postlethwait. Cambridge: Cambridge University Press, 2003.

de Certeau, Michel. *The Practice of Everyday Life*. Translated by Steven Rendall. Berkeley: University of California Press, 1984.

Derrida, Jacques. *Specters of Marx: The State of the Debt, the Work of Mourning and the New International*. Translated by Peggy Kamuf. New York: Routledge, 1994.

Dolan, Jill. *Utopia in Performance: Finding Hope at the Theater*. Ann Arbor: University of Michigan Press, 2005.

Du Bois, W. E. B. "Krigwa Players Little Negro Theatre." *Crisis* 32, no. 3 (1926): 134–36.

———. *The Souls of Black Folk*. New York: Signet Classic, 1995.

Dunn, Timothy J. *The Militarization of the U.S.-Mexico Border*. Austin: University of Texas Press, 1996.

"Edward Olmos—Biography." *The Ballad of Gregorio Cortez Newsletter* 1, no. 1 (Aug. 1983). Department of Special Collections, University of California, Santa Barbara.

Egginton, William. *How the World Became a Stage*. Albany: State University of New York Press, 2003.

Elam, Harry J., Jr. *The Past as Present in the Drama of August Wilson*. Ann Arbor: University of Michigan Press, 2004.

———. *Taking It to the Streets: The Social Protest Theater of Luis Valdez and Amiri Baraka*. Ann Arbor: University of Michigan Press, 1997.

Elam, Harry, and Kim Fowler. "Dreams of a City: The East Palo Alto Project." In *Performing Democracy: International Perspectives on Urban Community-Based Performance*. Ann Arbor: University of Michigan Press, 2001.

Etherington-Smith, Meredith. *Dali: A Biography*. London: Sinclair-Stevenson, 1992.

Faris, Wendy B. *Ordinary Enchantments: Magical Realism and the Remystification of Narrative.* Nashville: Vanderbilt University Press, 2004.

Faris, Wendy B., and Lois Parkinson Zamora, eds. *Magical Realism: Theory, History, Community.* Durham: Duke University Press, 1995.

Figueroa, José E. *Survival on the Margin: A Documentary Study of the Underground Economy in a Puerto Rican Ghetto.* New York: Vantage Press, 1989.

Finkelstein, Haim, ed. and trans. *The Collected Writings of Salvador Dalí.* New York: Cambridge University Press, 1998.

Flores, Juan. *Divided Borders: Essays on Puerto Rican Identity.* Houston: Arte Público Press, 1993.

Flores, William V., and Rina Benmayor, eds. *Latino Cultural Citizenship: Claiming Identity, Space, and Rights.* Boston: Beacon Press, 1997.

Gallardo, Edward. *"Simpson Street" and Other Plays.* Houston: Arte Público Press, 1989.

Gandy, Matthew. "Between Borinquen and the *Barrio*: Environmental Justice and New York City's Puerto Rican Community, 1969–1972." *Antipode* 34, no. 4 (2002): 730–61.

Garner, Stanton B. *"Angels in America*: The Millennium and Postmodern Memory." In *Approaching the Millennium: Essays on "Angels in America,"* edited by Deborah R. Geis and Steven F. Kruger. Ann Arbor: University of Michigan Press, 1997.

Geertz, Clifford. "Blurred Genres: The Refiguration of Social Thought." *American Scholar* 49 (1980): 165–79.

Geiogamah, Hanay. "The New American Indian Theater: An Introduction." In *American Indian Theater in Performance: A Reader,* edited by Hanay Geiogamah and Jaye T. Darby. Los Angeles: American Indian Studies Center, UCLA, 2004.

Goffman, Erving. *Frame Analysis: An Essay on the Organization of Experience.* Cambridge: Harvard University Press, 1974.

———. *The Presentation of Self in Everyday Life.* Garden City, NY: Doubleday, 1959.

Gómez-Peña, Guillermo. *The New World Border.* San Francisco: City Lights, 1996.

Gramsci, Antonio. *Selections from the Prison Notebooks of Antonio Gramsci.* Edited and translated by Quintin Hoare and Jeffrey Smith. London: Lawrence and Wishart, 1971.

Gray, Herman. *Watching Race: Television and the Struggle for Blackness.* 1995. Reprint, Minneapolis: University of Minnesota Press, 2004.

Greenfield, Alice. *The Sleepy Lagoon Case: A Pageant of Prejudice.* Los Angeles: Citizens Committee for the Defense of Mexican-American Youth, 1942.

Greenwood, Robert. *The California Outlaw: Tiburcio Vasquez.* Los Gatos, CA: Talisman Press, 1960.

Griffith, Lois. "Foreword: Life Action." In *Action: The Nuyorican Poets Café Theater Festival,* edited by Miguel Algarín and Lois Griffith. New York: Simon and Schuster, 1997.

Gutiérrez-Jones, Carl. *Rethinking the Borderlands: Between Chicano Culture and Legal Discourse.* Berkeley: University of California Press, 1995.

Hamamoto, Darrell Y. *Nervous Laughter: Television Situation Comedy and Liberal Democratic Ideology.* 1989. Reprint, New York: Praeger, 1991.

Hanson, Philip. "*Short Eyes*: Ethnic Identity in the Total Institution," *Gestos* 37 (April 2004): 51–67.

Hart, Steven Edward. "The Family: A Theatre Company Working with Prison Inmates and Ex-Inmates." Ph.D. diss., City University of New York, 1981.

Hatcher, Jeffrey. *The Art and Craft of Playwriting.* Cincinnati: Story Press, 1996.

Hernández, Carmen Dolores. *Puerto Rican Voices in English: Interviews with Writers.* Westport, CT: Praeger, 1997.

Hornby, Richard. "A Review: Bandido!" *OLLANTAY Theater Magazine* 4, no. 1 (1996): 175–78.

Hornor, Louise L., ed. *Hispanic Americans: A Statistical Sourcebook.* Palo Alto, CA: Information Publications, 1996.

Huerta, Jorge A. "Cherríe Moraga's *Heroes and Saints*: Chicano Theatre for the '90's." *Theatre Forum* no.1 (1992): 49–52.

———. *Chicano Drama: Performance, Society and Myth.* Cambridge: Cambridge University Press, 2000.

———. *Chicano Theater: Themes and Forms.* Ypsilanti, MI: Bilingual Press, 1982.

———. Introduction. In *"Zoot Suit" and Other Plays.* Luiz Valdez. Houston: Arte Público Press, 1992.

———, ed. *Necessary Theater. Six Plays about the Chicano Experience.* Houston: Arte Público Press, 1989.

———. "Professionalizing Teatro: An Overview of Chicano Theatre during the 'Decade of the Hispanic.'" *Theatre Forum* no.3 (Spring 1993): 54–59.

Huerta, Jorge A., and Nicolás Kanellos, eds. *Nuevos Pasos: Chicano and Puerto Rican Drama.* Houston: Arte Público Press, 1989.

Jameson, Fredric. *Brecht and Method.* New York: Verso, 1998.

Jenckes, Norma. "An Interview with Jose Rivera," *American Drama* 10, no. 2 (Summer 2001): 21–47.

Jenkins, Richard. "Ethnicity Etcetera: Social Anthropological Points of View." In *Ethnic and Racial Studies Today,* edited by Martin Blumer and John Solomos. New York: Routledge, 1999.

Kanellos, Nicolás. *Mexican American Theater: Legacy and Reality.* Pittsburgh: Latin American Literary Review Press, 1987.

———, ed. *Mexican-American Theatre: Then and Now.* Houston: Arte Público Press, 1984.

Kanellos, Nicolás, and Jorge Huerta, eds. *Nuevos Pasos: Chicano and Puerto Rican Drama.* Houston: Arte Público Press, 1989.

Kelman, Mark. *A Guide to Critical Legal Studies.* Cambridge: Harvard University Press, 1987.

Kondo, Dorinne. "Re(V)isions of Race: Contemporary Race Theory and the Cultural Politics of Racial Crossover in Documentary Theatre." *Theatre Journal* 52, no. 1 (2000): 81–107.

Kushner, Tony. *Angels in America: A Gay Fantasia on National Themes, Part One. Millennium Approaches.* New York: Theatre Communications Group, 1993.

———. "Theatre of the Fabulous." In *Staging Gay Lives: An Anthology of Contemporary Gay Theater,* edited by John M. Clum. Boulder, CO: Westview Press, 1996.

Latino Plays from South Coast Repertory: Hispanic Playwrights Project Anthology. New York: Broadway Play Publishing, 2000.

Latins Anonymous. *Plays.* Houston: Arte Público Press, 1996.

Lauria, Anthony, Jr. "'Respeto,' 'Relajo,' and Inter-Personal Relations in Puerto Rico." *Anthropological Quarterly* 37, no. 2 (1964): 53–67.

Lee, Josephine. *Performing Asian America: Race and Ethnicity on the Contemporary Stage.* Philadelphia: Temple University Press, 1997.

Lefebvre, Henri. *The Production of Space.* Translated by Donald Nicholson-Smith. Malden, MA: Blackwell Publishing, 1991.

Leguizamo, John. *Mambo Mouth: A Savage Comedy.* New York: Bantam Books, 1993.

Lockhart, Melissa Fitch. "Living between Worlds: An Interview with Guillermo Reyes." *Latin American Theatre Review* 31, no. 1 (1997): 117–21.

Marc, David. *Comic Visions: Television Comedy and American Culture.* 2d ed. Malden, MA: Blackwell, 1997.

Marqués, René. *La Carreta.* Río Piedras, PR: Editorial Cultural, 1955. Trans. by Charles Pildich. New York: Scribner, 1972.

Marrero, M. Teresa. "From El Teatro Campesino to the Gay 1990s." In *The State of Latino Theater in the United States: Hybridity, Transculturation, and Identity,* edited by Luis A. Ramos-García. New York: Routledge, 2002.

Mason, Jeffrey D. *Melodrama and the Myth of America*. Bloomington: Indiana University Press, 1993.

Massey, Douglas S., Jorge Durand, and Nolan J. Malone. *Beyond Smoke and Mirrors: Mexican Immigration in an Era of Economic Integration*. New York: Russell Sage, 2002.

Masur, Louis P. *Rites of Execution: Capital Punishment and the Transformation of American Culture, 1776–1865*. New York: Oxford University Press, 1989.

Mazón, Mauricio. *The Zoot-Suit Riots: The Psychology of Symbolic Annihilation*. Austin: University of Texas Press, 1984.

McConachie, Bruce A. *Melodramatic Formations: American Theatre and Society, 1820–1870*. Iowa City: University of Iowa Press, 1992.

McWilliams, Carey. *North from Mexico: The Spanish Speaking People of the United States*. 1949. Reprint, New York: Greenwood Press, 1968.

Melendez, Miguel. *We Took the Streets: Fighting for Latino Rights with the Young Lords*. New York: St. Martin's Press, 2003.

Menton, Seymour. *Magic Realism Rediscovered, 1918–1981*. Philadelphia: Associated University Press, 1983.

Mills, Fiona. "Seeing Ethnicity: The Impact of Race and Class on the Critical Reception of Miguel Piñero's *Short Eyes*." In *Captive Audience: Prison and Captivity in Contemporary Theater*, edited by Thomas Fahy and Kimball King. New York: Routledge, 2004.

Mirandé, Alfredo. *Gringo Justice*. Notre Dame: University of Notre Dame Press, 1987.

Monroy, Douglas. *Thrown among Strangers: The Making of Mexican Culture in Frontier California*. Berkeley: University of California Press, 1990.

Moraga, Cherríe. *"Heroes and Saints" & Other Plays*. Albuquerque: West End Press, 1994.

———. *The Hungry Woman*. Albuquerque: West End Press, 2001.

———. *The Last Generation: Prose and Poetry*. Boston: South End Press, 1993.

———. *Loving in the War Years: lo que nunca pasó por sus labios*. 2nd ed. Boston: South End Press, 2000.

———. *Watsonville: Some Place Not Here / Circle in the Dirt: El Pueblo de East Palo Alto*. Albuquerque: West End Press, 2002.

Moraga, Cherríe, and Gloria Anzaldúa, eds. *This Bridge Called My Back: Writings by Radical Women of Color*. New York: Kitchen Table Press, 1983.

Moreiras, Alberto. *The Exhaustion of Difference*. Durham: Duke University Press, 2001.

Muñoz, José Esteban. *Disidentifications: Queers of Color and the Performance of Politics*. Minneapolis: University of Minnesota Press, 1999.

Murray, Timothy, ed. *Mimesis, Masochism, and Mime: The Politics of Theatricality in Contemporary French Thought*. Ann Arbor: University of Michigan Press, 1997.

Najera, Rick. *"The Pain of the Macho" and Other Plays*. Houston: Arte Público Press, 1997.

Naremore, James, ed. and introd. *The Treasure of the Sierra Madre*. Madison: University of Wisconsin Press, 1979.

Nigro, Kirsten F. "Theatre on the Border." Paper presented at the 27th Comparative Drama Conference, Ohio State University, Columbus, April 2003.

Oboler, Suzanne. *Ethnic Labels, Latino Lives: Identity and the Politics of (Re)Presentation in the United States*. Minneapolis: University of Minnesota Press, 1995.

Olmos, Edward James, Lea Ybarra, and Manuel Monterrey. *Americanos: Latino Life in the United States*. Boston: Little, Brown, 1999.

Pagán, Eduardo Obregón. *Murder at the Sleepy Lagoon: Zoot Suits, Race and Riot in Wartime L.A.* Chapel Hill: University of North Carolina Press, 2003.

Parédez, Domingo Martínez. *El Popul Vuh Tiene Razón: Teoría Sobre la Cosmogonia Preamericana*. Mexico: Editorial Orión, 1968.

Paz, Octavio. *The Labyrinth of Solitude and Other Writings*. Translated by Lysander Kemp, Yara Milos, and Rachel Phillips Belash. New York: Grove Weidenfeld, 1985.

Piñero, Miguel. *La Bodega Sold Dreams*. Houston: Arte Público Press, 1985.
———. *Outrageous: One-Act Plays*. Houston: Arte Público Press, 1986.
———. *Short Eyes*. New York: Hill and Wang, 1996.
———. *The Sun Always Shines for the Cool, Midnight Moon at the Greasy Spoon, Eulogy for a Small Time Thief*. Houston: Arte Público Press, 1984.

Pizzato, Mark. "Brechtian and Aztec Violence in Valdez's *Zoot Suit*." *Journal of Popular Film and Television* 26, no.2 (Summer 1998): 52–61.

Ramírez, Elizabeth C. *Chicanas/Latinas in American Theatre: A History of Performance*. Bloomington: Indiana University Press, 2000.

Ramírez, Rafael L. *What It Means to Be a Man: Reflections on Puerto Rican Masculinity*. Translated by Rosa E. Casper. New Brunswick, NJ: Rutgers University Press, 1999.

Reyes, Guillermo. *Deporting the Divas*. In *Asking and Telling: A Collection of Gay Plays for the 21st Century*, edited by John M. Clum. Garden City, NY: Stage and Screen, 2000.

———. "Deporting the Divas," unpublished manuscript, 1996.

Rivera, José. *"Marisol" and Other Plays*. New York: Theater Communications Group, 1997.

———. "Poverty and Magic in *Each Day Dies with Sleep*." *Studies in American Drama 1945–Present* 7, no. 2 (1992): 163–66.

———. *"References to Salvador Dali Make Me Hot" and Other Plays*. New York: Theatre Communications Group, 2003.

Román, David. "An Interview with José Rivera." *Performing Arts* 31, no. 6 (1997): 6.

———. *Performance in America: Contemporary U.S. Culture and the Performing Arts*. Durham: Duke University Press, 2005.

Romero, Mary. "Introduction." In *Challenging Fronteras: Structuring Latina and Latino Lives in the U.S.*, edited by Mary Romero, Pierrette Hondagneu-Sotelo, and Vilma Ortiz. New York: Routledge, 1997.

Rosaldo, Renato. "Foreword." *Stanford Law Review* 48 (May 1996): 1037–1045.

Rosen, Carol. *Plays of Impasse: Contemporary Drama Set in Confining Institutions*. Princeton: Princeton University Press, 1982.

Rossini, Jon D. "*Marisol*, Angels, and Apocalyptic Migrations." *American Drama* 10, no.2 (Summer 2001): 1–20.

———. "The Pleasure of Reading: Cruz, Tolstoy, and the Pulitzer." *Gestos* 40 (November 2005): 63–77.

Saldívar, Ramón. *Chicano Narrative: The Dialectics of Difference*. Madison: University of Wisconsin Press, 1990.

Sanchez-Tranquilino, Marcos, and John Tagg. "The Pachuco's Flayed Hide: Mobility, Identity, and *Buenas Garras*." In *Cultural Studies*, edited by Lawrence Grossberg, Cary Nelson, and Paula A. Treichler. New York: Routledge, 1992.

Sandoval-Sánchez, Alberto. *José Can You See? Latinos On and Off Broadway*. Madison: University of Wisconsin Press, 1999.

Sandoval-Sánchez, Alberto, and Nancy Saporta Sternbach. *Stages of Life: Transcultural Performance and Identity in U.S. Latina Theater*. Tucson: University of Arizona Press, 2001.

Savran, David. "Ambivalence, Utopia, and a Queer Sort of Materialism," In *Approaching the Millennium: Essays on "Angels in America,"* edited by Deborah R. Geis and Steven F. Kruger. Ann Arbor: University of Michigan Press, 1997.

———. *In Their Own Words: Contemporary American Playwrights*. New York: Theater Communications Group, 1988.

———. *The Playwright's Voice: American Dramatists on Memory, Writing, and the Politics of Culture*. New York: Theatre Communications Group, 1999.

Seller, Maxine S., ed. *Ethnic Theatre in the United States*. Westport, CT: Greenwood Press, 1983.

Ševčenko, Liz. "Making Loisaida: Placing Puertorriqueñidad in Lower Manhattan." In *Mambo Montage: The Latinization of New York*, edited by Agustín Laó-Montes and Arlene Dávila. New York: Columbia University Press, 2001.

Sleepy Lagoon Defense Committee. *The Sleepy Lagoon Case*. Hollywood, CA: Mercury Printing, 1943.

Solano, Bernardo, and Allan Havis. *Nuevo California*. New York: Broadway Play Publishing, 2005.

Solis, Octavio. *Plays by Octavio Solis*. New York: Broadway Play Publishing, 2006.

States, Bert O. *Great Reckonings in Little Rooms: A Phenomenology of Theater*. Berkeley: University of California Press, 1985.

Steenland, Sally. *Unequal Picture: Black, Hispanic, Asian, and Native American Characters on Television*. Washington, DC: National Commission on Working Women of Wider Opportunities for Women, 1989.

Stern, Lynn E. "Nuevo California: On the Border of Art and Civic Dialogue. Case Study: San Diego REPertory Theatre." http://www.americansforthearts.org/animatingdemocracy/reading_room/case_studies/theatre.asp#sdrt.

Svich, Caridad. "Who Designates Arrival? As Latino Theatre Enters a New Phase, Its Playwrights and Practitioners Assess Their Evolution and Future." *American Theatre* 22, no. 4 (April 2005): 58–63.

Taylor, Diana. *The Archive and the Repertory: Performing Cultural Memory in the Americas*. Durham: Duke University Press, 2003.

Taylor, Diane, and Juan Villegas, eds. *Negotiating Performance: Gender, Sexuality and Theatricality in Latin/o America*. Durham: Duke University Press, 1994.

Valdez, Luis. *"Mummified Deer" and Other Plays*. Houston: Arte Público Press, 2005.

———. "Notes on Chicano Theatre." In *Luis Valdez—Early Works: Actos, Bernabé, and Pensamiento Serpentino*, by Luis Valdez and El Teatro Campesino. Houston: Arte Público Press, 1994.

———. *"Zoot Suit" and Other Plays*. Houston: Arte Público Press, 1992.

Valdez, Luis, and El Teatro Campesino. *Luis Valdez—Early Works: Actos, Bernabé and Pensamiento Serpentino*. Houston: Arte Público Press, 1994.

Vigil, James Diego. *Barrio Gangs: Street Life and Identity in Southern California*. Austin: University of Texas Press, 1988.

Vila, Pablo. "The Polysemy of the Label 'Mexican.'" In *Ethnography at the Border*, edited by Pablo Vila. Minneapolis: University of Minnesota Press, 2003.

Vorlicky, Robert, ed. *Tony Kushner in Conversation*. Ann Arbor: University of Michigan Press, 1998.

Westgate, J. Chris. "Toward a Rhetoric of Sociospatial Theatre: José Rivera's *Marisol*." *Theatre Journal* 59, no.1 (2007): 21–38.

Wolf, E. R. "Perilous Ideas: Race, Culture, People." *Cultural Anthropology* 35 (1994): 1–12.

Woodyard, George. "Rompiendo las Fronteras: El Teatro de Guillermo Reyes." In *Teatro y Territorios España e Hispanoamérica*, edited by Sara Bonnardel and Genvieve Champeau. Bordeaux: Maison des Pays Ibériques, 1998.

Worthen, W. B. "Staging América: The Subject of History in Chicano/a Theatre." *Theatre Journal* 49, no.2 (1997): 101–20.

Yarbro-Bejarano, Yvonne. *The Wounded Heart: Writing on Cherríe Moraga*. Austin: University of Texas Press, 2001.

Yarbro-Bejarano, Yvonne, with Tomas Ybarra-Frausto. "'*Zoot Suit* mania' sweeps LA, moves toward East." *In These Times* 3, no.11 (Jan 31–Feb 6, 1979).

Ybarra-Frausto, Tomas. "Rasquachismo: A Chicano Sensibility." In *Chicano Art: Resistance and Affirmation, 1965–1985*, edited by Richard Griswold del Castillo, Teresa McKenna, and Yvonne Yarbro-Bejarano, 155–61. Los Angeles: Wight Art Gallery, University of California, 1991.

Young Lords Party and Michael Abramson. *Palante: Young Lords Party*. New York: McGraw-Hill, 1971.

Index

Jon D. Rossini is an assistant professor in the theater and dance department at the University of California, Davis. He has published essays on Nilo Cruz, David Henry Hwang, and José Rivera in *Gestos*, the *Journal of American Drama and Theatre*, and *American Drama*.

Theater in the Americas

The goal of the series is to publish a wide range of scholarship on theater and performance, defining theater in its broadest terms and including subjects that encompass all of the Americas.

The series focuses on the performance and production of theater and theater artists and practitioners but welcomes studies of dramatic literature as well. Meant to be inclusive, the series invites studies of traditional, experimental, and ethnic forms of theater; celebrations, festivals, and rituals that perform culture; and acts of civil disobedience that are performative in nature. We publish studies of theater and performance activities of all cultural groups within the Americas, including biographies of individuals, histories of theater companies, studies of cultural traditions, and collections of plays.